BURSTING
THE
WINESKINS

A marvellous story: honest, human, yet almost a modern *Acts of the Apostles*. Michael Cassidy's teaching on renewal is extraordinarily helpful and balanced. A book that will surely bring reconciliation and spiritual refreshment to many Christians.

David Watson

Michael Cassidy is a bridge-builder, for he heads a multi-racial team, combines evangelistic and socio-political concerns, and is open to both the ecumenical and the charismatic movements, while retaining his critical judgment about both. Although he recounts some sensational happenings, I think and hope he is not implying that he regards these as normal Christian experience. I admire his honesty (joy and pain, Pentecost and Calvary), his courage (speaking out when others would have been silent), his humour (he is always serious but never solemn) and his independence (he refuses to be pigeonholed). Probably no reader will agree with the whole of his book, but every reader will be stimulated by it, as I have been.

John Stott

Michael Cassidy's book is extremely timely. It has appeared just when an increasing number of Christians from across the denominational spectrum are seeking ways to go deeper with God and to get in touch with the supernatural power that the Holy Spirit wants to release in their lives. Cassidy's experiences and insights provide balanced guidelines for such a spiritual search. I can see *Bursting the Wineskins* as one of the truly significant books of the eighties.

C. Peter Wagner

BURSTING THE WINESKINS

Michael Cassidy

HODDER AND STOUGHTON
LONDON SYDNEY AUCKLAND TORONTO

FOR OLAVE

who has
tasted new wine
and helps others to
do likewise

British Library Cataloguing in Publication Data

Cassidy, Michael
  Bursting the wineskins.
  1. Holy Spirit
  I. Title
  231'.3   BT122

ISBN 0-340-32641-7

CONTENTS

No one puts new wine into old wineskins;
if he does, the wine will burst the skins,
and the wine is lost, and so are the skins;
  but new wine is for fresh skins.

Mark 2:22

The new wine is there. But the old wineskins of
rigidity, of inflexible denominationalism, of
hide-bound traditionalism and of Christian
factionalism are often blocking the flow with
lethal corks. The new wine being created by
the work of the Spirit within the old wineskins
must be poured out and released, thereby
allowing God to bring fresh wineskins into
being. But first the old wineskins must burst.
Only this way will a thirsty world be able to
drink.

Bursting the Wineskins: pp. 232–3

FOREWORD

The work of the Holy Spirit, as witnessed to in this book by my brother, Michael, is a very practical experience of the inner work of the Holy Spirit, especially as it affects daily relationships among God's people. Therefore, the presentation of my brother in the pages of this excellent book is a witness rather than a theological thesis.

In evangelism and in the daily living of God's people, the Holy Spirit is not only the Initiator and the effective power, but He also is the Author. This is why it is always difficult for those who are compelled, inspired and guided by the Holy Spirit to write about His work.

However, Michael writes from practical experience and that is the strength of this volume. For myself, I find *Bursting the Wineskins* a very faithful witness to the power, the guidance and the balancing of the Spirit's ministry in us.

It is always very difficult to keep the balance between the tremendous and unusual manifestations of the Holy Spirit in the lives of those who open up to Him, and His work in keeping things in order among brothers and sisters. One group takes one extreme and another group takes another. Yet others are afraid of writing about the work of the Spirit because they fear the potential misunderstandings which this can bring. Of course, misunderstanding has nothing to do with the intentions of the Spirit Himself but does have a lot to do with how we react under the impulse and impact of the Spirit in our own experience. So, in most cases, the confusion lies not only with how people whom God blesses react, but also with how they explain what they have felt and experienced from His great work.

The balancing factor in this work on the Holy Spirit, as

Michael writes, is the Lordship of Jesus Christ. He is the centre and it is He whom the Spirit glorifies. He takes the profound and most thrilling things of Christ and applies them in the lives of ordinary people like ourselves. And in glorifying Christ, the Holy Spirit then shows His power. It is not power for self-demonstration but it is power to enlighten, and to prompt and to make the community of believers move forward, giving glory to God.

If I change and simplify the image, I would say that the Spirit's work is to bring out the radiant character of God's love through Jesus Christ for us all to see and experience in fullness.

I have, therefore, been much impressed, blessed and inspired by this tremendous work on the Holy Spirit, and I pray that those who read it will likewise be blessed in many ways. For instance, those who on the one hand tend to go to extremes by pushing one particular experience will discover the balancing power of the Holy Spirit in the person of the Lord Jesus Christ. On the other hand, those who fear the workings of the Spirit will understand that without Him the Lord Jesus stays a stranger and His work remains a mere story to be read about rather than a dynamic experience of God Himself through that same Spirit who brings power into the believer's life. Such people will take courage from this book as they discover the Holy Spirit is the only one who can make the things of Christ a living reality in our daily lives.

There is another category of person who will be helped by this book. I am thinking of those who see His work as affecting only our emotional life and feelings so that one seems always in the triumph of the third heaven! These will discover that the Holy Spirit is absolutely down to earth in the daily living of each day, so that when things go wrong in relationships, they can be disentangled by His power in the love of Christ.

The cross of course is very central in the work of the Spirit. It wasn't until the Holy Spirit came and filled the hearts and minds of the disciples that the cross was lit up and became the very centre of the Good News. Before that it was a tragic event. Again this insight is well presented in this book.

So I pray that as the Spirit of God fills the hearts of those who read, we will discover together the depth of that great work on the cross that Jesus Christ did, out of which Heaven opened and blessing came flooding into the hearts of men and women.

May God bless you as you read this tremendous work of grace and this witness to the work of the blessed Spirit of God.

FESTO KIVENGERE
Bishop of Kigezi, Uganda,
and East African Team Leader
of African Enterprise

AUTHOR'S PREFACE

This book is not an autobiography. It is, however, one person's story and quest relating to the person and work of the Holy Spirit. It is a testimony really. I share it because I suspect many others are caught up in a similar quest and perhaps my own flounderings and struggles may shed a little light on someone's path of progress. If that happens, I will feel rewarded indeed.

I am thinking especially of those who live in that theological twilight between a rather rigid evangelicalism and a full-blown Pentecostalism. I am thinking of those who long to know more of the Spirit's fullness but who for one reason or another have not been able to identify unequivocally with the Charismatic Renewal in its present stage of development.

I am also writing for charismatics who know they have much to teach the rest of Christendom but who are not always aware how much there is to learn from other sections of the Body of Christ.

Put differently I could say that my intention is to address on the one hand those whose fears of charismatics have paralysed them into an unhappy and perhaps frustrating isolation from the fresh winds of the Spirit and on the other hand those whose enthusiastic involvement in the Renewal or in Pentecostalism has isolated them from the wider Body of Christ with its important insights and correctives.

I hope also that the book will encourage many who may not be in any so-called 'camps', or bearing any of Christendom's labels, but who simply want to move forward in the faith and in their discovery of the Spirit's blessings.

Let me also say that I write as a layman rather than a theologian and my hope, therefore, is that this volume will not only be an encouragement to many clergy but to many thinking lay people as well. I have sought to keep reasonably down to earth and personal while at the same time not avoiding a modest measure of theological reflection. After all, the issues around the work of the Holy Spirit have a strong theological component and some degree of theologising therefore cannot be avoided. However, the heavier bits I have put in Appendices where they may be explored by the more theologically-motivated readers.

My appreciation goes to Derek Crumpton, David Bosch, Phillip and Charmian le Feuvre and to my colleagues in African Enterprise, especially John Tooke and Bill Winter, for extensive counsel and suggestions relating to different sections of the book. Their wisdom has meant much. I am also much indebted to Rob Warner and Edward England of London who have helped me pilot the book through its final stages into published form. Enormous secretarial labours were performed by Bertha Graham, Pat Stockdale and Hazel Hodgson while Malcolm Graham put in many hours of proofing. Myrtle Beck, Brenda Peterson and Colleen Smith helped me in many miscellaneous ways and especially with the finishing touches. One also owes much to many other friends and writers whose thinking has been absorbed almost unconsciously into one's own. In this I think especially of Bishop Stephen Neill. Above all, I want to thank my dear wife, Carol, who constantly prays for me, supports me and also helps me keep my feet on the ground. She also makes many sacrifices in order for me to give myself to projects such as this book.

My prayer in sending forth this little volume is that it will constitute a contribution, however modest, to that blessed Pauline process of 'maintaining the unity of the Spirit in the bond of peace'.

Michael Cassidy

Pietermaritzburg, Natal. July 1982

Chapter One

A WALK IN THE FIELDS

First be reconciled to your brother, and then come
and offer your gift.

Jesus – Matthew 5:24

The late afternoon sun had not yet set over the majestic
Drakensberg mountains when I set off on that memorable
walk through the fields of the Fyvie's farm near Bergville. It
was one of those hauntingly lovely South African evenings
when all of nature seems to beckon through the haze of gentle
light to the heart of man telling him that God is alive and
well.

Carol and I had escaped to John and Beth's farm for a
quiet weekend of rest and change. John and Beth were
playing tennis and Carol was bathing the children, so I
escaped down into what in South Africa we call mealie fields.
'Corn' it is to the rest of the world.

The cows were drifting up to the sheds for milking and
some ducks were winging their way home as I got down into
the fields. Here and there I disturbed little groups of par-
tridges which would screech away from almost under my feet
with great flappings and commotion. And in the distance, set
against the backdrop of the evening glow, were the majestic
Drakensberg mountains pressing their jagged and serrated
silhouette up to eleven and nearly twelve thousand feet.

All was peaceful and quiet and it was good to be away from
the hustle of town life and the constant pressures of ministry
and travel.

As I meditated and prayed, a very clear and distinct thought entered my mind. It came very much out of the blue but with the force of a whisper from on high. 'Before that conference next August, you must get yourself right with Jim and Mary.'

That was the first inkling I was to have that the South African Conference on the Holy Spirit – dubbed the Renewal Conference – was to be of importance to me. In fact I had scarcely even decided definitely to go, because I did not quite see renewal gatherings as part of my 'scene'. But I had tentatively decided to go because I didn't want to contribute to any more dividedness in the South African body of Christ than was already there.

But now came this word about something I had to do before getting there. I had to set right a relationship with some friends. It was a relationship which had gone wrong.

Jim and Mary had been close and dear friends. Perhaps more than that. But as can sometimes happen among Christians, we had fallen out and become alienated for a complex set of reasons which not even we ourselves fully comprehended. But there it was. We were alienated. And we had been so for some seven years.

This had been a source of great pain and grief to my spirit – indeed it had stuck on the landscape of my own soul like a great rock of obstruction which refused to yield or give place even to the clearing processes of time. 'Here am I,' I often thought, 'preaching reconciliation to all and sundry, yet I have a relationship in my own life where reconciliation is yet to take place.'

Yet the curious thing is that back in 1971 I seemed to have received a twofold guidance in this respect – firstly to abandon the relationship for the time being and not to try to restart it, and secondly to forgive *from the heart* (Matt. 18:35).

Not that I didn't need much forgiving myself, because I did, perhaps more than I could admit. But I for my part had to forgive from the heart those wrongs, real or imagined, which I felt had been done to me. That from the heart bit was the problem. It's easy to say we forgive people, and just

verbalise the concept, but to make it truly *from the heart* is
another matter. The trouble is that unless forgiveness is from
the heart, it is like burying a hatchet but leaving the handle
exposed so one can seize it again for further use at a later
stage.

Another curious phenomenon in all this is that ever since
this sad rupture, I had regularly and repeatedly dreamed
about Jim and Mary. In these dreams we were always
reconciled, in friendship and love. These dreams had gone on
constantly over the years.

Then one night, some time in mid 1976, I had another of
these dreams. It was particularly vivid. I woke realising that
in some curious way these nocturnal experiences had been
bringing healing to the wounds and pain of my heart and that
the forgiveness I now felt was indeed not just verbal but truly
from the heart. I had no real explanation for this, nor any real
place in my theology, yet I knew it was so. God was doing
something and saying something to me – IN MY SLEEP!
Beyond that I knew that the love I had previously felt for my
two friends was now truly rising afresh in my soul. Perhaps I
should make contact again.

But now, here I was, in my mealie field, nearly a year later,
and I had done nothing about it.

As for this conference, who knows what that would be all
about? And what was the link anyway between my two
friends in the States and a Christian gathering in far away
Johannesburg?

The sun had well and truly set over the Drakensberg
mountains and it was getting dark as I pensively wended my
way back through the mealie fields and up to the farm house.

Chapter Two

SIGNED, SEALED AND
DELIVERED

No one can say 'Jesus is Lord' except by the Holy
Spirit.

St Paul – 1 Cor. 12:3

In the weeks which followed, I inevitably had to give some
thought to what our African Enterprise stance generally and
my own specifically was going to be on this charismatic*
conference which was bearing down on us. African Enterprise was the missionary organisation I had started in 1961 to
evangelise in the cities of Africa.

We for our part were pretty firmly in what one might call
the evangelical† camp and our views on the work of the Holy
Spirit were straightforward and orthodox.

We believed that the Holy Spirit, as the Third Person in
the Trinity, is co-equal with God the Father and God the Son
and 'He proceeds,' as the creed says, 'from the Father and the
Son'. We knew that the Trinitarian formula had developed
both out of Jesus's teaching and the disciples' own experience. Before Jesus had come they had known 'God *above*

* Charismatic: This adjective, derived from the Greek word charismata,
  meaning 'things of the Spirit', is widely used to describe those movements
  in the Church which stress the work of the Holy Spirit.
† Evangelical: This term describes those Christians who limit religious
  authority to the Bible and who stress the New Testament doctrines of
  conversion, new birth, and justification by grace through faith alone.
  Evangelicals also hold to the full inspiration of the Bible as the word of
  God.

them', with the heavens declaring His glory and the firma-
ment showing His handiwork. Then when Jesus came they
knew 'God *with* them'. Had Jesus not said 'He who has seen
me has seen the Father' (John 14:9)? Finally after Jesus's
Resurrection and Ascension, they had known 'God *in* them'
in the person of the Holy Spirit. Here was God in a Trinity of
persons and yet a unity of substance. Here was God as
Father, Son and Holy Spirit.

Then as a team of evangelists, who had not only read our
Bibles but observed the spiritual processes of hundreds of
people coming to Christ over the years, we knew that the
Holy Spirit has a clear ministry not only before and at, but
after conversion.

BEFORE CONVERSION

Before conversion, He it is who illumines the seeking mind
and draws the questing soul. In fact I had often stressed to
clergy in talks on evangelism that one of the most key
Scriptures to grasp in the whole evangelistic enterprise is that
'No one can say "Jesus is Lord" except by the Holy Spirit' (1
Cor. 12:3). The process of revealing Christ as Lord to the
inquiring mind is one superintended by the Holy Spirit of
God. This means that no person has ever taken Christ as
Lord without the preceding work of the Holy Spirit revealing
Him as such. That illumination of the mind is a supernatural
thing. The natural man cannot discern by himself that Jesus
is Lord. These are things which he cannot know, as St Paul
says, 'because they are spiritually discerned' (1 Cor. 2:14).

This came home powerfully to me during an evangelistic
mission in the city of Ladysmith in 1965. A man came night
after night to the meetings. He was travelling from Rhodesia
(now Zimbabwe) to Durban and had stopped en route in
Ladysmith to do some business. Something detained him
and he had to be there a week, while our mission was on. His
Christian wife back in Zimbabwe had been praying fervently
for a long time that he should become a Christian. Now he
found himself locked up for a week in this quaint little town

with nothing on in the evenings, except of all things, an evangelistic campaign!

So, for want of anything better to do, poor man, he came to the town hall night after night.

Midway through the week he asked to chat with me and we went out to coffee after one of the meetings in a sleazy little roadside café. The little town was no longer boring. It had in fact become the scene of quest. A deep desire had developed in him in the previous few days to find Christ for himself. But it was as if there was a fog over his mind. Nothing I could say, no illustration I could adduce, no scripture I could quote, no explanation I could bring seemed able to remove the fog.

In the end I realised there was nothing more to say. The Holy Spirit would have to do His illuminating work. God the Father would have to draw him by His Spirit to the Son. I remembered Jesus had said: 'No one can come to me unless the Father who sent me draws him' (John 6:44). Likewise Jesus had said it was the job of the Holy Spirit 'to convince the world concerning sin and righteousness and of judgment' (John 16:8). And did not even the Old Testament contain the reminder that it is 'not by might, nor by power, but by my Spirit, says the Lord' (Zechariah 4:6)?

So my seeking friend, with his praying wife, would just have to keep seeking until the Spirit brought that final illumination without which 'no one can say "Jesus is Lord"'.

Then came the last night of the campaign. The town hall was packed. As the service ended, I saw my friend barrelling down the side of the hall towards me. His face was aglow, his eyes radiant, his smile like the Cheshire Cat of *Alice in Wonderland*.

'I see,' he said, 'I see – it's all so clear. How could I have been so blind? It's as if scales have been removed from my eyes. Praise God, I see!'

Yet I had said nothing new or fresh that night in my sermon. But his seeking heart had finally experienced that glorious illumination which is the Spirit's special work in us *before* conversion.

Years later he came up to me at a businessmen's meeting in Durban. He was still aglow. He was still going strong!

AT CONVERSION

Then there is the work of the Holy Spirit *at* Conversion. From the time of my own conversion at university in England in 1955, I had been fully persuaded that it was the Holy Spirit who was the agent in new birth and that it was the Holy Spirit who Himself indwells the believer at the time of his new birth.

I remembered back to that gentle English morning in a little Cambridge bed-sitter when, with the help of my friend Robert Footner, I had said 'Yes' to Jesus Christ and invited Him into my heart by faith. I remembered the overwhelming realisation at the end of that momentous day that Jesus had taken up residence in my heart. Life could never be the same again. I had no theology to tell me what had happened except that I had responded to God's promise in Revelation 3:20 and so had He! 'Behold, I stand at the door and knock; if any one hears my voice and opens the door, I will come in.' I had opened – He had come in.

My October 1955 journal records the feelings which gripped my undergraduate heart:

As I realised the true wonder of that promise, things began happening with an almost alarming and wonderful rapidity. It was as though I was having a radio wave of joy filtered into me – a new surge of wonderful life – and above all a new and hitherto unexperienced feeling of God's presence – all this in a day, in a few hours. That evening I heard a sermon which for once meant something to me. For the first time I understood what it all meant. I understood what it meant to 'have' Christ. I understood the words of the blessing 'the peace of God which passeth all understanding', because for the first time in my life I was experiencing true fellowship with God. After the service I leaped on to my bike and tore round to tell another of my friends all about it.

A week later I went to Church and saw a big placard at the
gate: 'If any one is in Christ, he is a new creation; the old has
passed away, behold, the new has come' (2 Cor. 5:17).
'Goodness,' I said to myself, 'even St Paul found what I've
found!'

I was almost as excited to read in a little book given me
shortly thereafter the testimony of Temple Gairdner, a great
Anglican missionary to Cairo. Shortly after his conversion,
he wrote: 'That sense of newness is simply delicious. It makes
new the Bible and friends and all mankind and love and
spiritual things and Sunday and Church and God Himself.
So I've found.'

Yes, they were heady days indeed – tasting the delicious-
ness of that sense of newness.

But what had in fact happened? I mean, theologically and
biblically what had taken place in my life?

Luckily the Cambridge Inter-Collegiate Christian Union
had weekly Bible studies – one in every individual college
and one centrally for all Christian students. At one of the
college studies the celebrated and saintly Dr Basil Atkinson,
one of England's most formidable Greek scholars and one of
the university's great characters, spoke on John Chapter 3
and the experience of new birth as Jesus put it to Nicodemus.

How well do I remember the great Basil opening up the
Word and expounding it with a perpetual beam which
turned his entire face into a sort of celebration. Somehow his
smile seemed to link up in a great circle with laughing
crinkles flowing left and right from the edge of his eyes!

'The Holy Spirit is the agent of the new birth,' he said.
'Just look at verses 5 and 6: Jesus said, "I say to you, unless
one is born of water [that refers, ruled Basil, to John the
Baptist's baptism of repentance which Nicodemus would
have known about] and THE SPIRIT, he cannot enter the
kingdom of God. That which is born of the flesh is flesh, and
that which is born of the Spirit is spirit."'

'So you see,' said Basil, 'when you open your heart to
Jesus, he comes in in the person of the Holy Spirit and
indwells you.' Flipping in his Greek Testament to 1 Cor.

3:16, he read: '"Do you not know that you are God's temple and that God's Spirit dwells in you?" Or take 2 Cor. 1:22: "He has put His seal upon us and given us His Spirit IN OUR HEARTS as a guarantee." When we are born again by the agency of the Holy Spirit, He enters our hearts and is there as a seal or guarantee that we belong to God.'

I remember another of Basil's favourite texts in this connection. It was Ephesians 1:13: 'In Him you also, who have heard the word of truth, the gospel of your salvation, and have believed in Him, were *sealed* with the promised Holy Spirit.'

'That word "*seal*",' he pronounced, 'refers in the Greek to the seal which oriental traders would put on their purchased products as a sign of purchase. The trader would buy some merchandise at the beginning of his day's business. But not having a supermarket trolley to cart it all round with him, he would put his own distinctive seal on the merchandise. It showed everyone else it was a purchased possession. Then he would leave it in an appropriate place and return later at the end of the day to collect it and take it home as his own.'

'So you see,' beamed Basil, as he could see truth coming home to us on the wings of illustration, 'this is why St Paul uses this Greek word for "seal" to describe what God does by His Holy Spirit at the time of our conversion.

'He "seals" us, to use the words of Ephesians again, "with the promised Holy Spirit, which is the guarantee of our inheritance until we acquire possession of it, to the praise of His glory" (1:13–14). The giving of the Holy Spirit is God's sign and seal that we are redeemed and purchased possessions of God and it also signifies to our own hearts that we belong to God and that His promised inheritance of eternal life is already ours, even though we may have to wait till that Final Day before taking full possession of it.'

This all made sense to me. It fitted my experience. I knew Christ had come into my heart in the person of the Holy Spirit at the time of my conversion. And I believed then, as I believe now, that this is the experience of every true believer at the time of new birth, whether he or she is powerfully aware of it or not. In the Spirit and by the Spirit we are signed, sealed and delivered!

It seemed even clearer when a few weeks later I discovered Titus 3:5–7 where Paul says to Titus, his convert and 'child in the faith', 'He saved us, not because of deeds done by us in righteousness, but in virtue of his own mercy, by the WASHING OF REGENERATION and RENEWAL in the HOLY SPIRIT, which he poured out upon us richly through Jesus Christ our Saviour, so that we might be justified by His grace and become heirs in hope of eternal life.'

If the Holy Spirit entered our hearts at the time of conversion, it was no wonder then that Paul prayed for the Ephesians that 'the eyes of your hearts' should be enlightened to know 'what is the immeasurable greatness of His power in us who believe' (Eph. 1:18, 19). Perhaps many of us, at the time of our conversion, need both prayer and teaching to grasp the implications of the Holy Spirit within. We too need the eyes of our hearts opened, (a beautiful and suggestive phrase) to grasp the immeasurable greatness of that power which is now at work within us from the time of conversion.

Chapter Three

AFTER CONVERSION

Blessed Assurance, Jesus is Mine
Fanny Crosby

I was so enamoured with Basil's first Bible Study on Nicodemus that I decided to keep going to the CICCU Bible Studies each Wednesday in our college. The CICCU was the Cambridge Inter-Collegiate Christian Union whose members had got their loving clutches on me within hours of my arrival in Cambridge. Their personal evangelism was thorough, sustained and full of care even though their zeal sometimes scared the wits out of fellow students, and their notices all over the college boards and via the college mail boxes, alerted every student willy-nilly to the regular weekly Bible Studies.

I remember seeing a cartoon in the university paper of two undergraduates looking up at a notice board with one cheerful old hand saying to the baffled freshman: 'No, CICCU, you fool, not Kikuyu!'

Anyway, CICCU or Kikuyu – it mattered not to me, so long as I could keep going to those weekly studies. Soon they took us into the book of Romans. In much of it I was totally lost and my interpretation left much to be desired. For example, when I read 'no human being will be justified in His sight by works of the law' (Romans 3:20), I took this as divine confirmation that I had been right to change my degree course from law to languages! After all, by the law would no human being be justified!

But soon we were in Romans 8. At once it became one of my favourite chapters in all the Bible. Amongst other things it spoke again to this matter of the work of the Spirit, especially after conversion.

First of all, it is the Spirit (called 'the Spirit of life in Christ Jesus' – vs. 2) who has set us free from the law of sin and death. Secondly, we are to 'live according to the Spirit' and set our minds 'on the things of the Spirit' (vs. 5). To do this is 'life and peace' (vs. 6) in contrast to the 'death' which results from setting the mind on 'the flesh', or the old nature (vs. 6). Thirdly, Paul tells us that we are 'in the Spirit' if the Spirit is in us. 'You are in the Spirit if in fact the Spirit of God *dwells in you*' (vs. 9). More than that. 'Any one who does not have the Spirit of Christ does not belong to Him' (vs. 9). In other words the mark of belonging to Christ at all is possession of the Spirit.

This principle of the indwelling Spirit in the life of every true believer I saw underlined further in the very next verse (vs. 11). 'If the Spirit of Him who raised Jesus from the dead *dwells in you*, He who raised Christ Jesus from the dead will give life to your mortal bodies also through His Spirit which *dwells in you*.' Three times in three verses – 'The Spirit dwells in you'. And this is spoken to all the Roman believers. How could anyone argue with this?

RECEIVING THE SPIRIT?

I underline this because it was against the backdrop of this scriptural teaching that I was later to find myself very confused by the phrase 'receiving the Holy Spirit' which constantly recurs in Charismatic writings. Had I not received the Holy Spirit? How then could I or any believer be challenged or prayed for to receive the Holy Spirit?

For example when I later read Dennis Bennett's book *Nine O'Clock in the Morning* I found him constantly speaking of praying for believers to receive the Holy Spirit. Then suddenly on page 115 there was a footnote: 'Receiving the Holy Spirit or being "baptised in the Holy Spirit" does not mean getting the Holy Spirit, but "receiving" or "making welcome", permitting the Holy Spirit to fill more areas of our lives and to flow out from us to the world.'

My thought then, against the backdrop of what seemed to me clear scriptural teaching, was this: 'If receiving the Spirit subsequent to conversion does not mean getting Him in one's life for the first time, it is probably better not to use the phrase.'

Then again on page 138, Bennett reports on a meeting in England:

> After making sure that all present had personally accepted Christ as their Saviour, I began to pray for those who asked – a few for healing or other needs, but mostly praying for them to receive the Holy Spirit. Once again the miracle began to happen, as Christians, ALREADY IN-DWELT by the HOLY SPIRIT [emphasis mine] began to trust Jesus to inundate them with His power of freedom so that the riches stored in them could break forth to the world.

Having read that paragraph I again wondered to myself, 'If they were already indwelt by the Holy Spirit, does the phrase "receiving the Spirit" really clarify or confuse the issue?'

Anyway this is to jump the gun a bit as back in 1955 hardly anyone in the mainline Churches had even heard the word Charismatic or been exposed to any such writings. But we did know we had received the Holy Spirit at our conversion and that He was the decisive factor in growth and progress after conversion.

I quickly discovered several other dimensions of His post-conversion ministry. One of these, the granting of assurance of salvation, is very clear in Romans Chapter 8 which opened up to me in CICCU days. Very soon after my conversion I began to experience the reality of verse 16: 'It is the Spirit himself bearing witness with our spirit that we *are* children of God'. No one had to tell me I was a child of God and that I

belonged to Christ as His son. That conviction and that
realisation were brought home to me and communicated to
my theologically untutored heart by some power other than
man. I couldn't understand it. Then I heard Romans 8:16 in
a Bible Study and it all clicked. Yes, it was the *Spirit* bearing
witness with my spirit that I was a child of God. Some weeks
later when Billy Graham visited Cambridge for a mission I
sang for the first time: 'Blessed Assurance, Jesus is mine'. I
knew that through the Holy Spirit.

THE WORD OF GOD

Then there was something else. The Holy Spirit communicated to me – it must have been, because it came through
with more than the persuasion of man – that the Bible was in
some very special sense 'the word of God'. In the first weeks
and months after my conversion I used to ascribe divine
authority only to the Gospels and to Jesus's own words, but
not to the Epistles. Then suddenly one day I knew, just knew,
that the whole Bible was in some special sense the Word of
God.

Not long afterwards (i.e. late in 1955) a great controversy
erupted in England with letters flowing fast and furious to
The Times on the issue of biblical authority and inspiration. It
all stemmed from Billy Graham's visit, as a so-called
'fundamentalist', to the intellectual corridors of Cambridge.
And whenever Englishmen get mad at each other *The Times*
has to take up the slack and yield itself as battlefield. I
followed it all closely and dived into Gabriel Hebert's book
on *Fundamentalism and the Church of God* and then into James
Packer's reply *Fundamentalism and the Word of God* plus many
others. I certainly didn't want the fundamentalist label, but I
did want to hold on to the Spirit-given conviction that the
Bible is the Word of God.

In another of those college Bible Studies I discovered
2 Timothy 3:16: 'All scripture is inspired by God.' And I
believed it. Then I found 2 Peter 1:20–1: 'No prophecy of
scripture is a matter of one's own interpretation because no

prophecy ever came by the impulse of man, but men moved by the Holy Spirit spoke from God.' And I believed it. Then I landed on Jesus's words in John 16:13–14: 'When the Spirit of truth comes, He will guide you into all truth . . . He will glorify me, for He will take what is mine and declare it to you.' John 14:26 spoke likewise with Jesus's words: 'But the Counsellor, the Holy Spirit, whom the Father will send in my name, He will teach you all things, and bring to your remembrance all that I have said to you.' I saw this as referring to the Apostle's inscripturation of Jesus's words as God's truth. And I believed it.

Was I naïve? Some might say so, but to me the conviction was one given not by man but by the Spirit of God. And even though, since that time, I have read many scholars who have resisted or attacked this high view, my mind has not changed, because I felt I knew this by revelation of the Holy Spirit.

One other point. In those far-off days many people taught us undergraduates many things about the work of the Spirit after conversion – in sanctifying us, in guiding us, in helping us grow, in strengthening us, in bringing liberty, in exalting Christ, in enabling others to respond to Christ and in bringing forth the fruit of the Spirit, as spoken of in Galatians 5:22 and elsewhere. But no one ever mentioned the Gifts of the Spirit of 1 Corinthians Chapters 12 and 14. It seems evangelicals avoided this subject. At least no one ever spoke of it to me. It was only about eight years after my conversion, when I was a student at Fuller Theological Seminary in California, that I began to wonder why.

Chapter Four

FIRST INKLINGS

We must in no way hinder the Spirit of God
Charles Troutman

I was saying a little while back that when this Renewal Conference loomed on the horizon for August 1977, I was not only given a personal priority of dealing with a broken relationship but also presented with the challenge of what stand to take both personally and as leader of an evangelical agency.

As I indicated, our stance in African Enterprise had been pretty straightforward, down-the-line, true-blue evangelical.

But it was inevitable, with an interdenominational ministry committed to the whole Body of Christ, that both individually and corporately we should have already by that time had some exposure to the Charismatic Renewal. Perhaps this is one of the special privileges of interdenominational ministries that one is constantly exposed to a wide range of viewpoints and perspectives. These inevitably constitute a creative disturbance to one's own theological status-quos, unless one shuts off all influences from those outside one's own ecclesiastical ghettoes.

I have always personally resisted Christian ghetto-living as both stultifying and suffocating. I have always praised and thanked God for my conservative evangelical heritage through CICCU and Inter-Varsity and Fuller Seminary and so on. But for some reason of either perversity or adventure, I have never wanted to close myself off from other influences, whether ecumenical, Charismatic or Catholic. If a thing is true, it's true, whoever has found it. Said Bishop Don Jacobs once to me in Nairobi: 'Michael, let every Christian be both your brother and your teacher.'

Perhaps that is why I easily responded to another bishop friend, Stephen Neill, one of my special patron saints, when on numerous occasions he has said to me: 'Now, here's a book I want you to read. You won't agree with all of it, but then why should you?' He taught me it was important to read books with which one disagrees. 'Can't be one-channel learners,' he would stress.

And of course that kind of outlook is very much in the English academic tradition on which I was raised. It is also part of the life-style of the Anglican Church of which I am a member. Anglicans, of whatever theological persuasion, evangelicals not excluded, have to live in a theological market place right within their own denomination. So each person, and especially those who have clear or definite theological convictions, has to work these out and spread them or defend them, according to inclination, against all comers. So theological pluralism doesn't frighten Anglicans. And it has never frightened me. In fact I enjoy it. Is it this which has opened Anglican and Episcopalian hearts across the world so readily to the renewing and refreshing winds of the Holy Spirit?

TRUTH

Yet my strong evangelical instincts, and deep commitments to biblical truth, as I understood it, always held me in check from quick embraces of some new Christian fad or from easy acceptance of the slogan that 'Doctrine divides and love unites'.

'Why,' I thought, 'should the New Testament contain so much doctrine if it is actually unimportant?'

I remember hearing Grady Wilson, the great comic of the Billy Graham team, and also a great evangelist, tell the story against himself of the fellow who came up to him after an evangelistic meeting in the Southern States and said: 'Gee, Dr Wilson, we sure like your preachin' – 'cos you don't give us no theology, no teachin', no doctrine, no nuthin!!'

I could laugh at that, but never go for it. To me right theology and doctrine were vital. Another dear friend down the years, Francis Schaeffer, had taught me 'Truth matters'. At the Berlin Congress on Evangelism in 1966 I had rejoiced in his affirmation:

> Historic Christianity rests upon truth – not truth as an abstract concept, nor even what twentieth century man regards as 'religious' truth; but objective truth. . . . Historic Christianity rests upon the truth of what today is called 'brute facts' and not just upon an unknown experience of men in past ages. . . . Behind the truth of such history is the great truth that the personal, infinite God is objectively 'there'. He actually exists: and Christ's redemptive and finished work actually took place at a point of time in real space-time history. Historic Christianity rests upon the truth of these things in absolute antithesis to their not being true.[1]

And this is just as applicable to the work of the Holy Spirit as to the Resurrection, or the Ascension, or the New Birth, or whatever.

So I wasn't willing to be swept off my theological feet by any Tom, Dick or Harry claiming some special new experience of the Holy Spirit.

YALE

Even so, I couldn't in integrity or honesty close my mind or eyes to certain happenings around me and across the world.

The first inklings I personally had of something beyond my rather orthodox evangelical understanding of the Holy Spirit was when a friend, David Fisher, who had been at Yale University in the early 1960s, came out to Fuller Seminary in California and told us of some sort of revival going on among the students in the Inter-Varsity group there. This wa Yale's counterpart to the CICCU at Cambridge. David saic numbers of the students were also 'speaking in tongues' – whatever that meant. I knew it was in the Bible somewhere, but those passages I had skipped over.

He reported that some sort of infilling of the Holy Spirit had taken place in several of them and that not only were certain gifts being manifested, but there was a new love and joy among them and a new evangelistic zeal. Beyond that they had been emboldened to mount a twenty-four-hour prayer vigil for one of their startled chaplains who had been taken to hospital with a serious illness. The chaplain, now even more startled, had been released by the hospital the next day!

Inevitably these happenings had sent a seismic shock through the ranks of the Inter-Varsity national leadership. What were they, as a respectable evangelical group to do?

On 22 January 1963 Dr Charles Hummel, one of the Inter-Varsity Christian Fellowship's (IVCF) national leaders, arrived nervously on campus to look at the whole business. He had been taught that the gifts of the Spirit were given only in the first century to establish the Church. Now this view was being challenged, not by some theologian with another view, but by EVENTS.

He later wrote:

> From all I could see, both the exercise of these spiritual gifts and their results were quite biblical, although contrary to my own theological convictions. . . . I left the campus with praise for the Lord's work in the Yale Christian Fellowship and its broadening influence on the campus. I also went away with the questions which were to pursue me for years.[2]

That was somewhat my own reaction to David Fisher's story as he told it. My stance was exactly that of the IVCF leadership who now witnessed other campuses being similarly touched. Said Hummel:

IVCF leaders had a theological bias against the
ment, yet we wanted to welcome any new work God
t be doing. How could we deny the significance of the
t that many were exercising these unusual gifts accord-
g to Biblical teaching and with beneficial results to
student lives?[3]

Charles Troutman, General Director of IVCF, now came
into the act with a memorandum to all IVCF field workers. A
summary paragraph said:

> If this is a movement of God for all His children – even
> though it may be abused – then we want to be part of it. If
> this is not a movement of God, we want to help those of our
> brethren who have become enmeshed. If there is a mis-
> placed emphasis, we want to bring a balance. We must in
> no way hinder the Spirit of God from working in indi-
> viduals as He wills.[4]

SUMMER 1963

This sort of cautious but gentle openness encouraged my
friend David to go off the next summer to Latin America to
learn more about some of the reported happenings there. But
not before he had introduced me to Harold Bredesen, a
Lutheran pastor who was a friend of his.

Bredesen startled me further with a story of a personal
experience which had come his way. He testified to a new
release of the Holy Spirit which had apparently transformed
his life and ministry. Flowing out of this experience had come
some very remarkable happenings, one of which has stuck
vividly in my mind ever since he narrated it.

He had been at a breakfast meeting in a New York hotel.
There he had met a young woman who testified to a dryness
in her spiritual life. Bredesen responded by saying that his
own devotional life had taken on a new depth 'through
speaking in tongues'.

The girl was totally mystified and asked what that was.

'It means speaking in a language that God gives you,' Harold had replied.

The girl asked whether he could do it whenever he wanted to and Bredesen replied in the affirmative. 'Would you like me to pray for you this way now? I won't embarrass you,' he promised.

I was fascinated. 'What happened?' I asked. 'How did the girl respond?'

'Well,' said Harold, 'I'd no sooner asked her the question than I began to feel a prayer language welling up in my heart for her and I began to pray out the sounds with my head bowed. When I had finished and opened my eyes, the girl was almost ashen in colour.'

'Why . . . why . . . I understood you,' she gasped. 'You were praising God and speaking a very old form of Arabic.'

I listened goggle-eyed as Harold went on to report how the girl then shared with him that she was the daughter of an Egyptologist and that she herself spoke several forms of Arabic and had in fact studied archaic Arabic. She even complimented him on his accent.

'You spoke it like a Bedouin! Where on earth did you learn old Arabic?'

Harold told her he had never learned it. It was the language God had given him for that moment to impact her as a needy and perhaps slightly sceptical human being. And God had done it in a manner which would be incontrovertible to her mind.

It was certainly pretty astounding to mine. I had never heard anything quite like it. Did God still do this sort of thing in the twentieth century?

I would have to reserve judgment.

In the meantime I signed up as a summer worker with the Billy Graham Los Angeles Crusade. Billy Graham had already exercised a massive influence on my life. For one thing my friend Robert Footner, who had led me to Christ, had himself been won under Graham's ministry at Harringay in 1954, so I was a second-generation Graham convert. Then, a few weeks after my own conversion, had

come Dr Graham's controversial mission to Cambridge.
That had really set me on my feet. On top of this, my own
call to evangelism had taken place in the bowels of Madison
Square Garden after one of the New York Crusade meetings
in the summer of 1957. So Billy Graham was a special sort of
hero to me. And the Los Angeles Crusade was the cherry on
the top. The whole summer was a glorious challenge and a
mighty blessing. The final meeting, with 200,000 people
present in the Coliseum, was one of those moments I will
never forget.

But the Charismatic question was not forgotten and could
not be because another of my very close friends, Edward,
who had been deeply involved with both Inter-Varsity and
the Graham Association, suddenly got all caught up, boots
and all, in the Renewal.

One smoggy afternoon, a good friend from the Billy Graham Crusade headquarters called me into his office.

'Mike, what's going on with Edward?'

'What do you mean?' I responded apprehensively, as I
could see he was a bit put out.

'Well, we have had a complaint. Someone phoned his
house about Crusade business and was told he couldn't come
to the phone as they were all in a prayer meeting and there
had just been a prophecy or something in tongues which
someone was busy interpreting. What do you make of that?'

He looked mystified.

'Oh, brother, don't ask me,' I replied, 'I'm just as baffled
as you.'

Some weeks later Edward resigned his connections with
both Inter-Varsity and with the Graham Association.

That shook me. Seems like this whole thing is dynamite, I
thought. Better take it easy.

Chapter Five

THE LESSON OF THE LION

We must insist from the beginning that we believe
. . . in a Spirit world which can and does invade the
natural or phenomenal universe.

C. S. Lewis

Then Dave Fisher came back from Colombia. The whole
place down there was popping, he said, with strange happenings of the Holy Spirit. One story, which he told in a
newsletter, focused on one Victor Landero, a onetime
bartender who had also managed a stable of prostitutes.

Landero, an uneducated ruffian, had been converted in
1957 through reading a Bible which someone gave him. He
immediately rid himself of both bar and brothel and began to
share Christ with all and sundry in a remote unevangelised
area upriver to which he had moved. There were no missionaries around to tell him or his converts what could or
couldn't happen in the twentieth century. They just read and
learned from Victor's Bible and believed what they read
there. And the book of Acts began to get re-enacted. The
miraculous became part of their daily lives.

David's newsletter told of one incident related to an
extraordinary dream Victor had. Years later I read the same
story in a book by Professor Peter Wagner of Fuller Theological Seminary, one of the world's senior missiologists.
Maybe I should let Peter tell more fully the story. A professor's book perhaps carries more weight than a student's
prayer-letter!

One night Victor Landero had a vivid dream of a certain hut in the woods which he had never seen before. A clear voice said to him, 'The people in that hut are dying without Christ because no one ever told them of Him.' It took some time to do it, but months later Victor started out through the woods with no idea where he was going. After only two days, he came into a clearing and saw the hut of which he had dreamed. He knocked on the door, met the family, and told them why he had come.

The woman of the house was speechless. Only three nights previously, she had dreamed a strange dream. She saw her house full of people with a stranger talking to them out of a book. The word 'gospel' came to her in her dream, although she had never heard the word before.[5]

David Fisher narrated how the woman had then gathered her family and friends that evening to listen to the message from this mysterious stranger. Virtually all responded by committing their lives to the Jesus of whom Victor spoke. Staying with them for some days, Victor grounded them in the first principles of their new-found faith. In due time this little group became a thrilling New Testament Church, not untypical of many others springing up in extraordinary ways.

Wagner goes on to report how Landero had spent many hours with the believers in this area praying to God.

One day something unusual happened. They were overcome with a sense of joy that they could not explain. They prayed through the night, and read the book of Acts to each other. After they had done this several times, spontaneously one of them spoke in tongues! Others soon began to do the same.

A type of charismatic movement had started in the Colombian forest, but it was a 'spontaneous combustion' process. Obviously, this particular manifestation of the Spirit had come down from heaven. It was not something that had been taught to them by other Christians.[6]

It didn't end there. Soon after the gift of tongues, says Wagner, came the gift of interpretation.

> One of the first messages received through tongues and interpretation was a clear command to persevere in what they were doing. They received it as the voice of God. Then they started praying for the sick and many were healed. A blind man received his sight. A paralytic began to walk for the first time. Young men saw visions, and old men dreamed dreams. Everyone was praising the Lord.[7]

This kind of thing challenged the directors of the Latin American Mission (LAM) to their boots. Like the Inter-Varsity directors they were facing not theological arguments but facts. What were they to do?

David Howard, director of the Colombian field of LAM, a man with no Pentecostal inclinations, later wrote:

> Slowly, God removed our scepticism, confirming the gifts of the Spirit by showing the fruit of the Spirit in the lives of the believers who received these gifts. . . . They showed more love, joy, peace, and other Christian attributes than many Christians who had known the Lord for years.[8]

Peter Wagner concludes his section on Landero and his Colombian friends saying:

> Howard and his colleagues exercised Christian patience and tolerance in what was for them an unusual and difficult situation. They have never regretted it, for the Spirit has continued to work in many extraordinary ways, and most of all, the Lord is adding daily to the Church such as should be saved.'[9]

KEN STRACHAN

Anyway, as far as I was concerned, Dave Fisher's stories about Landero were very interesting, especially because they tied up in my mind with what I had heard in my last term at Fuller Seminary from Dr Kenneth Strachan, the General Director of the Latin American Mission.

Ken Strachan was one of the twentieth century's great missionary statesmen and leaders and LAM was, and is, certainly one of the twentieth century's great missionary agencies.

Strachan knew he had cancer and was in the home-straight of his life. What a privilege therefore when we students heard he was coming in his sunset days to lecture on missions for a term at Fuller Seminary. I listened avidly to everything he said, drank in the lessons he had learned, and cultivated his friendship at a personal level.

Few visiting professors who came to Fuller Seminary in those years made such an impact on the students as Strachan. The dedication of the man, the humanity and godliness of his character struck all of us. But what impressed me most was his spiritual, intellectual and indeed theological integrity in the face of some of the unusual spiritual phenomena breaking out in these infant Latin American Churches, especially in Colombia. After all, visions, tongues, prophecies and healings had hardly been an integral part of his mind-set up to that point.

If I remember rightly his own view up to then had been that these phenomena belonged with the first century Church to authenticate its word, but they had all stopped with the end of the apostolic period.

Yet now he heard of them in his own missionary 'area' as it were, and in Churches over which he had, in at least some remote degree, a measure of jurisdiction and responsibility.

Strachan reported to us how he had had these miraculous phenomena rigorously investigated by trusted colleagues. The result was that he had been forced to alter his own presuppositions about what God was doing in the twentieth century.

Nor is this always easy. Many of us would rather cling to our views of the possible than let these be shaken even by any evidence to the contrary.

A friend of mine in Durban was once leaving a little restaurant after a party with a group of friends. As he put his hand to the door, prior to opening it and stepping out into the street, he heard a lion roar. He knew it had been a good party, but not that good! He also knew he was not hearing things. Yet beyond that he knew by every instinct and by all presuppositions and by all conditioning, that there are no lions in city centres, not even in South Africa!

So, although slightly mystified, he stepped boldly out into the street – and almost into the jaws of – well, you guessed it – a real, live, larger than life, African lion. At which point his presuppositional world did a 360-degree somersault in a thousandth of a second as he pulled off a gymnastic feat which would have been the envy of an Olympic gold medalist. This feat launched him backwards like a space capsule through the door of the restaurant where he fell shamefaced at the feet of his astonished friends.

Of course, at that moment he did not know of the circus in town or of the frenzied lion-tamer struggling frantically to locate the whereabouts of his lost and wayward star performer!

My point is that one does sometimes have to change one's presuppositions in the face of facts. And Victor Landero's story, plus the honest testimony and conclusions of Ken Strachan, had changed mine – even as, in another sense, a lion in a Durban street had affected my friend on his evening out.

Chapter Six

STIRRINGS AMONG THE BONES

So I prophesied as I was commanded; and as I
prophesied, there was a noise, and behold, a
rattling; and the bones came together, bone to its
bone.
(Ezekiel – Chapter 37:7)

The latter part of 1964 saw four of us from Fuller Seminary
set out for Africa as the newly formed African Enterprise
team. Our burden for urban evangelism in Africa was real
and deep. We couldn't wait to get started.

Our views on the work of the Holy Spirit were safely and
soundly evangelical, as I have said, although our hearts were
open to know and learn more of His mysterious ways.

After some eighteen months of full and hectic campaigning
in Natal and Lesotho, where we conducted a nation-wide
evangelistic endeavour just prior to that country's independence, the door opened for me to attend the World Congress
on Evangelism in Berlin in late 1966.

This mighty gathering called evangelical leaders from all
over the world to come together for reflection on the imperative of world evangelisation. The theme was 'One Race, one
Gospel, one Task'. No one there would have doubted the
importance of the Holy Spirit in the task of world evangelisation yet, novice though I was to the world evangelical
scene, it struck me as curious that so few Pentecostals were
present, although much fuss was made of the presence of the
controversial Oral Roberts. Either evangelicals weren't too

interested in pentecostals, or pentecostals weren't too interested in world evangelisation. I wasn't sure which way it was.

In any event I couldn't become too concerned about that as I was fully preoccupied with the uproar caused in the South African delegation and beyond it by my treatment of the topic assigned me – 'Political Nationalism as an Obstacle to Evangelism'. I had shown how both white and black nationalisms could impede evangelism. Illustrating this from my own South African experience, I stood squarely on the theological toes of certain Dutch Reformed South Africans present. They even demanded from the Congress authorities that my paper be expunged from the Congress record. My only consolation lay in the fact that the more they thundered, the more friends I gathered from all over the world, many of whom have stood by me to this day.

Anyway, when Dick Halverson of Fourth Presbyterian Church in Washington, D.C., spoke on evangelism and the release of the Holy Spirit as an overflow of fellowship, as seen in Acts Chapter 2, I found myself under conviction by that same Spirit to apologise to my two Dutch Reformed friends for reciprocating hostility after their volcanic reaction to my paper. My apology was well received by one and rejected by the other. "I want to vomit and go home", he expostulated.

Perplexing though all this was, equally perplexing on a different front was the experience of being cautioned by one evangelical leader 'not to touch the Charismatic Renewal with a barge-pole', while another took me on one side over breakfast and told me how his whole life and ministry had been revolutionised by an experience which he called 'the Baptism in the Holy Spirit'.

I left Berlin wondering more than ever why a deep commitment to evangelism, a Pentecostal fullness of the Holy Spirit and an authentic social concern should not come together. Had not the Bible put all these ingredients into one holistic package and marked them 'Mix well'? That's how it looked to me. Yet the mixing didn't seem to be happening.

Flying on to the States following Berlin, I met at least two or three other friends from Fuller Seminary days who not only professed a new experience of the Holy Spirit, but who were manifestly different in consequence. One of them, now a relaxed free and loving person, had been one of the most rigid, unbending, up-tight spiritual automatons I had ever known. To see him so positively altered kept the cogs of my soul churning.

SHRINE AUDITORIUM

One day during that time a friend invited me to one of Kathryn Kuhlman's services in the Shrine Auditorium in Los Angeles. He wanted to reinforce in me the belief that God could still heal in the twentieth century. Having some sort of 'in' with somebody, he obtained two tickets so we could sit on the platform. Clearly he supposed that seeing might be believing.

Of course there were the inevitable sub-cultural hurdles to negotiate. First of all the organ prelude seemed more appropriate to the spins and whirls of an ice rink than a religious service. The flashing smiles of the short-back-and-sides henchmen everywhere bordered for me on the superficial and contrived. Miss Kuhlman's palais-glide entry on to the stage with a Lawrence-Welk-type spotlight and organ swell was almost more than I could handle. And her peroxide hair and evening gown for 2.30 in the afternoon threatened to become the last straw. My stiff upper lip grew stiffer.

But then something began to happen. The presence of God became very real. It seemed He could handle peroxide and spotlights better than I. Warm and worshipful singing uplifted Jesus, the Son of God. Vital and heartfelt praying called on the Spirit of God to manifest Himself. Miss Kuhlman preached a clear and straight Gospel message with no frills. People committed themselves to Christ.

Then came the healing section of the service. Keep in mind that my mood was that of sniffing out the phoney. My spirit was sceptical. Yet testimony upon testimony was given of healings right there in the service – often accompanied by manifestly authentic amazement and astonishment at the happening. A variety of people from housewives to a Los Angeles traffic cop testified to seeing from eyes that had not seen in years or hearing from ears that had not heard and so on.

My spirit through all of this remained on the alert for the faintest trace of anything staged, pre-planned or contrived. And I did not see it. I simply saw person after person, young men and maidens, old men and children, reacting with an almost New Testamental spontaneity at the mighty works of God in their lives at that moment.

THE LAME WALK

Perhaps the happening which impressed itself upon me most vividly was one involving a seven-year-old boy whose legs had been faulty from birth. According to his mother he had never walked in his life without brace and crutches. Apparently he had seen Kathryn Kuhlman on television and had said to his mother: 'Mummy, take me to that lady. Jesus is going to heal me through her.' The mother, not a church-goer of any shape or description, was reluctant, but finally agreed at the child's insistence. They had queued from early that morning and had thereby secured good seats right near the front.

During the healing service Miss Kuhlman suddenly said: 'There is a crippled child somewhere down on my left whom Jesus is healing right now. Please come out from wherever you are and get your leg-braces off.'

There was a stir and a gefuffle over in the left front section of one of the side aisles and people began to try to lift a grotesquely handicapped little boy over the seats.

'That's right,' urged Kathryn. 'Now get him down and get those braces off.'

My eyes were wider than saucers. What if this didn't work? What if he fell down and damaged his already damaged limbs further? I quaked almost as much for Miss Kuhlman as for the child and his trembling mother.

I was hardly prepared for what happened in the next moment. The braces removed, the child was lifted to his feet and helped up the steps to the stage by the mother.

'Now let him go, ma'am,' said Miss Kuhlman, 'let him walk on his own.'

A frantic look in her eye, the mother obeyed. The little fellow stepped gingerly forward – at first shakily and then more confidently. Across the stage from one side to the other he went, then turned round and walked back, a spellbound incredulity etched movingly on his little face. The mother stood frozen, ashen and transfixed, her hands clutched over her cheeks as if holding them in place, while the tears welled up and overflowed.

'Now,' urged Kathryn. 'I want you to run – over to the other side of the stage and back again. Come on. Off you go.'

With one bounding movement the child raced across the stage, not seeing his mother faint behind him as he did so. He spun on his heals, turned round and raced back.

Being, as I said, on the stage, I had a grandstand view of this. Sir Laurence Olivier himself could not have pulled off an act like that. Indeed it was no act. At least, no act of man. It was, I recognised, an act of God. And I could not deny it. Nor had I any desire to do so.

'I have never seen him walk before,' rejoiced his now recovered mother through her tears.

There and then I came to believe not just academically but deeply and truly that God still heals today.

LAWRENCE HAMMOND

Mind you, I was not without some persuasion of this already as my mind went back to the first time I had been faced with this sort of phenomenon.

I had been some years previously in the New York area visiting Mrs Marion Johnson, one of the leading lights in what was then known as International Christian Leadership – an outstanding ministry to civic and political leadership founded by the great Norwegian visionary, Abraham

Vereide. They mounted the annual Presidential Prayer Breakfast. I had come to know Vereide in 1960 and by attending the Presidential Prayer Breakfast in 1961 had been introduced to many others in that great outreach which continues ever more effectively to this day.

Marion was thus one of my new-found friends. She had urged me to visit her in one of my vacations. She was always full of the Spirit's latest happenings in her life and in the lives of her friends.

'Oh! Michael, dear,' she expostulated in her effervescent and grandmotherly way, 'I must tell you about how the Lord has healed my dear friend Lawrence Hammond who lives in Chicago.'

The story was so extraordinary that I resolved to go to Chicago on my way back to Seminary in California and get it first-hand from the horse's mouth as it were.

When I finally reached Chicago some weeks later, Lawrence Hammond greeted me warmly and told me his story.

As I remember it at this time distance, it went something like this. He had been taken terribly ill with some kind of intestinal blockage and other problems. This landed him in hospital where his condition deteriorated horribly. His tummy had blown up to the size of a football and was grotesquely swollen.

The surgery which was decided upon did not apparently give much ground for hope. Having insisted on knowing his true condition, he had been told his chances were slender.

'I think they were mainly interested in me as a guinea pig for medical science,' he laughed.

Anyway he decided to call his episcopal minister to come to his bedside to anoint him with oil and pray over him. This was two or three days before the operation.

He waited patiently, but desperation mounted as no minister appeared. Finally, the day the operation was to take place the new little curate who had just come to their Church arrived in a state of jitters at his bedside.

'I'm terribly sorry,' he apologised as he put his hat down

on the bed. 'Rector is out of town and can't come, so they asked me to come over. But I don't know what to do. They never taught us about healing at Seminary and I've never anointed with oil and I don't know what to do.'

'My heart absolutely sank,' Lawrence said to me. 'I had set so much store by a visit from our minister as I knew he believed in healing. Now here I was with this poor young fellow, quite lost and at sea.'

'Well,' he went on, knowing he had me all goggle-eyed and transfixed, 'I simply asked the curate if he believed God could heal, to which he replied in the affirmative. Then I asked him to lay hands on me and pray. The little fellow, almost ashen in colour, reached out his hands towards my bulging stomach. Then as he touched me and before he could pray it was as if a three-thousand-volt electric current went through me. The curate got such a fright he rebounded from the bed and literally fell to the ground, knocking his hat flying off my bed as he did so. And there and then the physical swelling of my stomach visibly subsided, like air coming out of a balloon or a soccer ball.'

Lawrence's face glowed as he told the story. 'So I pulled all the plastic tubes out of myself and leaped from my bed shouting "I've been healed, I've been healed!" By this time the little curate was up off the ground and we sort of danced a jig round the ward. All this noise attracted the attention of the Jewish rabbi who was passing the ward. He had often seen me and knew the seriousness of my condition. As he perceived the spectacle and saw my normal-sized stomach and gathered what had happened, he rushed out the door and down the passage shouting "It's just like the Red Sea! It's just like the Red Sea!"'

So there they all were – the whooping patient, the dancing curate and the ecstatic rabbi – when several horrified nurses rushed in calling for order, calm and sanity.

'But he's been healed,' beamed the curate.

'Yes, he has, he has, he has,' bubbled the rabbi.

Anyway, the nurses, now joined by a doctor or two, finally got Lawrence back into bed.

'I told them,' reported Lawrence to me as I drank in the story, 'that I was not going to have the operation. After many protestations I agreed with them that they could take me upstairs for some further tests, but that was all. Their tests revealed my condition as seventy-five per cent NORMAL and surgery was no longer necessary.'

Lawrence went on to relate how his condition picked up five per cent a day in the next five days. He was then discharged as normal.

'What are you going to put on my medical report?' he asked the bewildered doctor as he stood at the door of the ward.

The doctor paused, reflected and then with a quizzical look on his furrowed brow replied: 'I will put "Healed – Source Unknown"!'

And that was that. Lawrence left the doctor and nurses to their agnosticism and stepped out hale and hearty into the world to tell one and all that Jesus Christ still heals today.

It was quite a story. Certainly it prodded me to reflect further on the God with Whom we have to do.

FAITH

I began to wonder why we do not see more of this kind of thing in today's Church. Perhaps it is because there are so few around with the faith of children. Beyond that, Jesus said 'According to your faith be it done to you' (Matt. 9:29).

A Church so conditioned by twentieth-century naturalistic presuppositions presumably sees very little of the overtly miraculous because it believes in the supernatural so little.

Dr Rodman Williams, a Presbyterian writer, puts it this way:

We are having to learn much . . . in matters of the Spirit. We now know that the world of extraordinary healing, mighty works of deliverance, and so on, ought never to have become alien to us. It surely was not thus to the primitive Christians. We now realise that we have been blinded by a modern world view that intellectually and empirically views all that happens or may happen as belonging to the realms of natural forces.[10]

That was just how I felt I had been. Blinded. I had been and was far more a creature of my time than I realised. I had been limiting God by screening out what He could and couldn't do.

Rodman Williams further articulates the realisation which began to dawn on me in the weeks and months following the Shrine Auditorium experience:

Despite at times its slow process and our frequent falling back, we are beginning to move ahead in this world reopening before our eyes. It WAS true after all, what we read in the New Testament. By the Spirit of God, people really were healed of all manner of diseases and ailments: they ACTUALLY were delivered from forces of evil beyond the reach of natural means. For such is happening again in our midst.[11]

What struck me increasingly was the realisation that perhaps there really is more available for the Christian community as a whole to appropriate. The power of God is there, but our little faith does not release it. The situation is thus one laden with vast possibilities and potential.

Was this what even the great Karl Barth was recognising when he wrote of the Christian community as the place where 'astonishing' and 'extraordinary' things may happen? Said he:

The Christian community can and must be the scene of many human activities which are new and supremely astonishing to many of its own members as well as to the world around because they rest on an endowment with extraordinary capacities.[12]

Emil Brunner, another theological giant, in his book *The Misunderstanding of the Church*, puts it this way:

> We ought to face the New Testament witness with sufficient candour to admit that in this . . . Spirit which the Church was conscious of possessing, there lie forces of an extra-rational kind mostly lacking among us Christians today.[13]

What Brunner is here recognising is that the modern Church's problem is basically one of lack. The powers and endowments stemming from the Holy Spirit seem to be in short supply. When they do appear, as they did for me in a new way in that Shrine Auditorium, they are strange to us. But they were not strange to the New Testament.

This is not to say that most of us are unfamiliar with the power of the Spirit working through the spoken word to convert and convict and transform. To that power my own personal experience and indeed my own evangelistic ministry bore testimony in modest measure. But the sort of intrusion or manifestation in deed, as in the healing of the crippled child, I had not seen.

Perhaps this is what Dr Brunner is also feeling for when he observes from the New Testament that:

> Word and Spirit are certainly very closely connected. . . .
> There exists even in the New Testament a certain tension between Word and Spirit. 'The Kingdom of God is not in word but in power' (1 Cor. 4:20). The apostle Paul freely admits that he won the Corinthians not through words of wisdom but through demonstrations of the Spirit and of power. Here is indicated a reality which can reveal itself apart from words, like that power of the Spirit which struck down Ananias and Sapphira and killed as though it had been a powerful electric current. . . . We shall never understand the essential being of the New Testament Church if we do not take fully into account these revelations of the Spirit. . . . The Spirit operates with over-

whelming, revolutionary, transforming results. It manifests itself in such a way as to leave one wondering why and how.[14]

He adds:

> Here the mighty energies of the Spirit are more important than any word, although these energies, insofar as they are those of the Holy Spirit, owe their origin to the Word of God. Present day evangelists and missionaries usually realise this fact far better than we theologians who not only undervalue the dynamic power of the Holy Ghost, but often know nothing of it.[15]

An astonishing confession. But perhaps we missionaries and evangelists should not exempt ourselves more than the theologians.

Before leaving for South Africa at the end of that 1966 trip in the U.S.A., I heard the reactions of several senior Church leaders and academics who were looking at some of the same data facing me. Dr John McKay, a former President of Princeton Seminary, commented: 'The uncouth life of Pentecostalism is often preferable to the aesthetic death of the main line churches.'

Dr Henry van Dusen, one-time President of Union Theological Seminary in New York, voiced his conclusion after a world tour when he saw many aspects of the world-wide Church: 'I have come to feel that the Pentecostal movement, with its emphasis on the Holy Spirit, is more than just another revival. It is a revolution in our day. It is a revolution comparable in importance with the establishment of the original Apostolic Church and with the Protestant Reformation.'

Dr Sam Shoemaker, the celebrated Episcopal leader from Pittsburgh, was on record with the conclusion that 'God is trying to get through into the church, staid and stuffy and self-centred as it often is, with a kind of power which will make it radiant and exciting and self-giving.'

Dr Phillip Hughes, a British leader, and then Editor of the Anglican magazine, the *Churchman*, came away after a visit to California saying, 'The breath of the living God is stirring among the dry bones of the major, respectable and old-established denominations.'

If men like this were coming to conclusions like that, well, who was I to stand aloof? I returned to South Africa with my mind somewhat 'blown', as the saying goes, and with the intensified realisation that I, along with all Christians, had to come to terms more fully with what was going on around us.

Chapter Seven

REBEKAH AND A WORD OF KNOWLEDGE

Let her be the one whom Thou hast appointed.
(Abraham's servant – Genesis 24:14)

Back in the full swing of evangelistic ministry in South and East Africa in 1967, '68 and '69, I took up a position of openness and goodwill towards the new pentecostalism. My stance was one much like that more recently articulated by the Canadian evangelical scholar, Clarke Pinnock:

The new Pentecostalism seems to this observer to be a genuine movement of the Spirit of God renewing His church. I speak as an observer, who though standing outside the new Pentecostalism proper, has learned to appreciate it from personal involvement in charismatic groups.... From these experiences I have emerged a stronger and better Christian.... I agree with Karl Barth that there may often be too little of the pneumatic in the church (i.e. that which relates to the Holy Spirit) but never too *much*. Therefore it thrills my soul to see multitudes of people allowing the Spirit to operate freely in their midst.[16]

So wherever I went I encouraged openness to these fresh breezes of the Spirit. I could not perhaps help people in any dramatic fashion into new discoveries of the Spirit's fullness. However, I could at least encourage them along the way, not only in terms of openness to a new release of the Spirit within but in terms of altered presuppositions about the operations of the Spirit as a whole.

For me one momentous nudge in this direction came from the curious direction of my romantic life! Like most young single men, including Christians, I had had my fair share of heartaches in this area and made my fair share of blunders. Relationships of promise seemed to grind to a frustrating halt – either with a check in my own spirit, or in my lady-friend's, or in both of us.

One time, towards the end of 1964, and shortly before leaving Fuller Seminary to return to South Africa, I was caught up in a particularly complex tangle. I was at a loss to know which way to turn. Driving along a side road in West Los Angeles, headed towards a speaking engagement in Bel Air Presbyterian Church, I pulled the car off the road. I had a few minutes to spare and felt a deep need of some word from God about this anguished department of my life.

My mind turned to Genesis – the story of Isaac and Rebekah. What was immediately quickened to my needy heart was the word of Abraham to his servant. 'You will not take a wife for my son from the daughters of the Canaanites, among whom I dwell, but will go to my country and to my kindred, and take a wife for my son Isaac' (Genesis 24:3–4).

What impressed itself on me out of this story was that God wanted me, like Isaac, to find my life partner in my own country and among my own kindred. That meant I was not to marry an American girl, but a South African one. This rather helpfully ruled out a somewhat spectacular slice of attractive options!

Above all, like Abraham's servant, I prayed: 'Let her be the one whom Thou hast appointed' (Genesis 24:14). I also rejoiced in the obvious lesson of the story that God could circumstantially cope with this side of things and lead one to the right person. How touching were the servant's words when he realised that the maiden Rebekah, who 'was very fair to look upon' (vs. 16) was indeed the one appointed for Isaac. 'Then I bowed my head and worshipped the Lord and blessed the Lord, the God of my master Abraham, who had led me by the right way to take the daughter of my master's kinsman for his son' (vs. 48).

There was also beauty here in the way Rebekah's family could recognise: 'The thing comes from the Lord' (vs. 50).

And so 'Isaac . . . took Rebekah, and she became his wife; and he loved her' (vs. 67).

From then on the story of Isaac and Rebekah had very special significance for me. It was a challenge to caution, faith and dependence. After all, a major mistake in this area of my life and my ministry would be over. That I knew. And the point had been well underlined for me by Charles and Honey Fuller, who founded Fuller Seminary and who had prayed much for me regarding this side of things – especially Honey. Whenever I saw her she would tell me she was praying for the 'right girl'.

'It must be the RIGHT girl, Mike,' she would say with emphasis, 'the RIGHT girl.'

She even wrote me periodic little notes to believe God and trust Him. I was to wait for His provision.

WAITING

That was 1964. But waiting was easier said than done. Headstrong and faithless as I often was, I floundered around in confusion, impatience, frustration, failure, and in mistaken flights of fancy which hurt both others and me.

One old Dutch Reformed saint encouraged me that in the case of Adam and Eve 'the Lord . . . brought her to the man' (Genesis 2:22). 'If He did it for Adam, He can do it for you,' said my friend with a great roar of Afrikaans laughter as we drove one day along the Cape coast. 'Just relax, Mike, the Lord will bring her right across your path. You don't have to hunt as the Gentiles do!'

The five-year period from 1964 to 1969 was inevitably particularly difficult in this respect. Not only were they extremely demanding years of ministry, but almost all my friends were married. And nothing would gel for me. It seemed God had forgotten about me. And I was getting into my thirties. Over and beyond that, we were doing ministry on most of the varsity campuses of South Africa and inevitably meeting some of the choicest and loveliest Christian girls in the country. In missions too we saw the cream of the crop. Not surprisingly my colleagues, especially Chris Smith, who was an incorrigible match maker, were always picking girls out for me; a gorgeous choir girl or a dynamic secretary, or a budding pianist, and trying vainly to get me matched up and on my way.

TO A HEAD

Things came to a head for me in our city-wide mission to Nairobi. This spanned the latter part of 1968 and early 1969. The pressures on all sorts of fronts were enormous. Compounding it all was a tremendous sense of loneliness which suddenly gripped my life. Genesis tells us that in His created order God saw that everything was 'good' – with one notable exception. 'It is not good that the man should be alone' (Genesis 2:18).

I think I can honestly say that most of the time through those bachelor years the sense of God's companionship was real and satisfying. But it would be failing in honesty not to admit that awful moments of loneliness would suddenly descend on one, perhaps at weekends or else right after an exhausting and demanding mission. At such times I would either fight a mighty spiritual battle or else drift back in confusion or disobedience into former relationships which were not working out.

One Saturday afternoon in early 1969, when all the rest of the team were preoccupied, I went for a long walk under the warm African sun.

'Lord,' I prayed, 'this is the last major mission I can go through without the companionship and help of a wife. Please undertake and supply for me. May your Spirit guide me to the right person.'

Our next major endeavour was to Cape Town University in August 1969. A year of preparation had gone into the effort and things looked good. Excellent cooperation between student groups, superb publicity and months of fervent prayer all suggested a great mission ahead.

My own spiritual and mental preparation had also been intensive, but against a developing crisis in my personal life. Struggling vainly to get a relationship with a long-standing girlfriend to work, I finally said just before leaving for Cape Town: 'Lord, if you want me to remain single and serve you as an unmarried man, so be it. I have failed too dismally in this matter and disappointed You and others too deeply and struggled too frantically. Won't you now just take over this whole area unconditionally. I give up. Nothing is working out. And I am just failing You, myself and others in trying to handle it my way. Over to you, Lord. Single or married, I am YOURS. Do with me as seems good to you.'

The relief in coming to this important point was great, although I could not but regret that it took me until I was thirty-two before it really happened. Cheaply and glibly I had said that sort of thing before. But within a couple of days of leaving for the Cape Town 'Varsity mission, I prayed it and meant it more truly and sincerely than ever before.

CHRIS

One day, about five or six days before the mission, Chris Smith and I were busy with a mob of Christian students stuffing envelopes for a major publicity mailing. The door opened and in walked a very beautiful girl. Almost immediately she commanded the attention of the room. She was introduced all round as Carol Bam, a local school teacher and one of the assistant missioners, no less. One of the other lady missioners, allocated as mission counsellor to one of the women's residences, had gone down with malaria and the students had chosen Carol Bam as substitute.

Chris, true to form and ever alert to the main chance, immediately gripped my arm and pulled me over to the side of the room. Speaking in a whisper and with one eye half cocked in Carol's direction, he mumbled: 'If you fumble the ball this time, old buddy, you've really had it.'

'Come on, you rascal,' I replied, 'keep quiet and lick that envelope.'

And that was that – until a few nights later when Chris

again spoke of Carol as we walked round a field and enjoyed a late night constitutional before bed. But this was Chris all over again. Another back-firing mismatch in the offing.

The mission got underway with huge attendances in the lunch-hour, sometimes as many as 1500 students and once with 2000, and then good attendances of 700 or 800 in the evenings. The assistant missioners in the residences reported amazing openness and many conversions.

One evening, assistant missioner Carol Bam reported to me that she had two high-powered agnostic friends whom she had come to know when she was working part time in the science labs at Cape Town University some years previously. They wanted to challenge me. Would I go out to coffee with them? So there we were – two missioners defending the faith against two ardent but enquiring agnostics. It was a good evening.

Then, on Saturday, the day after the mission ended, Mission Co-ordinator Mick Milligan of the student YMCA, the best student Christian group I have encountered anywhere, had us all out on a picnic. Carol Bam occupied herself with the Milligan children. This frustrated Chris Smith. She also talked about taking a new teaching job 'next year'. Time and again Chris's scheming eye would catch mine. In the end, just to oblige Chris and not telling him, of course, I asked this elusive teacher how she would enjoy a game of tennis. We set it up for Tuesday afternoon.

Then came Sunday.

Chris and I went out for a hike on Table Mountain, starting at Constantia Nek and following the trails from the rear side of the mountain. I remembered that General Smuts, that great South African Prime Minister, had always found inspiration on the great mountain. We were tired after a mightily demanding week.

Inevitably Chris brought up his now favourite subject – Carol Bam. He urged me to take her out. I refused. He implored me to pray about her. I looked blank. He finally said: 'Won't you even CONSIDER her?'

'OK. If it'll make you feel better I'll consider her.'

'When will this man lay off and give up?' I thought to myself.

We hiked for an hour or so, finally scrambling to a magnificent promontory from which a majestic view opened up of the Southern Suburbs down on the left flank of Constantia Nek and the ocean down near Hout Bay on our right.

Our legs dangled over an impressive drop.

'Mike, why don't we have a word of prayer together right here and now about Carol?'

What could I say? How could I decline? It would be another in a long line of similar prayers with Chris going back over many years. But I could not be a total cad.

'Surely no harm in praying,' I reflected. 'All right, old buddy. You win. I'll pray.' My enthusiasm was less than total.

So we did. With a gentle Cape breeze ruffling our hair and with one of the most beautiful parts of South Africa spread out like a painter's canvas below us, we prayed.

We clambered up from our perch and set off across some rugged terrain to rejoin the trail. I had gone about forty yards when it happened. The nearest thing to a telegram from on High which I ever received.

'This is the girl. Go ahead.'

I almost stopped in my tracks. Nor did I doubt or query for a moment. It was unmistakable in its inner intensity. It was so clear. So simple. It was the voice of the Spirit. It was for me the word of knowledge. It was God. I was being enabled to know, in the supernatural, something I could not know in the natural. After all I simply did not know Carol at all at that stage. But here was one of those promised whispers from the same God who had of old assured us: 'And your ears shall hear a word behind you, saying, "This is the way, walk in it"' (Isaiah 30:21).

Believe it or not, I did not say a word to Chris. I think I was too overwhelmed. It was too momentous a moment to share with anyone but the Lord Himself. I just pondered the whole extraordinary happening in my heart. But my spirit almost bounded down the mountain. Chris seemed not to detect that

I was 'tripping the light fantastic' and we returned to the car with my secret intact.

In my heart now was the deepened realisation that the Spirit of God can and does still in the twentieth century speak clearly, directly and unmistakably. But should I have marvelled? Are not the Scriptures plain? 'I the Lord do not change' (Malachi 3:6). 'Jesus Christ is the same yesterday and today and for ever' (Hebrews 13:8).

CAROL

That night I preached to a packed student service in the Mowbray Methodist Church. And there she was – half way back – in the central aisle. And I loved her. For I knew she was 'the one appointed' for me. I suspect my sermon took wings!

After the service, I walked to the hall for the coffee time. Coming up the path as I headed for the hall, and all alone, was assistant missioner Carol Bam. We walked into the hall together and chatted with students. It was good to have her standing at my side. Later a student said to me: 'When I saw you two side by side chatting to students, I thought you looked good together!'

Anyway, I said nothing to Carol. But I looked forward to that tennis date on Tuesday.

Early next morning, about four o'clock, I was suddenly wide, wide awake, almost as if shaken awake by some unseen hand.

And now again the Inner Voice. Just as clear.

'You must stop Carol taking that job.' 'Why Lord?' I responded in my heart. 'Because she will be with you in Johannesburg and the States next year.' Very direct. Very specific.

It was a strange word – but one whose meaning in terms of Johannesburg and the States would later become clear. For the moment I only saw it as further confirmation that we would by then be married. But the bit about stopping her taking the job added urgency to my already excited spirit.

I remained reflective till dawn, then rose, prayed with

vigour and went to breakfast with only one thought. I must see Carol quickly and urgently. But when? Her whole day was occupied with teaching. My evening was committed to a student bull-session in one of the residences. The phone rang. My bull-session was cancelled. My evening was free.

I rang Carol's home and left a message with her mother for her to ring me. The call came late in the afternoon. Would she come out to dinner with me that night, I asked.

'Yes, but I must be in early as I have a lot of marking to do tonight,' she responded casually.

'Cool cat,' I thought. 'She has a surprise coming.'

We chatted casually over dinner, my excitement mounting. I liked what I heard. And saw. And sensed. Yes, this was the girl. The girl for me.

'Let's drive down to Hout Bay,' I suggested. On the way to the car we passed Westerford High School. She chatted cheerfully and then stopped me bolt upright saying, 'You know I had a funny experience today. I had to go for a job interview here at Westerford School. They want me to teach next year and have totally rearranged the teaching schedule to give me the class and subject I want – Matric Biology. It seems they have gone to tremendous lengths to accommodate my preferences. But suddenly I had this strange feeling that I couldn't take the job. Most mystifying – when it's just what I want. So the head has given me two days in which to make up my mind. Today is Monday. I must tell him on Wednesday.'

The job. The job. That was the word. The Spirit's word – at 4 a.m. 'You must stop Carol taking that job.' Everything went click. It was further confirmation. I would propose at the first suitable moment. And I did. Half an hour later, walking on the beach.

Carol was thunderstruck. Totally thunderstruck. She had been through a very distressing romance and had recently been engaged. She had lost thirty pounds in the whole experience, I learned later, and she had taken herself into deep trauma in the whole affair. She had accordingly resolved when the thing had broken up six months previously never to consider marrying anyone till she had known them at least two years. The whole scenario of her recent trauma and resolutions raced through her mind in split seconds of bewildered reflection. Now here comes this crazy missioner who proposes not after two years but after two hours of the first date.

'Well,' she said with total astonishment etched all over her face, 'I can't say yes and I can't say no.'

Then with typical feminine indecision and procrastination, she kept me waiting another full forty-five seconds before saying 'Yes!'

We were engaged to be married.

Back in my room I dived into Genesis 24 – the story of Isaac and Rebekah. With overwhelming joy and gratitude I read the words: 'Then I bowed my head and worshipped the Lord, and blessed the Lord . . . Who had led me by the right way' (vs. 48).

I also picked up *Daily Light*. August 18 had been quite a day. I read the Scriptures for the day. They included these words. 'What god is there in heaven or on earth who can do such works and mighty acts as Thine?' (Deut. 3:24). 'Who in the skies can be compared to the Lord? Who among the heavenly beings is like the Lord? O Lord God of hosts, who is mighty as thou art, O Lord, with thy faithfulness round about Thee?' (Ps. 89:6, 8). 'There is none like Thee among the gods, O Lord, nor are there any works like Thine' (Ps. 86:8). 'Because of Thy promise, and according to Thy own heart, thou hast wrought all this greatness, to make thy servant know it. Therefore Thou art great, O Lord God; for there is none like Thee, and there is no God besides Thee, according to all that we have heard with our ears' (2 Sam. 7:21, 2).

It was a great reading. Our God lives. And speaks. And acts. And reveals by His Spirit. He is not silent.

And to think of that poor girl with malaria whose place Carol had taken on the mission team and to grasp that a mosquito had brought my future wife to me! My, that was some bite! Some plan! Some God!

I went to sleep rejoicing.

Chapter Eight

ISAAC AND THE WORD OF PROPHECY

Make love your aim, and earnestly desire the
spiritual gifts, especially that you may prophesy.
St Paul – 1 Cor. 14:1

Poor Chris. We kept him in the dark. Carol wanted this a complete secret till she was ready to tell her parents who might need, she felt, some preparation for the shock.

All week I kept up the act. My, how I acted! How I dissembled! I didn't know I had it in me to be quite such a capable liar! The game was almost lost when Chris spotted white beach sand which had blown into my car that memorable evening at Hout Bay.

'Hey, Mike, what's this? Looks like Chappaquidick,' he expostulated with a bellow of Yankee laughter as my mind raced for some suitably absurd explanation. But Carol would not let me let on. In the meantime I just lived in Genesis 24 in the Isaac and Rebekah story, reading it, rereading it and savouring its import.

The following Saturday Chris and I were driving into the centre of Cape Town to meet with Elizabeth Whitsett, one of our African Enterprise Board members from the U.S.A., when he started on me again. 'Mike,' he said, 'I just wish you'd consider dating that girl, Carol. I've just had her on my mind so much for you. In fact I've even put a specific entry in my prayer diary that "God should join Michael and Carol Bam together in marriage".'

'Chris,' I responded with feigned exasperation, 'you know why I won't date her? I'll tell you. You're just putting too much pressure on me. I just don't want to talk about the girl again.'

'Well,' said Chris, with an audible groan of frustration as he prepared to play his final card, 'there's just one thing I want you to do. Please. Just one thing. I want you in your devotions tomorrow to read Genesis twenty-four – the story of Isaac and Rebekah. I've had it so much on my heart as somehow specially for you.'

Of course I almost burst inside with a combination of my own frustration at not being free to tell him, till Carol gave me the green light, plus my own joy at this yet further confirmation in terms of Isaac and Rebekah.

'All right brother,' I replied all poker-faced, 'just for you, tomorrow I'll read Genesis twenty-four about Isaac and Rebekah. Now let's close the subject and think about this luncheon.'

That afternoon, Carol and I slipped away for the weekend to a beautiful farm in Franschhoek, at the foot of the Hottentot's Holland mountains. Some dear friends who owned it had opened the way for us to go. It was virtually our first unhurried time together. And how delicious it was. Just to be together, walking through the vineyards, thinking, talking, dreaming, praying. How good God had been!

Next morning, very early, I rose and went out on to the mountainside for prayer, reflection and quiet.

Then just as strangely as some of these other things had happened, yet just as real, I suddenly felt the presence in a remarkable way of Charles and Honey Fuller. How they had exhorted me! And how they had prayed for me! How they had held on in faith! And now it was as if the veil of heaven, for they had both gone to be with the Lord, was being pulled back and we were all being permitted several mysterious moments of fellowship together. The sense of the experience lay in a communicated joy and relief and gratitude to God on their part that I had finally found the person of His choice for me – the one appointed – as they had prayed.

I later shared this experience with Dr Dan Fuller, their son, who lectures at Fuller Seminary.

'Dan, I don't understand the theology of the thing at all. But there you are. That's what happened.'

With a warm grin across his theologian's face he simply said, 'Strange things *do* happen. Very strange things.'

DISCLOSURE

On Sunday evening at the end of that weekend Carol and I returned to Cape Town where I had to speak at a students' follow-up meeting. Carol had by now agreed that I should no longer keep our secret from Chris. It was now six days since we had become engaged and we were becoming positively used to the idea. Now I could confidentially tell Chris, although we decided not to make it public till my ministry in Cape Town was over.

Before going to the student service I dropped Carol off to go ahead while I raced by Chris's room and captured his prayer diary. Finding the entry about Carol and me I simply wrote: 'Answered: Genesis 24:48' in bold red ink, scored it with a line above and a line below, pocketed the diary and set off for the service.

When it was over I suggested Chris come out with me for a drive as I was tired and wanted to escape for a while. We drove up to the top of Signal Hall which commands a majestic view of Cape Town, parked the car and surveyed the sparkling sea of lights, the marked semi-circle of empty darkness delineating the gentle curve of the famous Table Bay.

After a few moments I slipped my hand in my pocket, pulled his diary from it, and tossed it nonchalantly into his lap.

'What on earth is this?' he asked screwing up his eyes to see in the dark.

Then slowly, incredulously, he alternated his eyes from my wicked grin to his little book and then fumbled dumbly through to the page which carried his special entry.

There across it were the words: 'Answered: Genesis 24:28' (the verse tells of Abraham's servant bowing his head and worshipping and blessing the Lord for leading him 'by the right way'). It was a moment we would never forget. Chris simply exploded, like a sort of Vesuvius suddenly deciding it had been quiescent too long and that the moment had arrived for a good old-fashioned eruption. Midst laughter and banter, midst praise and prayer we reflected on the whole extraordinary saga. Truly our God is an amazing God. Is He not worth following and serving to the ends of the earth?

ELISSE

But now to the part of the story which constitutes the major reason for sharing this whole experience in such detail.

The weeks which followed were rich and memorable. Halcyon days indeed. It was life on the wing. In a dozen different ways, especially from the Scriptures, the Lord confirmed the rightness of it all. We announced our engagement on my thirty-third birthday, 24 September, and set the wedding date for 16 December (1969).

Some weeks later I had to leave for a brief period of ministry and report-back in the United States. During that time I was taken one day by my old friend, Ed, for lunch with a couple called Paul and Elisse Larsen who lived in Pasadena and whom I had briefly met some three years previously.

Paul and Elisse had long been involved in the Charismatic Renewal. According to Ed, Elisse had 'a well-matured prophetic gift'. I wasn't quite sure what he meant although back in 1966 in a prayer time following a meal at the Larsens', Elisse had burst forth in an extraordinary word of exhortation and revelation which was in the first person singular as if God was Himself directly speaking. At the time it seemed clearly that the word was for me, and everyone later was in accord with this. But how to integrate the happening into my current theological framework I wasn't sure. After all, I had not heard at any time in my growth and training along the way of the Lord speaking directly, other than in the Scriptures. Indeed I knew this sort of thing was suspect in many circles. And of course, even if genuine it was open to dangerous abuse. That I have seen many times since then.

OLD TESTAMENT

Whether or not prophecy in this sense could still happen outside the Scriptures, one certainly sees plenty of it inside the Scriptures, especially in the Old Testament. Time and again we find the Old Testament telling how the Spirit of the Lord would 'come UPON' one of the prophets who would then speak as from God.

Thus 'the Spirit of the Lord came upon Jahaziel . . . and he said, "Hearken, all Judah and inhabitants of Jerusalem and king Jehoshaphat: Thus says the Lord to you, 'Fear not, and be not dismayed at this great multitude; for the battle is not yours but God's'"' (2 Chron. 20:14–15).

Likewise Ezekiel testifies: 'The Spirit of the Lord fell upon me, and he said to me: "Say, Thus says the Lord"', and the message is communicated. The servant of God then delivers the Word and Ezekiel reports on it a few verses later saying, 'I was prophesying' (Ezekiel 11:5, 13).

Seemingly Ezekiel understands prophecy to take place when the mind and will of God are being conveyed through a human agent to God's people. The prophet hears or discerns the will and word of God and declares it. At that moment he is prophesying.

When we come to Isaiah and Jeremiah it is little short of astonishing how clearly they are able to reiterate: 'Thus says the Lord. . . .' or to testify unequivocally 'Thus said the Lord to me' (e.g. Jer. 13:1, 14:1, 15:1, 16:1, 17:19, 18:1, 21:1, 25:1).

On the other hand, we also know from the same book of Jeremiah the awesome responsibility of claiming to exercise such a gift and how the false use of it is an abomination to God and a fearful hazard to His people.

Again, from Jeremiah: 'Thus says the Lord of hosts: "Do not listen to the words of the prophets who prophesy to you, filling you with vain hopes; they speak visions of their own minds, not from the mouth of the Lord."' (Jeremiah 23:16). So it was possible even in the Old Testament for people to make supposedly prophetic utterances which were false and not authentically from God.

Another startling word: 'I did not send the prophets, yet they ran; I did not speak to them, yet they prophesied' (Jer. 23:21). Here is another picture of false prophecy and of wasted religious activity outside the will of God and out of accord with the divine mind.

More frightening yet: 'I have heard,' says the Lord, 'what the prophets have said who prophesy lies in my name, saying, "I have dreamed, I have dreamed!" How long shall there be lies in the heart of the prophets who prophesy lies and who prophesy the deceit of their own heart. . . . Behold, I am against those who prophesy lying dreams, says the Lord, and who tell them and lead my people astray by their lies and their recklessness, when I did not send them or charge them: so they do not profit this people at all, says the Lord' (Jer. 23:25–32).

I was not unfamiliar with this passage by 1969 and so the possibility of the counterfeit, which I have recognised even more markedly since that time, was not lost on me.

On the other hand, the question remained. Was there still in our day any genuine prophecy remotely comparable to that of which the prophets of old spoke? And what did the apostle Paul mean, for example, when in 1 Cor. 14:1, he says 'Make love your aim, and earnestly desire the spiritual gifts, especially that you may prophesy'?

Did that refer only to preaching as my orthodox evangelical teaching had always led me to believe? And could one say of preaching, as Paul does of prophecy in 1 Cor. 14:22, 'Prophecy is not for unbelievers but for believers'? If not, then perhaps prophecy is something which may not exclude preaching but which can on occasion go beyond it.

And what is Paul on about when he writes: 'Let two or three prophets speak, and let the others weigh what is said. If a revelation is made to another sitting by, let the first be silent. For you can all prophesy one by one, so that all may learn and be encouraged' (1 Cor. 14:29–31)? Paul ends this great chapter as he began it – on the primacy of prophecy. 'So, my brethren, earnestly desire to prophesy, and do not forbid speaking in tongues' (vs. 39).

It had been a perplexing set of wonderings in my heart ever since the first experience with Elisse in 1966. And now I was back with her again – and of course all full of the great happening with Carol which had so recently taken place.

After lunch we retired to the living room. Coffee over, Elisse suddenly said, 'Tell us, Mike, how you met Carol.'

I began to narrate the story in brief and had only got a few minutes into it when Elisse who had been listening in a relaxed way suddenly began to give the almost physical impression of someone welling up like a spring or a bottle about to overflow. I didn't quite know what was happening. Quietly Ed said: 'Mike, let's just be still for a moment before the Lord.'

Then, with her eyes closed, Elisse began to speak out in a strong but deliberate voice:

Son of Abraham –
  Son of Abraham –
    Son of Abraham ——
I have called you Isaac
And I have brought a Rebekah unto you,
                Isaac, my son.
I have snatched her out of a
snare and a trap of Satan and have given her unto you.
And as you heard in this thing and were
obedient, so you will hear even again my voice,
and regularly in other things, like a bell.
I will cause you to ride on the highways of the Earth.
Trust that which I am putting in your heart.
And there are some shakings that shall come upon you,
Yea, everything around you that can be shaken will be
  shaken,
And what remains will be of my Spirit.

In the midst of the battle, stand still in quietness and
   peace,
For this day I have kindled my fire within you.

My reaction after this was firstly one of awe, for I had said
nothing at all to Elisse about the years and years of Isaac and
Rebekah background with its climactic significance in recent
months when both Chris Smith and I had independently felt
so powerfully led into the story. Of course I was also greatly
excited at yet more confirmation about Carol. On the other
hand I was fearful about the shakings. Unbeknown to me our
team was due in the following two years to enter such a set of
convulsions as would leave the ministry almost destroyed.

During this time of convulsion all I had to hold on to were
these prophetic words plus the accompanying assurance that
God was somehow in it all for His purpose. Otherwise I
would have given up. But on 23 November 1969, in the
Larsens' home, I was not to know any of that. My preoccupa-
tion was with the marvellous word of confirmation about
Carol, and the utter mystery of its being couched in the Isaac
and Rebekah categories with which I had been living so
intensely throughout that time.

Later Elisse told me that every time I mentioned Carol's
name in the post-lunch discussion the name Rebekah leaped
overwhelmingly into her mind until finally she had to burst
forth in that prophetic word.

APPLYING PRINCIPLES

Inevitably, of course, apart from the personal side, was the
theological. For here incontrovertibly to my mind, was the
operation of yet another supernatural, charismatic gift. And
if it could happen once authentically, it could happen again.
Not only could but should.

One of the things which intrigued me was that this sort of
prophetic utterance was not something I expected and was
not part of my pre-suppositional world, as it were, in any
significant way. My exposure to such things had been mod-

est, to say the least, and I was not therefore spiritually pre-programmed to be favourable. It was therefore another big surprise. But not one I could ignore.

On the other hand I stood in need of that sort of divine confirmation, given the speed with which my relationship with Carol had developed. How marvellous, therefore, that God in His graciousness had granted such confirmation with such clarity through His Spirit's working!

And so this thought pressed itself in upon me even more deeply. Was not the modern Church often short-changing itself, screening out by presupposition, pride and prejudice aspects of the fully supernatural heritage which was not only part of its birthright but should be part of its normal life?

After all, so many of these things are in our theoretical theologies or in our lectures on the early Church or the book of Acts. But are our theologies not meant also to be operational and functional not simply in terms of their central teaching and experience of salvation and the new birth, but in terms of their outworking in the Spirit's daily equipping of us for life and ministry?

Somehow it seems we have talked ourselves, often quite eloquently, into an acceptance of something less than what was the norm in the early Church. Thus Charles Williams in his sensitive little volume *The Descent of the Dove* can lament that 'the languages and habits of heaven seemed for a few years, a few decades to hover within the church after a manner hardly realised since, except occasionally and individually'.[17]

But did God intend it to be thus? In any event it is undeniable that millions of believers in our time are beginning to give a negative answer to that question. God did not mean it to be thus, they say. John Taylor in *The Go Between God* recognises this and concludes:

> The whole weight of New Testament evidence endorses the central affirmation of the Pentecostalists that the gift of the Holy Spirit transforms and intensifies the quality of human life and that this is a fact of experience in the lives of

Christians. The longing of thousands of Christians to recover what they feel instinctively their faith promises them is what underlies the whole movement.[18]

My conclusion after this experience with Elisse was that at the very least something supernatural and of God had taken place.

But was it prophecy?

NEW TESTAMENT TEACHING

Obviously Old Testament prophets as such are not going to be duplicated in the same way in the modern day. After all, Scripture is written down and the canon of both Testaments is closed. On the other hand prophecy and the prophets form an obvious line of continuity between Old and New Testaments, the Old Testament prophetic line not ending with Malachi, the last of the Old Testament writers, but with John the Baptist. Said Jesus: 'For all the prophets and the law prophesied until John' (Matt. 11:13).

In John the Baptist we see a combination of proclamation and prediction as He declared that there was both wrath to come (Luke 3:7) and grace to come through Jesus, the Baptiser in the Holy Spirit (Luke 3:16).

As such John stands as the link between the two Testaments.

So what about the New Testament ministry of prophecy? For example, if we are to desire especially to prophesy, as Paul says in 1 Cor. 14:1, what is he asking us to desire?

Perhaps the answer comes partly as we see the makeup or composition of the word and partly as we see how the Bible uses it (see Appendix B).

The word 'prophet', from the Greek *prophetes*, is made up of two Greek parts – *pro* (meaning 'before' or 'for') and *phemi* (meaning to speak). So the prophet is one who 'speaks before', in the sense of proclaiming ahead of time, or the one who 'speaks for', in the sense of speaking for God.

This would suggest that prophecy includes both the pre-

dictive element in the sense of foretelling, and the proclama-
tory element in the sense of telling forth the will of God. Both
of these elements are obviously present in the Old Testament
prophets.

But what of the New Testament? Bullinger's Greek lexicon
says of the word *propheteia* (prophecy) that it means 'speaking
forth utterance inspired by the Spirit of God, referring either
to the past, present or future. Prediction is not the main
feature, but a showing forth of God's will.'

In Elisse's words to me, both ingredients were present.
Confirming Carol as the partner of God's choice and will was
primary, yet the predictive element was there also, as a
general word about my future ministry ('I will cause you to
ride on the highways of the earth') as well as advance notice
of an impending crisis ('Everything around you that can be
shaken will be shaken').

In broad terms my own reflections on the New Testament
data tell me that prophecy is that process whereby a believer,
under the inspiration or special anointing of the Holy Spirit,
may declare forth or confirm the will of God, relating to
either the past, the present or the future in such a way as to
edify and upbuild Christians or on occasion convince and
convict the outsider.

One friend summarised it for me saying: 'Prophecy happens when someone who has listened for the word and will of
God declares it.' For me that gets closest to it.

I have set out some of the New Testament data on this in
Appendix B if the reader would like to explore this a little
further.

Suffice it for now to say that that morning back in 1969,
with all that had preceded it, was evidence enough for me
that God had not only spoken through His prophets of old
but that He still speaks today.

The issue in one sense is – did God speak? – or – does God
speak?

My conclusion is that He *does* speak.

Chapter Nine

GATHER TO ME MY FAITHFUL ONES

One man's piety is another man's poison.
Richard Lovelace

Maintain the unity of the Spirit in the bond of
peace.
St Paul – Eph. 4:3

When I was a student at Fuller Seminary in the early 1960s there were a number of Scriptures by which God challenged me significantly. They became part of God's mandate to me for my life.

One of these was Psalm 50 verse 5: 'Gather to me my faithful ones.' It was not that I felt I by myself could do this or that God was laying such a mighty injunction upon me alone. I simply recognised that the Scriptures here revealed a deep desire in the Divine Heart that His people should be *together* – together with Him and with each other. And I saw in this Scripture an injunction – no doubt to all God's people – but at that moment quickened to my own heart and finding a response of resolution in my own will. There and then I decided that I would like to be part of that process, seemingly close to the Lord's heart, of drawing Christian believers together.

The appalling fragmentation of the Church struck me as a scandal. What could the world possibly make of us as we tore each other down, competed, criticised, worked at cross-purposes and carried on a sort of religious trench warfare?

This is the jolly procedure of lobbing theological or other sorts of grenades at each other from the safety of our own religious trench, which is just another name for an extra deep rut. We then block our ears while the thing explodes with shattering consequences in the other trench of our fellow Christian soldiers just over the way! What kind of an army is that? What sort of teamwork is that? What sort of enemy would be impressed by that? Certainly no football, baseball, rugby or cricket team could function that way. But the Church often does. And the tragic, often paralysing consequences are plain for all the world to see.

I remember as a child playing soccer one day during a break between classes. I was just about to score an easy goal, both the goalkeeper and backs being out of position, when I was knocked down from behind. I went flying. The ball went flying. And my dramatic goal was never scored. However, imagine my consternation when I found that the fellow who had knocked me over was on my own side!

And that is how it often is in the Church. When one is about to attempt a goal for God – a great campaign, a new outreach, a special endeavour – one is knocked over, by one's own side, from behind! Never from the front. Christians tend to be allergic to frontal assault. They prefer the verbal dart – from behind. And it's not the Marxists, Moslems, atheists, free-lovers or secularists who knock you over either. It is other Christians.

This spectacle made me resolve that whatever the hazards, and I was not unaware of them, we would commit ourselves in our own style of ministry in African Enterprise to a cooperative approach with all those who could sincerely subscribe to the historic creeds of the Church. Our own message would remain unswervingly evangelical in its content and in its attempted faithfulness to biblical revelation, but we would also try nevertheless to be catalysts and contributors to the process of 'gathering the faithful ones' unto their Lord.

After all, not only would this strengthen their effectiveness and add new credibility to their witness, but it was also integrally related to the work of the Holy Spirit. For the injunction of Scripture is to 'maintain the *unity of the Spirit* in the bond of peace' (Eph. 4:3). In fact St Paul goes further and says that 'if there is . . . ANY PARTICIPATION IN THE SPIRIT. . . , complete my joy by being of the same mind, having the same love, being in full accord and of one mind' (Phil. 2:1–2).

He sees *any* participation at all in the Spirit as carrying with it this imperative of Christian accord, fellowship and cooperation. Earlier in that same epistle he comes on even more strongly. 'Only let your manner of life be worthy of the gospel of Christ, so that whether I come and see you or am absent, I may hear of you that you stand firm in one spirit, with one mind striving side by side for the faith of the gospel' (Phil. 1:27). Clearly Christian conduct which is worthy of the Gospel is to be marked by unity and cooperation in the Gospel, and those who sincerely seek to follow the biblical Christ are both to 'stand firm' in the Gospel and strive side by side for it 'in one Spirit' and 'with one mind'. In short there is to be a true 'partnership in the gospel' (Phil. 1–5). The reason for this, as we see in Jesus's prayer in John 17, is 'that the world may believe'. It is quite simple. Christian disunity, rivalry and isolation from one another makes the Gospel unbelievable to the world and quenches the work of the Spirit. Indeed if we are 'eager for manifestations of the Spirit' (and who is not?), then according to the Apostle we are to 'strive to excel in *building up* the church' (1 Cor. 14:12). Multitudes of Christians excel in tearing down the Church. How many excel in building it? But if we want to see the Holy Spirit released and manifested, that is where we are told to excel – 'in *building up* the church'. Specialists in construction. That's what we need. Not destroyers.

DIVERSITY

My observation of things back in the early '70s has been well summarised by New England theologian, Richard Lovelace, in his book *The Dynamics of Spiritual Life*. He writes:

The instruments through which God works in the church are human beings. If our hearts and minds are not properly transformed we are like musicians playing untuned instruments or engineers working with broken and ill-programmed computers. The attunement of the heart is essential to the outflow of grace. . . .[19]

He goes on:

There are many lines of estrangement in the modern church which are readily dissolved by the application of a balanced understanding of spiritual dynamics. For one thing, different groups within the church are at odds with one another because their models of the Christian life, its beginnings and its fullness, are so diverse. One group of genuine believers can never remember a conscious conversion to faith in Christ; another insists that a datable experience of being 'born again' is essential; a third says that a second distinct experience of 'the baptism of the Holy Spirit' is necessary for Christian maturity. When we 'test the spirits' in the lives of representatives among these groups, we often find an equal level of spiritual vitality – or deadness – in each sector. The Christian life is being offered in diverse packages, but what is inside is the same – newness of life in Christ. Nonetheless, the different groups enjoying this life are readily offended by one another's packages. One man's piety is another man's poison. What is needed to reconcile these models is a 'unified field theory' of spirituality.[20]

In other words, these different groups need to get together, because each has strengths and weaknesses and each has something to give and something to learn from the others.

There is also the problem of language and vocabulary. Adds Lovelace:

Remember that genuine experience of Christ has generated several different theological languages during the church's history. Because of human limitations and the grandeur of the subject, no single language has been adequate to convey this. Reporters on Christian experience who describe it in a language strange to us may only be viewing the same thing from another perspective. We need to listen with care and sensitivity for the distinctive notes of true Christianity expressed in unfamiliar patterns.[21]

One of the things for which I have always been thankful in our style of cooperative evangelism in African Enterprise is that it has enabled us to meet almost all sections of the Church of Christ and to discover that no one has all the truth or all the darkness. We all have a bit of each. Moreover as our evangelism so often required that we talk to people who never talked to each other, we increasingly became persuaded in the early 1970s how wonderful it would be if we could organise an opportunity for some of these people to meet and relate and share – in fellowship.

Imagine if ecumenical social activists, evangelical pietists and neo-evangelical evangelists could all confer. Imagine if Pentecostals and non-pentecostals, Charismatics and non-charismatics could share their riches. Would such an encounter not bring all of us closer to the full-orbed truth of Christ and His word?

DURBAN '73

Great then was my delight when towards the end of 1967 the Spirit of God placed in our hearts the burden and vision for a South African Congress on Mission and Evangelism which would seek to draw together South African Christians from all backgrounds to look at the vital issues of mission and evangelism in our complex crucible.

The Congress took over five years to bring to fruition and it was only in March 1973 that it finally happened.[22] But it was not fully representative. The Pentecostals for the most part were not there. Nor were the Dutch Reformed. The involvement of both in a major ecumenical experience in South Africa had to wait till the giant South African Christian

Leadership Assembly (SACLA) in July 1979. As for the Charismatic Renewal, in 1973 in South Africa it was only a trickle or a stream, not the mighty river it has since become.

However what we learned in mounting the Durban Congress, which became a watershed in a number of ways for the South African Church, was just the sheer difficulty of getting Christians together. Yet what richness and spiritual blessing there was once this happened and once everyone was over their fears, hang-ups and caricatures about each other.

For example as we moved into high gear in planning, one South African evangelical actually went to the Billy Graham Headquarters in Minneapolis to try to dissuade senior aides there from encouraging Dr Graham to come. Reason? Some ecumenicals were to be involved in the South African gathering.

Another North American leader phoned me about the ecclesiastical mix and said: 'You can't do it this way. We won't have it.'

'What kind of theological imperialism is this?' I thought.

'Brother,' I said, quite calmly, 'we are doing it this way!'

Yet another leader, a prominent non-charismatic, wrote: 'You can't include David du Plessis, the big Pentecostal, on your programme.'

Another polite contradiction: 'Brother, we *are* including David du Plessis. Sorry to disappoint you.'

Then there were social activists who said 'You mustn't have Billy Graham.' Others objected to Hans Ruedi-Weber of the WCC. And so it went on. All the Peters saying: 'No, Lord, keep me away from my Cornelius!'

Yet, surprisingly, once they were all together the world did not cave in! In fact, it went on more merrily than ever!

One evangelical went up to Hans Ruedi-Weber at the Durban Congress and said: 'Does the World Council know that you are giving such evangelical Bible studies?'

'But they pay me to give such studies,' replied Hans Ruedi with a twinkle.

'Ah yes,' murmured the mystified delegate, moving away into the crowd.

I was near the North American leader who had opposed David du Plessis' participation just after David had finished his major talk. The opposer had been waiting tensely for a plug on tongues. Instead came a mighty and anointed evangelical address on 'Forgiveness'. Nothing about tongues at all!

'Wow!' he whispered to his neighbour, 'I didn't know Pentecostals could talk like that.' His damning had been based on distance. He was down on what he was not up on – which is my wife's definition of prejudice!

Several very hot social gospellers and political activists gasped when they heard both Billy Graham and Leighton Ford plead that the personal Gospel be 'fleshed out' in compassionate social concern.

As for Billy Graham's evangelistic rally which took place with 50,000 people present midway through the Congress, one Catholic priest who had never been in on an evangelistic rally, let alone seen 4,000 enquirers respond to an evangelistic invitation, burst out: 'Oh, may it be a milestone for South Africa!'

Yes, this was richness indeed. At every level – theological, social, political, evangelistic and Charismatic – Christians learned from each other.

FORGIVENESS

When it came, in the Congress, to our special area of concern for this book – namely the work of the Holy Spirit – there was value indeed in hearing a range of viewpoints in fellowship.

David du Plessis began by noting how for years the Person and work of the Holy Spirit had been neglected and ignored, but now a 'great change' had come, with most denominations giving prominence in their councils and assemblies to this great theme.

Du Plessis stressed how he saw 'forgiveness' as a key prerequisite in terms of the fullness of the Holy Spirit!

There came a day when God challenged me to go to my

brethren in other churches. 'But Lord, they are dead!' He said: 'Yes, but I never sent any disciples to bury the dead. I sent them to raise the dead.' – 'But they're enemies.' God said: 'I have given you an invincible weapon against your enemies. *Love* your enemies.' I said: 'How can I love people who do things of which I cannot approve?' God said: 'Forgive them. Forgive them.' I said: 'Lord, I can't forgive them. How can I justify their teachings, their actions, their deeds?' He said: 'I never gave you any authority to justify anybody. I only gave Christians authority to forgive everybody.'[23]

David went on to tell how he also felt called, to the alarm of some of his friends, to minister to Catholics but with the Lord's exhortation:

Don't minister to Catholics if you cannot love them. And as long as you condemn them you are not loving. You cannot love if you don't forgive. The more you love, the easier it is to forgive and the more you forgive the easier it is to love. Love is a fruit of the Spirit and an unforgiving spirit ruins your love, but a forgiving spirit increases the fruit of the Spirit. . . . My friends, my life was completely revolutionised from the day I began to practise forgiveness.[24]

FULLNESS

When it came to the difference between receiving the Spirit and being baptised in the Spirit du Plessis noted that Jesus came and said to a theologian: 'You must be born of the Spirit.' But he didn't say how.

When he came to the woman at the well, he didn't use that theological term at all. There he said: 'I can give you a drink of living water which will satisfy you for ever. Everlasting life. You'll have a well in you.' Then on the day of the feast he explained how this could happen: 'If any one thirst, let him come to me and *drink*. He who believes in me . . . "out of his heart shall flow rivers of living water" (John

7:37–8). Out of you, not in you. Note too, he did not say 'out of your head', but 'out of your heart'. In other words, 'out of your innermost being will flow rivers of living water', not out of your head. It's your heart he's talking about.

David then stressed his view that it is in the new birth and conversion that we come to Christ and 'drink', as it were, of 'the water of life, freely'. That is when we become sons and heirs. That is when the Spirit comes *into* a man. But when you come to baptism, water is put not into us, but ONTO us or upon us. No baptised baby drinks water. Therefore, concluded David:

> Baptism in the Spirit is the Spirit upon you, but a drink is the Spirit within you. I'm so glad to tell you I know thousands of beautiful Christians who have indeed had a drink, and have a well within them, and are therefore sons and daughters of God, even though they claim no baptism in the Spirit. I don't call baptism in the Spirit the infilling. I call the drink the infilling. A baptism is not into you, it's upon you. So today if you want a drink, Jesus alone can give it to you. If you want the baptism, Jesus is the only baptiser. Nobody else. That's where you get the blessing and that's the Pentecostal message.

This fascinating, though controversial and, to many, unorthodox understanding of this doctrine intrigued Congress delegates and paved the way for several testimonies, two of which interested me particularly.

BILL BURNETT

First came Bill Burnett, then Anglican Bishop of Grahamstown, and late Archbishop of Cape Town till his early retirement from that post in 1981. He admitted an element of surprise at finding himself giving a 'testimony'. 'It doesn't seem properly Anglican,' he noted with a twinkle, 'it doesn't sound quite British!'

Burnett then went on to relate that in his own experience it seemed to be more God searching for him, than he for God. 'If my search had been what counted, I think I'd still be crawling around on hands and knees,' he said. He then related how he had been baptised 'in a fit of absent-mindedness, sent to a Church school, meaningfully confirmed, regularly dosed on injections of grace, and finally converted at seventeen while reading a book.' A call to the ministry followed.

However, whether in preaching, putting out theological statements, working for better race relations, or struggling for Church unity, something always seemed to be missing – the power of the Spirit of God. He began to long for a fresh empowering through the Holy Spirit. On Sunday, 13 March 1972, it happened.

Said the Bishop: 'It was curious. I had no desire to be Pentecostal at any time. I knew nothing about it in point of fact. I wasn't aware at the moment it happened of even a sense of need. I had just come from a retreat where I had had loving communion with God. But on Saturday, March 12th, I was preaching in a church school in Grahamstown on the text: "The love of God is shed abroad in our hearts by the Holy Spirit who is given to use". I felt my heart warmed somehow or other. Then after Holy Eucharist next day in the same chapel, I retired home for a quiet Sunday. I was reading a Sunday newspaper. Not very edifying literature. There was just a quarter of an hour before lunch. Somehow I felt a tug to go to my chapel and while I was there I just began to pray in silence, as was my custom, and to sense the presence of God so that He could do with me whatever was in His will. On this occasion I simply offered to Him every part of my body I could think of.

'Before I could get through the catalogue, somehow, quite unexpectedly, the Holy Spirit fell on me. I didn't know quite what was happening. Quarter of an hour was up by then and I had to go to lunch. But after lunch I couldn't rest. I had to go back to the chapel where I was blessed anew and refreshed. I rejoiced and then found myself praising God in a wonderful new way. I didn't know what it was, I was simply praising God! I was also full of joy, and delight and full of his love. That was why I was praising God because his love had simply filled me to overflowing in a way I'd never known before. Of course I knew before that God loved me. I knew that at my conversion, but somehow it hadn't been the same full blessing of his love.'

Bishop Burnett told of the great difference this experience had made in his life and ministry. 'It has brought,' he said, 'a new freedom to love and a new joy in prayer. No longer is prayer talking to the wall or the eiderdown. It really is a fellowship and a dialogue in prayer, a rejoicing and a delight. And, what's more you can go on and on and on! I find also a new power over sin, a new power in proclamation, a new ability to forgive.'

This testimony intrigued me no end because Bill Burnett had been my chaplain at high school, so I knew him from way back. And, no doubt about it now, he was a changed man. Indeed his influence since that time has been mightily used under God to accelerate a major impetus of renewal in the Anglican Church of South Africa.

Shortly after Burnett's experience, the Archbishopric of Cape Town became vacant.

'Too bad about this Pentecostal thing,' said many Anglicans, 'he would have made a good archbishop. But that's disqualified him.'

Others, more daringly, whispered, 'Do you not think that just possibly this new experience in the Holy Spirit may have happened to EQUIP HIM FOR THE JOB?'

It was a wild idea. Almost unthinkable. A Charismatic archbishop. The thing seemed virtually a contradiction in terms.

In the event Burnett was swept into the position by one of the quickest, easiest and most uncontested archepiscopal votes in the history of the Anglican Church in South Africa.

TOM HOUSTON

A very different sort of testimony, and to me equally valid and important, came from the British leader, Tom Houston, a Baptist. He testified that his search for the fullness of God had been a 'series of failures'. In twenty years of searching, Tom said, he had tried the Hudson-Taylor way, the George Muller way, the Charles Finney way, the John Wesley-Nazarene way, the East African revival way, the Keswick way and for four years the Pentecostal way. He had even had what some termed the Baptism in the Spirit!

The end result of all this was the realisation that the ultimate fullness of God is only for God! The important thing which emerged for Tom was not that he should have all of God, but that God should have all of him, whether for emptiness or for fullness.

Said Tom:

I suddenly realised I was after the wrong thing – that I couldn't have an experience that would make me God. And as I searched for the fullness of God I realised I was seeking to feed my pride. Tom Houston was to be God's gift to the Church, God's gift to the pulpit. That had to go. Having tried all these ways I came back to realise that what was important was not what I had of God but what God had of me. Indeed his search for me became truly important. If I was to go back over my life, I could show again and again that the spiritually significant things in my life took place when He reached down and, unsought, did that which was remarkable in my experience. I was converted that way. Nobody spoke to me, nobody followed me up, nobody gave me follow-up literature. I had none of these things. God just reached down when I was a boy and grabbed me.

Now what does it all add up to? It all adds up to the fact that the initiative was always His. There is never a time when God is not working in my life or in the work to which He has sent me. He doesn't go to sleep like the gods Elijah talked about. What is required of me is response in two basically simple ways: first of all the response of an up-to-date repentance so that there is nothing in my life about which I am not in the open, with God and my fellows; and secondly the response of faith to what I know of Him – as Father, Son and Holy Spirit.

Tom then underlined du Plessis' emphasis on forgiveness as it related to the Spirit's fullness. To Tom the greatest thing about the power of the Spirit was that He brought the capacity to forgive into the believer's life. 'If you forgive, it opens things up. If you don't, it seizes things up.'

This surely, said Tom, was the heart of Pentecost.

This can be seen from so many angles. Here was Jesus, who had been judicially murdered. Fifty days later His men go onto the streets and say to the people: 'You did it.' They did not mince words. But they did not go on to say: 'Pilate should be put from office; we should impeach Caiaphas; something should be done about Herod.' They went and said unequivocally, 'You did it!' Then they preached forgiveness. And what else could Peter do? For when Jesus came back, He came back loving and forgiving. Peter, sick at heart with his sin, was reinstated with love and forgiveness by the Lord. How could he have any other message when he got up to preach at Pentecost? That was the miracle of Pentecost. It had never happened before, where a party whose leader had been judicially murdered went onto the streets and preached forgiveness to those who had done it. No wonder there were three thousand converted in one day.

We also know, that we cannot have forgiveness in a cup for ourselves. We can only have forgiveness as in a channel or pipe when the other end is open and forgiveness is flowing through us to others. When that is happening we will see evangelism which really works![25]

COMPLEMENTARY

As I said, this was a very different type of story. Yet what struck me most was not the difference in these three stories but their complementary nature. Du Plessis, Burnett and Houston were all saying important things and listening to the three men one had a powerful sense of the Spirit's deep and overflowing work in all of them. All were testifying with different vocabularies to the Holy Spirit as the author of new life and grace to their lives. All three were dynamic men of the Spirit, though their testimonies varied. All three were and are still being mightily used by God. Works of grace and rivers of new life flow from all three. And besides, was it not splendidly healthy to learn from different Christians who could share their quest and experience with such integrity and honesty?

As far as I was personally concerned I began in the Durban '73 congress to find one little clue in this whole enquiry which became increasingly important – the life, vitality, fruit and evidence of the Spirit's presence are more important than the labels, semantics and vocabulary attached to the phenomena.

On the other hand, we couldn't avoid struggling with the theology of it all and that process continued for me after the Durban Congress was over.

The congress experience, with its multiplicity of Christian viewpoints, also persuaded me more than ever that true togetherness in the Christian Church was worth striving for as the matrix out of which could come not only the Spirit's release and greater manifestation, but also the greatest forward movement of mission and evangelism.

As David Watson, the prominent Anglican evangelist, has said:

> Unless renewal precedes evangelism, the credibility gap between what the church preaches and what the church is will be too wide to be bridged. It is only when the world sees the living body of Christ on earth that it will be in any way convinced of the reality and relevance of Christ himself.[26]

Chapter Ten

HELPS ON THE WAY

The eminently humble person, though he be
inflexible in his duty and in those things wherein
God's honour is concerned . . . yet in other things
he is of a pliable disposition . . . ready to pay
deference to others' opinions, loves to comply with
their inclinations, and has a heart that is tender
and flexible, like a little child.

Jonathan Edwards

By the time 1974, '75 and '76 rolled round, I found myself
caught in an interesting and sometimes confusing web of
currents and crosscurrents in terms of my own odyssey.

Plodding my way along in a rather pedestrian fashion, I
found myself pushed forward by one set of observations and
held back by another. It was like walking through the maze
at Hampton Court Palace and finding that the blockages and
the beckonings were about equally distributed! Not only that
but Charismatic and Pentecostal positives seemed offset by
almost as many negatives, while evangelical caution, conser-
vatism and theologising often proved more of a friend than a
foe and more of a balancing help than a restraining hindrance.

In a sense the insights and blind spots of each constituency
contributed positively and negatively in about equal measure as I sought to progress. It brought home afresh the
fallibility of both, the rich discoveries of both and the need of
each for the other.

As I reflect back, the catalogue of helps and hindrances fell out pretty much as follows in the next two chapters.

LIFE AND GROWTH

First of all, against a backdrop of a culturalised and often over-cerebral Evangelicalism and Ecumenism, I saw tremendous vitality and growth in Churches and people touched by the Charismatic Renewal. As David Watson has noted, 'Many Christians today are weary of reports, reforms, reunion schemes, discussions, dialogues and debates. We spend our time talking to ourselves while the world plunges headlong into suicide and despair. And it is in this context that the primary need for a dynamic spiritual renewal by the Holy Spirit of God becomes obvious and urgent. We lack the fire and passion which has always been the mark of the Spirit's presence.'[27]

Over and against the dead formalism of many mainline Churches was the spectacular growth of the Pentecostal movement world-wide. For example in Latin America its growth has been prodigious. It is said that in Chile and Brazil the Pentecostal Church is growing faster than any other Church anywhere and possibly faster than any other Church at any other period in Church history. Chile has one million Pentecostals out of a population of 7½ million. Chile's Church membership in 1932 was only 10,000. This represents a hundredfold increase in 50 years. When Manuel Umana, a Chilean Pentecostal pastor, died, his funeral was attended by 100,000 people. In Brazil, one branch of the Pentecostal Church established 227 congregations in nine years' work. In Sao Paulo there is one Pentecostal church building which holds 25,000 people. In Colombia there are reportedly more than 10,000 Catholic Charismatic prayer groups. And in Seoul, Korea, is the world's largest single congregation, the 160,000-member Full Gospel Central Church, pastored by the Pentecostal Dr Paul Yonggi Cho. 'Look for men and women who are Spirit-filled,' he urges, when explaining some of the keys to the incredible phenomena of his congregation.

Turning to the U.S.A., a Gallup Poll, conducted by *Christianity Today* (January–February 1980), reveals that 19 per cent of all adult Americans (i.e. over 29 million) consider themselves to be Pentecostal or Charismatic Christians.

These 29 million Pentecostal-charismatics are found in almost equal percentages (18–21) in the Roman Catholic, Baptist, Methodist and Lutheran denominations, and are similarly scattered among many smaller denominations and independents, and, of course, the 'classical' Pentecostal denominations formed since 1906. . . . About one quarter of those who reckon themselves to be Pentecostal-charismatic are Roman Catholic and two-thirds are Protestants – corresponding approximately to the proportion of each in the American populace.[28]

The explanation for this surging growth is suggested by a non-charismatic theologian in the Church of Christ, Jack Cottrell: 'The charismatic movement can be seen as the attempt to fill an emotional, experiential vacuum left in an American Christendom that has become more liberal and more rationalistic.'[29]

Adds Roman Catholic theologian, Kilian McDonnell: 'Churches do not seem to be offering spiritual depth. People go where they can (1) be fed and (2) find community. . . . People want to experience God, not simply to know that He exists.'[30]

In my own country of South Africa it was always a source of interest to me to observe how much certain Churches have abominated the Pentecostals as incorrigible 'sheep-stealers'. However, it is a characteristic of sheep that they tend to go where there's food.

The attractiveness of spiritual life and growth also became evident in the little parish Church I attend in Hilton, Natal. It was once almost lifeless and with very low membership. Now it is bursting at the seams. This did not come about through intense theological discussion which, incidentally, I would welcome more than disparage. The fact, however, is that it came about through Charismatic Renewal. Nor is this to imply that there are no longer any problems, but at least they are the problems of life, not the problems of death.

Dr Jim Packer of Regent College, Vancouver, has put it this way:

> Though theologically uneven (and what spiritually significant movement has not been?) the charismatic renewal has drawn many people who are weary of that which only ministers to and appeals to the mind. After all, man has a heart too, and whoever bypasses that fact will in the end lose out. Even stiff upper lips can hanker to shout the occasional 'Hallelujah'.[31]

UNDERGROUND ECUMENISM

Some people see the Charismatic Renewal as the most unifying thing in Christendom today. I'm not sure I would go that far. In South Africa a wider and in my judgment more significant range of Christian leadership was brought together in SACLA (South African Christian Leadership Assembly) on the basis of an open Evangelicalism rather than on the basis of the Renewal platform. Perhaps that is a pointer to a new way ahead for the world Church. Moreover, in other parts of the world I see people from a wide range of backgrounds clustering in Renewal gatherings while cleavages in the overall body of Christ still remain deep and pervasive. Here and there the Renewal has in fact been more divisive than unifying.

Even so, I would not want to minimise the very real gains and progress which have come in many parts of the world through allowing the Holy Spirit greater freedom amongst His people.

I recollect one interesting experience shortly before Mission '70 in Johannesburg which was a very large interdenominational evangelistic endeavour led by African Enterprise in 1970. I was speaking in the leading congregation of a Pentecostal denomination which had thus far stayed out of the mission.

At the end of my message I was startled by an outburst in tongues from one member of the congregation. It was one of my first experiences of such a thing. Moments later an interpretation was given. It was a stern rebuke which included these words: 'I am wanting to do a great work in this city, but I cannot because my people are setting one another at naught.' The effect on the congregation was astonishing. A great spirit of repentance swept over the people. And the following week the whole denomination entered the mission!

The Anglican Church in South Africa provides another interesting case study. For years there has been a deep cleavage between this body (The Church of the Province of South Africa – CPSA) and another smaller, more self-consciously evangelical body called the Church of England in South Africa (CESA). The exchanges on everything from disputed properties to theology have in the past been bitter and acrimonious. CESA has for over a hundred years bewailed how unevangelical the more Anglo-Catholic CPSA is.

However, the Charismatic Renewal has had such a dramatic effect on the Church of the Province as to make it almost unrecognisable from the denomination I knew fifteen years ago. Its movement in what I would call by my lights a more evangelical, biblical and evangelistic direction has been dramatic and clear-cut. Whereas fifteen years ago it almost ostracised evangelicals, it now makes them bishops! As the Holy Spirit, who guides into all truth, has had greater sway, He has in fact led the whole denomination back into the Bible in a whole new way and made it far easier for more traditionally evangelical bodies to relate in fellowship than ever before. What the Evangelical Fellowship of Anglican Churchmen (EFAC) – an evangelical pressure group – failed to do, the Charismatic Renewal has done – and in a short time.

The situation with Roman Catholics is even more dramatic. It would have been almost unthinkable fifteen years ago for evangelicals and Roman Catholics to have true fellowship together, let alone cooperate in evangelistic endeavours. Yet I can think of missions we have conducted both in Latin America and Africa where Roman Catholics, who have been mightily touched by the Charismatic Renewal, have joyfully participated with us and often been almost indistinguishable from other evangelicals.

Dr Ralph Martin, a Catholic Charismatic leader, asserts that 'literally millions of Catholics have been renewed or converted to a significant relationship with Jesus as Saviour and Lord, and to a life of holiness and service empowered by the Holy Spirit.'[32]

One of the fruits of the Catholic Renewal, so Martin feels, is:

> a heightened awareness of the evangelical heart of Roman Catholic Christianity. . . . I would say that the Catholic Charismatic Renewal is broadly characterised by a basic conversion or reconversion through which millions of Catholics have encountered or accepted Jesus Christ as the Saviour who takes away the sin of the world, our sin, and as Lord. . . . There is a tremendous widespread blossoming of the reading of Scripture and of giving testimony in evangelism.[33]

It is also fascinating that Martin prefers to talk about what is happening as an 'evangelical awakening' in the Catholic Church rather than as a 'Charismatic Renewal'. He adds:

> I personally feel more comfortable being called 'a Catholic evangelical' than a 'Catholic charismatic'. The focus in my life, as it is in most of the renewal movement, is not on the gifts of the Holy Spirit but on conversion to the person of Christ and entrance into a life of faithful service to Him.[34]

Significantly he recognises that a struggle over the basic Gospel message is going on right now in the Roman Catholic Church.

> Liberal Protestant thought has made serious incursions into the Roman Catholic Church. It is my hope that the

charismatic renewal and the evangelical emphasis growing out of it will be able to contribute to the strengthening
of the orthodox understanding of the Gospel in the Catholic Church. I believe this struggle for the basic Gospel is
an area of common ground between Protestant and Catholic evangelicals. . . . I look forward to the time when we
Catholic evangelicals have more contact with our Protestant evangelical brothers and sisters: we desire to serve the
same Gospel and the same Lord.[35]

Protestant Michael Harper rightly looks at this sort of
phenomenon with thanksgiving. He even speaks of cases of
inter-communion and notes that the world of Catholic
officialdom is often sticking rigidly to the rule-book while
behind the scenes an 'underground ecumenism' is operating
where many of these rules are being totally ignored. He
quotes Bernard Shaw's play *St Joan* where Robert, a law-
abiding conservative, turns to a certain Poulengey and says:
'What! You are as mad as she [Joan] is.' Poulengey answers:
'We want a few mad people now. See where the sane ones
have landed us!'

Underground ecumenism may seem to some the product
of madness and a dangerous ecclesiastical aberration. But
to others it seems a work of the Holy Spirit. The 'sane'
ecumenists and experts on canon law have got us nowhere
very much, perhaps the 'insane' will achieve something
where others have failed.[36]

Of course some evangelical critics will argue that Catholic
Charismatics have not by and large turned from their views
on Mary, the Saints, the Mass, papal authority and so on.
But this type of doctrinal reformation does not happen
overnight, least of all after centuries of conditioning, and
some time must be allowed within Catholicism for a certain
amount of additional theological thinking on certain issues
highlighted by both the Reformation and the Renewal. In the
meantime it is less than charitable or honest not to recognise

the mighty movements of the Spirit which are at work within contemporary Catholicism. And if the Spirit of God has so obviously gone over there to our Cornelius (having presumably been there all along, though less obviously to us Protestants) who are we with Peter to say 'No, Lord', as Jesus pushes us into relatedness?

PRAYER AND WORSHIP

Another positive feature of Pentecostal and Charismatic witness is the commitment to prayer. This has often impressed me.

For example in our mission to the city of Pietermaritzburg in South Africa in 1975, many people paid varying degrees of lip service to the importance of prayer, yet it was the Pentecostal Churches which formed a chain of prayer which ran twenty-four hours a day, seven days a week, four weeks a month for an astonishing six months! Small wonder that we saw such an amazing response as we did during that challenging endeavour.

Others I have come across have also noticed this. Pentecostal and Charismatic ventures are generally born in hours of prayer, while projects born in other sections of the Church tend more to be born of talk and organisational expertise.

Then there were the occasional experiences which came my way of Charismatic worship. I had been raised on a varied diet of Ancient and Modern (more ancient usually than modern) plus the standard fare of evangelical hymnody, and I must confess there were times when I wearied of singing theology to other singers or of singing lofty exhortations to – well, I'm not sure who – myself presumably – e.g. 'Rescue the Perishing, Care for the Dying' etc. Not that singing about God is to be decried, but what struck me about Charismatics was that they sang TO God. They addressed Him in their singing and worship and really 'connected' with Him. There was in song a personal realising of fellowship with the Father and the Son through the Spirit. By abolishing excessive anxiety over the clock, time was allowed for people to express their feelings and attitudes until a real sense of communion with God had been achieved in the meeting.

But there were other things with which to contend and many of these were not so positive.

And to some of these I now turn, not only to underline to Charismatics that they still have a few things to learn, but to remind evangelicals they still have many things to teach!

Chapter Eleven

OVER THE OBSTACLE COURSE

> Enthusiasm tramples over prejudice and
> opposition, spurns inaction, storms the citadel of
> its object and like an avalanche overwhelms and
> engulfs all obstacles. It is nothing more or less than
> faith in action.
>
> Henry Chester

The path to greater fellowship with Pentecostals and Charismatics was for me, as I suspect it is for others, not without its pitfalls. In fact at times I felt I was busy negotiating an obstacle course.

Some of these obstacles were admittedly tossed into my path from the wobbly fringes of the Movement and not from its purified and mature centre. That I know. But they were obstacles nevertheless and one's skills at spiritual hurdling were accordingly extensively tested.

Actually, one incisive Charismatic friend who read the first draft of this chapter warned me that if I presented all this as typical I would have the whole Charismatic constituency taking up cudgels against me. But he reassured me that it would, of course, all be done in love! For which assurance needless to say, I blessed both him and the gentle and loving army of waiting warriors with their theological hatchets!

Anyway, being a rather devout coward who is far from anxious to be cudgelled, even in love, let me quickly affirm my recognition that in mushrooming new movements of spiritual life there will always be excesses from those who go off beam, either in weakness or zeal or through old Screwtape's machinations, or because of the flesh. All historians of renewal and revival know this. And I know it too.

On the other hand, my experience was my experience. I can't get away from it and it is this which I am relating. And the fact that I initially thought some of these things to be typical only goes to show how easily the exceptions can be thought to prove the rule! Let the exceptional brothers and sisters take note!

PARTY PRESSURE

The first obstacle, however, was neither particularly Pentecostal or peculiarly Charismatic. It is found throughout the Church and is perhaps inevitable wherever there are groupings of any sort, whether social, political or religious. I am thinking of group pressure.

In my experience it came in a sense from two sides – or if you like from two parties, the evangelical and the Charismatic. Was I imagining things? I don't know. It seemed real anyway, put it that way.

It all reminded me somewhat of that animal absurdity who appears in those delightful children's stories about Dr Doolittle. The creature has a head at each end of its body. It is called a Pushmepullyou! It is the contorted consequence of being pulled in two different directions! That's how I often felt when exploring this issue.

Of course many would deny these tugs and pulls, affirming grandly that they know only the pull of God's Word! They are not affected by party loyalties. But others would no doubt admit with me the power of this phenomenon.

You see, on the one hand, I felt a deep loyalty to the evangelical party, as it were, and on the other hand I felt the pull of the Charismatic bandwagon. On the one hand I did not want to lose acceptance with my evangelical friends but nor did I want to become a Charismatic catch to be fêted on the Pentecostal testimony circuit as a scalp won from the other side. Basically I was resisting being a feather in anybody's cap. I just wanted to find deeper life in Christ.

I think these conflicting pulls highlight two problems in Christendom. The first is that we all tend to find our security in a circle of like-minded people rather than in Christ. We want and need acceptance and we sympathise with poor old Peter when we learn on the Gentile issue how he compromised the truth in his own search for it by 'fearing the circumcision party' (Gal. 2:12).

The second problem, which is the obverse side of the party-fear coin, is party pressure. This is what the party itself does to its membership to make it toe the line – or else risk rejection. So if the first problem is fearfulness in the individual, the second is fearsomeness in the party!

Commenting on Evangelicalism – but the remarks as far as I am concerned are just as applicable to other parties (e.g. Charismatics, Pentecostals, Anglo-Catholics or ever-so-reformed Reformists) – one writer has said:

> Evangelicals fail to achieve the rich diversity that is displayed by independent men of other convictions; their goal is conformity and they tend therefore to spend their energies on being like others rather than carving their own ideas out of the raw stuff of life. This makes for dullness.[37]

The writer goes on to ask whether Evangelicalism (and again I insist on the relevance to all 'parties') has not developed into 'a closed system' marked by three classic characteristics. The first is a comprehensive way of looking at life which claims to solve all problems and right all wrongs. The second is a refusal to allow itself to be modified by newly-observed facts, preferring rather to absorb the impact of those facts by a well-developed casuistry. The third is to disarm the newly-initiated person of his critical faculties once he has stepped inside the system. In this system emotional heat turns disagreement into betrayals and heresies.[38]

All of this results in timidity about spiritual pioneering, in fearfulness about conclusions which are not pre-packaged by the party and ultimately, unless checked, in that deformity which is the sad consequence of inbreeding. It also, by the way, leads many religious parties to chuck out their best men – the best being those who dare to risk a little independent thinking? Anglicans have been quite good at this and amongst the worthies we have dumped are John Wesley, who has given us a major denomination and General Booth who founded the Salvation Army! The Catholics did something similar with a certain Martin Luther!

I remember one classic personal experience of this type of pressure. In 1973 I was invited by the Commission on World Mission and Evangelism of the World Council of Churches to attend a small dialogue symposium in Geneva on Evangelism. My assignment was to present a paper on Evangelism from an evangelical perspective.

Following this Geneva experience a number of evangelicals in Southern and East Africa concluded this was the moment to write me off. After all, to set foot in Geneva was almost the ultimate evangelical heresy.

Said one prominent evangelical: 'Michael has sold his soul to Geneva.' A university Christian group, which was thinking of inviting us for a mission to their campus, at once abandoned the idea! The fact that I had been in Geneva to bring an *evangelical witness* appeared not to have entered their minds!

Although I have reservations about aspects of current ecumenical theology, on the other hand I could only see this kind of party pressure as counterproductive and simplistically judgmental.

Likewise in exploring the work of the Spirit I felt myself caught in certain party pulls, the one seemingly saying 'Don't forsake us – or else' – and the other seemingly saying 'Please embrace us – or else!' Somehow it made the exploration of truth just that much more difficult.

SUBCULTURE

Another obstacle on the course was what I might call the Pentecostal subculture. I suppose for me this was the problem of distinguishing form from essence. What was essential to the movement and what were trappings? In any event subcultural trappings at times almost prevented me seeing the wood for the trees.

Extravagant praying, boisterous exuberance, groaning prayers and often plain noise in the few meetings to which I was exposed became obstacles to my spirit.

One high-powered Pentecostal sister was once praying in our office and the whole street must have heard her.

The late Dr Edgar Brookes, distinguished historian, scholar, parliamentarian and then Chairman of African Enterprise (South Africa), was coming up the stairs to our office as the thunderous prayer proceeded.

'The Lord couldn't have failed to hear that,' he whispered to me with a naughty twinkle.

Then there was also the matter of hands in the air. And hugging too.

For some years it was all a bit much.

Let me illustrate out of someone else's experience. A certain Methodist pastor in Texas was invited to a Renewal weekend. He presumably went because he was seeking personal renewal. However, the problem to him was the 'trappings'.

Tongue in cheek, he tells his tale:

> We sang a lot during the weekend. Not just plain songs, either, but songs that usually included some motions or actions. We were told to smile broadly, stomp our feet, touch our neighbour and most of all raise our hands. I got to thinking about my own hesitation to elevate my arms. It is not a comfortable position. Nor is it natural. Nor is it common. It is a position that shows vulnerability. Hands up! is . . . what cops say to robbers etc. So on a purely subjective level I could see how others who resisted holding their hands up could feel like someone about to be held up or arrested![39]

For my part I used to sense in certain prayer meetings that I was almost being watched to see if I would raise my hands or not, thereby indicating my Charismatic *bona fides* or lack thereof. If you raised your hands you were charismatically there. You had arrived. You were amongst the initiated. You could be accepted without reserve. After all, it was the public sign, like raising your hand in class when the teacher asks who has been a good boy and done his homework.

My Texan pastor friend also tells his reaction at the camp to all the hugging which was required. He says: 'Those who go in for that sort of expression see it as a sign that the walls are tumbling down. I'm not much of a hugger and am not always thrilled to be a huggee . . . but those huggers are like steam-rollers who plough right through my fence.'

Personally I do not now have a hugging hang-up! In fact I quite enjoy it! I have crashed the hug barrier, as it were. But some more sensitive souls, who are still tiptoeing towards a deeper experience of the Holy Spirit, can be both figuratively and literally stopped in their tracks by suddenly being engulfed midway through divine service in the arms of the local butcher.

Incidentally, I remember once seeing a dear friend of mine, an American black, hugging a white South African politician. I never saw such a struggle between black power and white fear in my life!

Perhaps all this relates to a Charismatic tendency at times to measure internal states by external signs along with an insensitivity to the feelings of quiet, shy or reserved people. And so, either feeling that they have been delivered from that type of reserve, or forgetting that they were ever marked by it themselves, they periodically batter down the tender defences of the seeking or uninitiated.

The Texan pastor put it this way:

> We were given fair warning early in the weekend that our dignity would have to go. Maybe you should know that our church is made up mainly of Germans and their descendants, some of whom are upset if you find them in the hospital without a robe on! Dignity is one of their cardinal virtues, especially in church. So the drive to get rid of dignity stalled right away on these Teutonic defenses.[40]

I guess my point is that subcultural baggage, which may or

may not include subtle though often unconscious manipula-
tion, is more of a hindrance than a help. It is an obstacle in
the course, though foolish is the man who allows it to become
insuperable.

POWER MANIA

Another obstacle to me was what seemed often to be a
spiritual power mania in Charismatic and Pentecostal
circles. Not that I would deny the divine promise or the
human need of the Spirit's power. Much that I have already
said earlier would show that.

However the thing can get off beam. One amusing, though
perhaps unusual experience, came my way in a meeting of
Pentecostal businessmen. In all sorts of ways it was a thoroughly splendid and edifying exercise. However, I once
again felt that noise was often mistaken for power and
volume for victory. The idea that God might have normal
hearing appeared not to have entered anyone's mind.

It came to a head for me when one ardent brother, whose
rasping and crackling vocal chords suggested he was no
stranger to the testimony circuit, screamed out: 'We don't
need theology' ('Amen' roared the crowd) – 'We don't need
hermeneutics' ('*Amen*' re-roared the crowd) 'WE-JUST-
NEED-THE-P-O-O-O-O-W-E-R OF GOD!' (More
Amens, hoots of holy laughter, plus sustained clapping as the
brother beamed seraphically and triumphantly at the multitude).

It was the kind of populist rhetoric which was funny to
hear but hard to swallow!

I turned to my neighbour, who was, I might say, a
prominent and highly-regarded Pentecostal leader from
Latin America and whispered: 'I have rarely heard a man in
greater need of both theology – and – hermeneutics!'

Thankfully, he nodded in vigorous assent. And winked!

My relief was great. I could continue to explore the realm
of the Spirit without having to embrace that kind of excess!
Besides, when populist Pentecostals set the Spirit's power
over against theology or hermeneutics (the science of inter-

preting the Bible correctly), they not only create unnecessary complications for thinking people, but they also add substance to the oft-heard accusation that the Renewal Movement is theologically lightweight and exegetically erratic. I don't think that is by any means generally true, but there is no point in fuelling an impression one would presumably want to dispel. My friend Derek Crumpton, a leader in the South African Renewal, says I probably hit an untypical 'immature lay zealot' in that experience. Possibly. If he was such he shouldn't have been addressing a National Convention!

There is another thing here. It is the idea that weakness and the fullness of the Spirit do not go together.

Michael Griffiths has aptly noted:

> The power of the Holy Spirit did not make an apostle into a kind of superstar evangelist. Paul could say he was 'so utterly, unbearably crushed that we despaired' (2 Cor. 1:8) and were 'afflicted at every turn – fighting without and fear within. But God . . . comforts the *downcast*. . . .' (2 Cor. 7:5–6). He learns that God's power is 'made perfect in weakness' (12:9). We can scarcely argue that these men did not know the blessing for biblically this is the authentic apostolic experience. We should be careful when our stereotype of the Spirit-filled leader does not measure up to his being 'in weakness and in much fear and trembling' (1 Cor. 2:3), and where his 'bodily presence is weak, and his speech of no account' (2 Cor. 10:10). God's power is not intended to make men powerful, but rather to display God's transcendent power in the scruffy earthenware of dedicated but frail human vessels.[41]

In like vein Michael Green notes how the Corinthian Charismatics were always out for power and always seeking shortcuts to it. Yet Paul's reply was to boast not of his power but of his weakness through which alone the power of Christ could shine.

Paul knew all about the marks of an apostle, in signs,

wonders and mighty deeds (2 Cor. 12:12) but he knew that the power of an apostle or of any other Christian, came from the patient endurance of suffering such as he had with his thorn in the flesh, or the patient endurance of reviling and hardships which he was submitted to in the course of his missionary work (1 Cor. 4). The charismatics had a theology of the resurrection and its power; they needed to learn afresh the secret of the cross and its shame . . . which yet had produced the power of God (1 Cor. 1:8).[42]

The point, as it seemed to me, was that one had to proceed in search of the Spirit's power in the realisation that it would always be just that – the Spirit's power. Not our own. It is crucified power. The treasure is held in an earthen vessel. And one which also needs theology, hermeneutics and all!

Besides, there is something rather engaging about any sort of self-effacing denial of power. The other day I passed a tiny little French Citroen which looked just about on its last legs. The sticker on the back, however, warned: 'Beware! This is a French Nuclear Power Zone.' In that self-effacing banter on the bumper, which in truth spoke more of weakness than of power, there was something more attractive than the extravagant self-advancing claim of some new multi-cylindered wonder to be the fastest, the best and the most high-powered ever to have hit the roads.

To me the Christian who is conscious of weakness actually often manifests more truly the appeal of Christ than the one who projects a self-conscious awareness of great spiritual power!

DOCTRINE DIVIDES

A related hassle for me was an oft-heard Pentecostal cliché that 'doctrine divides but experience unites'. Of course, the slogan is not void of truth, but it is a half-truth and as such almost as perilous as outright falsehood.

I remember once being invited to preach in a Pentecostal Church and being informed by one of its laymen: 'We keep away from doctrine. It is so divisive.' The implication was 'And, brother, you'd better too!'

Perhaps he meant that they kept away from talking about Baptism, or the millenium and they didn't want me to push any doctrine of bishops on them! – or maybe my advisor was trying simply to get away from churchiness – I'm not sure. But in any event, this sort of thing set off my alarm signals a good few times.

The fact is that my evangelical heritage had underlined, as I indicated earlier, the importance of truth. The Bible, especially the New Testament, would not have contained so many pages of 'teaching' if 'doctrine' was of no consequence. . . .

Interestingly, Richard Quebedeaux reports that 'there are now even a few Unitarian-Universalist Charismatics'.[43] His word 'even' obviously expresses surprise that those who are professing a new fullness of the Holy Spirit should continue uncritically in views manifestly out of line with the New Testament. For is not the Holy Spirit the 'Spirit of truth' (John 15:26) and the One who 'will guide you into all the truth' (John 16:13)?

WE'VE GOT IT

Another hurdle to negotiate is the tiresome impression some Charismatics and Pentecostals convey that they have got it, that they are a sort of spiritual aristocracy and everyone else is in the category of a second-class citizen. Maybe many groups and individuals are guiltless at this point but it is a not uncommon impression and it is an obstacle whenever it rears its head.

I remember in one city bumping into a Christian friend. He was so full of smiles, joys, overwhelming miracles round every corner that I quickly felt my inadequacies and insecurities surfacing! Was he telling me all this to elevate and inspire me or to cast me into the slough of despondency by showing up the startling contrast between all the supernaturalism round him and all the naturalism around me?

One of his points for rejoicing was put this way: 'You

know, Mike, I praise God because in this town He is dividing out the true from the false Christians.'

'Oh!' I said, somewhat startled, not being aware, you see, of this dividing process. 'And, brother, how do you know the true from the false Church?'

'Well, the true Church is made up of those who love Jesus.'

'And how do you know who loves Jesus?'

'Well, you know – those who SAY they do.'

This rationale astonished me. After all, every Christian in town would probably claim, once nailed to the wall, that they loved Jesus, although that vocabulary might not be their natural choice. However, my friend's facility at sorting out the true from the false constituted for me a snare and a delusion. In fact, he picked out one pastor in particular as epitomising the false, whereas I knew him to be a man of deep and genuine, even if modestly unorthodox, piety.

'Well, dear brother,' I said with admirable restraint, 'I know only one way God judges who really loves Jesus and it is Jesus Himself who verbalised it: "If you love me, you will keep my commandments." So if you know who is keeping the commandments and who is not, then I guess you know who loves Jesus and who does not and who is true and who is false. I'd say that was a kind of complicated assignment!'

Anyway, he was very loving and gracious and also admirably restrained, because I too was being a bit provocative! He gave a good old-time laugh, looked at me quizzically, said he'd have to think about it, and went on his way rejoicing!

NO POLITICS, BROTHER

Another thing which bothered me, especially in the context of apartheid South Africa, was the difficulty of being accepted by Pentecostals and Charismatics while seeking at the same time to be true to the socio-political implications of the Gospel. We will say more on this in a later chapter, but suffice it for the moment to indicate that this constituted a real headache for me.

'Michael is political,' my Pentecostal friends would say. 'He opposes apartheid and the Government.'

This sort of remark reveals one of those theological eccentricities so characteristic of many conservative Christians in South Africa – namely to label as political those other Christians who oppose apartheid while withholding the label from those who support it! To oppose the system is to be political, to support or tolerate it is not.

To me the social sins of structural injustice and racial discrimination are little different in seriousness from the personal sins of adultery, dishonesty or drunkenness. Are we to repent of one category of sin and not the other?

The trouble was compounded by the fact that almost all my theologically conservative friends were also political conservatives who tolerated and indeed often supported the South African status quo. They seemed to me to have domesticated God to the support of discriminatory politics.

On the other hand their contrary accusation might be that I was seeking to domesticate God to the opposition party and to my own viewpoint. But I think I have been rescued from that hazard, being, as I am, rather persuaded that God is not headed for the ballot box of any one party. He is on His own side – in favour of holiness, justice, goodness and compassion, wherever these are manifested in private and public life, and against impurity, injustice, evil and heartlessness.

Remember that story of the two nineteenth-century sailors – one French and one English – who were discussing their respective national navies?

Said the Frenchman: 'I can't understand how it is that the English navy always seems to win its battles.'

'Well,' said the English sailor, 'before we go into battle we pray.'

'But we pray too,' insisted the Frenchman.

'Ah, yes, but we pray in English,' replied the other with a bland smile.

However, while we dare not turn God into a cosmic Englishman, Afrikaner or black freedom fighter who is there to promote our private nationalisms, neither dare we remove Him from a compassionate love for the world and from full involvement in the whole arena of human life, including the socio-political. If He is concerned about how one person relates to another, will He not be concerned about how one group relates to another? If He is concerned that 'not one of the least of these little ones' should be caused to stumble, then surely He is concerned if whole groups or nations of people are caused to stumble through oppressive systems.

Anyway, as I said, more on this later. Suffice it for the moment to note that this was an obstacle on the course for me.

SUBJECTIVISM

I suppose I would have to say that another obstacle to me was the highly subjective and often apparently untested criteria for guidance through visions, prophecies, dreams or mental pictures. This is sensitive territory and I do not want to be cavalier or sceptical about phenomena which I know can indeed be authentic. But on many occasions in Church services or Charismatic gatherings I have been disturbed in spirit by the ease and almost gullibility with which the message behind such supposed phenomena has been received by the faithful as authentic.

I guess my fear relates basically to an undiscerning intrusion of subjectivism untempered by the insights, cautions and controls both of the word of God and of the spiritually mature leader.

Apart from anything else, any person with unhealthy or erratic ambitions for spiritual power and authority can easily achieve an undue and improper domination of a group by manipulating them with over-regular reports of dreams and pictures into a position of spiritual subservience and awe. Every congregation and fellowship is full of emotionally dependent people who are all too susceptible and ready to be impressed by this sort of style.

It will be remembered that Paul wrote the Colossian letter and John his first epistle in order to counter sincere but deluded claims to direct divine revelation from certain brethren 'who would deceive' (1 John 2:26), or 'delude with beguiling speech.' (Colossians 2:4)

Richard Lovelace, the historian of church renewal already referred to, and a strong sympathiser with Charismatic Renewal, has made this observation:

It seems difficult to frame a very strong biblical argument for limiting prophetic utterances to the apostolic period. And yet the Church in later eras has repeatedly found that when it goes beyond the canon of Scripture to recognise new revelations, it soon finds itself dealing with severe problems. Outbreaks of fanatical enthusiasm in church history have always been accompanied by a belief in contemporary revelations of the Spirit. . . . Some Reformation groups which began by stressing the contemporary revelation of the Spirit soon ended by treating the Scriptures as an addendum which was more or less unnecessary once a Christian obtained direct access to the mind of God through the Spirit.[44]

It is to be noted that the Reformers and Puritans guarded against overly subjective revelations and enthusiasms by stressing the *objectivity* of the written Word within the context of their doctrine of the Holy Spirit. On the other hand they recognised that illumination by the Spirit was necessary for the understanding and application of Scripture.

The great Edwin Hoskens in his commentary on the Gospel of John says apropos of Scripture and the work of the Spirit (see John 16:12–15):

Jesus is the way in which the disciples must be led by the Spirit. He is also the truth to which they must be guided. The author (John) is therefore concerned to impress upon his readers the danger of false conceptions of the work of the Spirit. The inspiration does not detach men from the truth that is in Jesus and set them free to wander into new realms of truth, apart from the sanctuary of God. . . . The Power of the Spirit does not consist in secret and mystical revelations but in the external preaching of the Gospel which makes them revolt from the world and attaches them to the Church. And His action does not consist in delivering new truths to the disciples but in providing a larger, deeper and more perfect understanding of the teaching which Jesus has given them.[45]

These are important words of caution which many leaders in the Renewal have in fact already sounded themselves. In so doing they have prevented what are probably relatively isolated excesses from developing into a trend. However, what is hopefully uncharacteristic nevertheless occurred often enough along my own personal path to constitute an obstacle.

What I have outlined in this chapter is the obstacle course, or part of it, which faced me as I sought to understand more of what God had shown to Pentecostals and Charismatics.

Less motivated, I might have been paralysed by the group pressures, stymied by the subculture, offended by the power mania, frustrated by the apparent indifference to doctrine, squeezed out by the exclusivism, alienated by the apolitical stance or frightened off by the rampant subjectivism. Certainly I often wished the obstacle course were less arduous.

But on the other hand, I was all along encouraged by the vitality and life and reality which I saw in these circles, especially when set alongside the often lifeless and barren deserts in other sections of Christendom. The Renewal seemed to me to be not the ultimate expression of the Church, nor the final repository of biblical truth nor even the purest form of Christian life, but it was the sounding of a gong, a trumpet call, a clarion clang of a bell, calling out to the Church at large that the ministry of the Holy Spirit must receive more attention, that there is new life and power and love to be found in His release and that His gifts are there to be used and appropriated by the twentieth-century Church as part of its needed and necessary equipment for service in our time.

And so for these reasons, with the obstacle course modestly negotiated, I decided to attend the first South African Renewal Conference on the Holy Spirit – set for the Milner Park Arena in Johannesburg in August 1977.

Chapter Twelve

MILNER PARK AND A SECOND TOUCH

There is a place in the life of the church for
mountain-top experiences.
Caesar Molebatsi of Soweto

You will recollect my saying at the beginning that I had this
strange sense that God wanted me to deal with an alienated
relationship before going to the Renewal Conference. I knew
I had to get right with Jim and Mary but had postponed
doing anything about it over the four months since that
sunset walk in the fields at the Fyvie's farm near the
Drakensberg mountains. Should I write? Or phone? Or do a
tape? Or what? Undecided, I did nothing. Besides that, there
were so many other distracting pressures.

Finally about a week before the conference I decided I
would just have to write to Jim and Mary after it was all over.
The Lord would make allowances for how busy I had been!

Just then a phone call came from Kenya saying I should
rush up to Nairobi to meet my colleague Bishop Festo
Kivengere, leader of our East Africa team, in order to discuss
some emergency matters in connection with our refugee
work. It was now six and a half months since the brutal Idi
Amin had murdered Archbishop Janani Luwum who was,
incidentally, Chairman of African Enterprise in Uganda.
After Janani s death Festo had had to flee into exile as it
seemed he was next on Amin's hit list. Then came the deluge
of refugees to our Nairobi office and our East African team

had scarcely paused for breath, especially Festo who had catapulted hither and yon all over the world, sharing about Uganda's plight. The continuing flow of refugees from all sections of society, especially the students and professional people, had created endless new challenges plus some dramatic new headaches. Now I had to hurry to Nairobi to consult with Festo about a new one. It was Wednesday. The Renewal Conference was to begin the following Monday. Certainly and unquestionably there was now no time to write the oft-postponed letter to Jim and Mary. The Lord would understand!

Anyway, we began to attend to the Uganda problems which occupied us day and night for several days. During the time I was contacted by some local Pentecostals who had some overseas friends they wanted me to meet. One was a leader from Canada.

He asked what I was doing.

'Well,' I said, 'I'm involved in a project up here with Bishop Festo Kivengere.'

The man looked blank. The name of an evangelist whom I thought to be a household name in Protestant Christendom meant nothing to him.

I was just ruminating on the implications of this ignorance when the dear man asked: 'Is he an Anglican bishop?'

'Yes, indeed,' I replied.

'And is he born again?' came the cheeky retort.

'Yes, brother,' I said, scarcely concealing my incredulity at such a question about one of the world's leading evangelists, 'Festo is born again.'

But as I walked away from the conversation I couldn't suppress in my spirit the renewed and horrifying realisation of the encapsulated nature of most Christian living. Half the Christian world just does not know how, where or whether the other half lives. The well-intentioned questions of my new acquaintance were a sad commentary on the state of things.

A POWERFUL DREAM

I went to bed late and tired on Friday night and slept soundly. But about 4 a.m. I had yet another of those vivid, clear and penetrating dreams about Jim and Mary. I told early in this story how these dreams had recurred regularly for five or six years since I had become alienated from this couple.

Once again, as in the past, I saw myself in the visual images of this dream becoming reconciled to them. I awoke, totally alert and intensely conscious of God's presence. And of His injunction. It was about that letter.

I bounded out of bed, put on the light, sat down at the desk and finally wrote the letter which would seek to heal a seven-year breach.

About 7 a.m. I called Festo in his hotel room and said I'd like to breakfast with him and share something.

Over bacon and eggs I shared the early-morning experience and the initiative taken. 'But what if it is rejected or turned down?' I asked, wondering if I could sustain such a rejection.

'Well, brother,' said Festo with his inimitable twinkle, 'you have entered the Calvary arena. Whatever happens, you have done the right thing in the light of Calvary love. Leave it to the Lord.'

Our Ugandan refugee matters were dealt with by Sunday night and on Monday morning I flew back from Nairobi to Johannesburg, wondering what the week would bring forth and relieved beyond words that I had finally and belatedly obeyed the Lord in taking the reconciling initiative about which He had spoken to me so many months before. 'Do something about that relationship before the Renewal Conference,' had been His word. At last after about four months, I had acted, but with just two days to go till zero hour! Such are the ways of human procrastination and stubbornness.

ANOTHER WORLD

I was met at Jan Smuts airport, driven to Milner Park and deposited safely in the speakers' lounge for lunch.

Yes, believe it or not, I had even been asked to speak. Hope for South Africa was my subject. But this was another world.

Faces which constituted the familiar evangelical landmarks were missing. Instead we had the Pentecostal and Charismatic faithful. The globe-trotting David du Plessis, Bob McAllister of Rio, Cecil Kerr of Northern Ireland, Dan and Al Malachuk of Logos Books, Larry Christenson, Derek Prince and Francis MacNutt – ('Who's he?' I asked of one horrified Charismatic who wore that same look manifested by me with the Canadian brother who had never heard of Festo Kivengere!!) I hardly dared say I'd never heard of any of the other big wheels except David du Plessis, whom I'd met back in 1971 and brought to South Africa for the Durban Congress in 1973.

I had also met Derek Prince once – at an airport. But he had seemed preoccupied, rushed and reserved. 'Guess he doesn't like evangelicals,' I'd decided defensively as I slipped into a negative view. I didn't know Derek was a shy man. No time for me to find out. Judgment was easy. Fellowship hard. I also knew he had certain controversial views. But that does not constitute grounds to break fellowship.

Sitting there in the speakers' lounge over coffee, I felt within a little nudge from the Spirit. 'Go over and greet Derek. You've been distant. Deal with it. Go and greet him.' So over I went and said hullo. It felt good and he was very friendly.

As the conference got under way that night I was at once struck by the tremendous sincerity, buoyancy, warmth and devotion which characterised the worship and the singing. These people weren't just singing some nice theology to who knows who or exhorting each other in song (e.g. 'Trust and Obey') but were really connecting with their Lord in true and moving adoration. As one looked around the auditorium there were many who were indeed 'lost in wonder, love and praise'. It was exhilarating and in marked contrast to the often impoverished and sterile worship of other sections of the Church.

I recollected the comments made to me about PACLA by Archbishop Bill Burnett, formerly my chaplain at high school and later Archbishop of Cape Town. PACLA was the Pan African Christian Leadership Assembly, of which I had been programme chairman, and it met in Nairobi in December 1976.

'Weak in worship,' Archbishop Bill had said, and now I really saw and understood and 'felt' what he meant. I also saw that worship takes time and needs time. It is not singing three songs in a row and having a quick prayer. It involves allowing the sheer majesty and greatness and goodness of God our Father to break in on our inner beings and draw them out in worshipful adoration.

Dr James Packer has expressed 'unambiguous approval' of many features of the Charismatic Renewal when biblically assessed. One of them he notes as:

> its insistence that each Christian be thoroughly involved in the Church's worship; not necessarily by speaking in the assembly (though that kind of participation, when orderly and well done, must surely be approved) but primarily by opening one's heart to God in worship and seeking to realise for oneself the divine realities about which the church sings, prays and learns from Scripture.[46]

It struck me there and then, and I have not altered my view an iota since then, that the Church generally and evangelicals specifically have so very much to learn from Charismatics about worship in the Spirit and in truth.

Nor is this simply of relevance in terms of finding new richness in worship itself. It is also, I believe, of direct relevance to the whole process of Evangelism which is such a special area of evangelical concern.

Commenting on the apparent richness of worship in the first-century Church at Antioch, Michael Green notes not only that it was 'while they were worshipping the Lord and fasting' (Acts 13:2) that the prophetic word was given which set Paul and Barnabas aside for their first momentous missionary journey, but also that their unity in worship was probably a factor in their numerical growth. Green adds: 'The attractive power of a congregation at worship is hard to exaggerate. The unity, the intensity the variety of the worship should raise questions in the mind of the stranger which it is the task of the preaching to explain.'[47]

Of course all this is not to deny the presence at times of excess in modern Charismatic worship (which may not match what happened at Antioch) but only to assert and reassert that the positives far outweigh the negatives. In part it comes back to John McKay's comment mentioned earlier of preferring 'uncouth life to aesthetic death'. I would hasten to add that in my own experience I have witnessed little of the uncouth in Charismatic settings. I have, however, witnessed much aesthetic death elsewhere.

EXPECTANCY

The conference proceeded uneventfully and happily for me from Monday night to Thursday. I was struck by the very powerful sense of God's presence in almost all the proceedings and by the spirit of expectancy towards God. People saw Him as one mightily and intimately involved with His people. He was active. He was alive. He was there. Right there. And He could act now. Right now.

This sense of immediacy about God's activity struck me as a most positive dimension of Charismatic faith. Certainly it reflected more to me of the New Testament atmosphere and of the spirit of the early Church. Too often other sections of the Church are operating like the schoolboy who described faith as 'believing in something which you know isn't true'! These people believed it was true and acted as if they did. It was infectious.

GRAIN OF WHEAT

On Thursday morning, 1 September, I found myself a nice safe seat way back out of sight – the sort of seat no one but God would have noticed.

I was very reflective about the whole experience. What did it all say or mean? Here was I in a full-blown Renewal Conference, but as a sort of side-line cheerer for the Renewal Movement who approved of the game but couldn't quite get into it, yet who periodically dashed onto the field for a few mischievous moments before running back for the evangelical grandstand where I felt a bit safer!

Yet I must not sell myself or the grace of God too short. It had not all been fear and caution, because through all the preceding years of openness I had also experienced a strange sense of the sovereign purpose, planning or even strategy of God in allowing that fresh effusion of the Holy Spirit to elude me while it seemed to come so readily and easily to so many around me.

I had accordingly rested in slightly perplexed peace on the subject knowing that 'the Spirit . . . apportions to each one individually as He wills' (1 Cor. 12:11). Perhaps it was this important and meaningful sense of divine sovereignty which for years had also kept me interested yet detached, hungry yet content, open yet cautious, committed yet agnostic, deeply yearning yet curiously unmoved.

So there I was. Bob McAllister of Rio was preaching with extraordinary power on the importance of discerning the Body of Christ. The challenge to see Christ in my brother and my brother in Christ had struck home afresh and renewed in me more deeply than ever a commitment to the Church world-wide in all its facets.

The speaker sat down. Then Derek Crumpton, the conference coordinator, moved to the microphone to close the meeting. In a transitional and apparently throwaway line he said: 'Unless a grain of wheat falls into the earth and dies, it remains alone; but if it dies, it bears much fruit' (John 12:24). Just a verse of Scripture and well known to me at that. Later he told me: 'I still remember that moment. I had had that Scripture so strongly impressed on me that I knew it had to be spoken out, even if it appeared out of context.'

And so in obedience he spoke it out. At that moment, and totally and unexpectedly, I felt as if a surgeon's knife went through me. Something deep and painful and crucifying and new was happening in me in those very moments. I could not restrain the tears. The grain of wheat which was my life had to die in new and deeper and truer ways if it was to bring forth fruit pleasing to God. Somehow I had to get out of the way more and let God be God. Maybe it was a matter of getting the self more underground and hidden and out of sight like the grain. I knew God wanted more of me.

He wanted all of me. But the world, the flesh and the devil were still clutching at portions of territory in my life. It was painful to face. I had the Spirit, but did the Spirit have me?

I don't know how long the struggle continued. Half an hour. Maybe more. During that time loving brothers and sisters cared for me and prayed with me. Then the Spirit of peace and quiet praise began to overtake me. I wondered what it was all about. At the least I was sure that getting right with Jim and Mary had paved the way for this breakthrough.

In the middle of the whole experience I had the distinct sense of the Lord whispering that I should not fear to share this with the greater constituency of evangelicals in South Africa and in the wider world, especially the Lausanne movement for world evangelisation which was born out of the great 1974 world congress in that city. Although I was part of its continuing committee, I was not sure how such an opportunity of sharing would come my way. I would have to wait and see.

Another somewhat disturbing word came through to me. It related to my own plenary address to the conference that night. 'Remind them that Soweto is only eight miles away.'

Soweto is the great, sprawling and tragic creation of urban apartheid. Situated on the edge of Johannesburg, it stands not only as one of the great human sores of South Africa but as a symbol of black frustration, despair, pain and struggle. The *South West Township* – SO-WE-TO. Not a very prepossessing name. Nor a very prepossessing place.

And now here was the Spirit of God right in the middle of one of the most momentous spiritual experiences of my life bringing to my mind a social reality and a political tragedy of almost epic proportions and saying that neither I nor the South African Church should forget it.

It seemed I was to remind evangelicals of Pentecost and remind Pentecostals of politics! What an assignment! No wonder my spirit blanched. Indeed I quietly protested to my Lord. The sense of the Spirit's response was at once impressed on my soul: 'Unless a grain of wheat falls into the earth and DIES. . . . You must die to your will and the desire to please.' My willingness for such a death was being immediately tested. I was a reluctant debutant.

The thought of perhaps having to jar the conference with that sort of challenge had little appeal to me. But the Spirit's word was also in line with black expectations for me. For a couple of days blacks had been coming up to me and saying: 'We are praying for you, Mike, and for your message.'

I couldn't help reflecting that of the many sins of which we had all been exhorted to repent, no one had yet really hit racism. That night just before I stood up to speak, one leading black reached forward from behind me, clutched my upper arm and whispered: 'Courage, Mike, courage!' It was helpful.

HOPE FOR SOUTH AFRICA

The rest of the day following my seering experience in the morning had proceeded much like any other. No dramatic new experiences. No overwhelming sense of God's presence. Just quiet work on putting my message finally together. My subject was 'Hope for South Africa'.

I delivered the word with relative freedom and with a clear sense of what had to be said. I indicated in my opening comments my concern that 'in the great euphoria of these precious days' we should not allow ourselves to 'dangle too far above the complicated and ravished soil of South Africa today'. If we did, we would 'allow the intoxication of these days to open up an unbridgeable gulf between this great and glorious conference and the tortured tragedy of a city eight miles away called Soweto'.

I went on: 'At the outset I have to say this, that humanly speaking (and these are the key words – humanly speaking) I see no hope. Humanly speaking the tunnel is stygian dark to the eye. Humanly speaking I believe that we have through our political life-style sown a wind and we must, if human events take the normal course, reap the whirlwind. Every human law of history tells me that this is so. Humanly speaking, if we live in a moral universe, as I believe we do, then the judgments of history must surely overtake us. Humanly speaking thirty years of official discrimination cannot but produce a political convulsion of shattering and mind-boggling proportions. So humanly speaking I feel the situation in our land today is absolutely hopeless. Seeing what I see and hearing what I hear and knowing what I know from various people, I cannot say otherwise and still be true to myself. . . .

BUT GOD . . .

'And yet, and yet I want to say before this gathering that I AM HOPEFUL. I am full of hope in my heart tonight . . . because of two tiny but atomic words . . . BUT GOD. So Acts 2:23 says: "This Jesus, delivered up according to the definite plan and foreknowledge of God, you crucified and killed by the hands of lawless men. BUT GOD raised Him up." Then there is Acts 10:28: "You yourselves know how unlawful it is for a Jew to associate with or to visit any one of another nation; BUT GOD has shown me that I should not call any man common or unclean." Again Acts 10:40: "BUT GOD raised Him on the third day and made Him manifest."

'In those two words,' I went on, 'I see the tremendous hope we have for this land because they speak of Divine initiative, a Divine intervention in history.'

I went on to elaborate that there was hope for South Africa because of two particular historical precedents – firstly because there was hope for Israel in Egyptian bondage, and secondly because there was hope for Judah in Babylonian captivity.

On the first historical situation I concluded that 'in spite of the perversity of many of our Pharoahs, in spite of the despair of many of our own people, in spite of the reluctance of many of our men of God, yet God is going to work and He is going to bring us through. If not by the loving and constant courtship of the Holy Spirit, then by the persuasion of seven or even seventy-seven plagues of Egypt if need be. But He will bring us through.'

As to the second historical situation, what could one do but find even more encouragement and hope because here we have now, not simply a rabble group of slaves, but an apostate people who in spite of rebellious deafness to their prophets' pleas for justice and for purity of worship, had nevertheless found hope and mercy even while under the historical dynamics of divine judgement. Said Ezra: 'Even now there is hope . . . in spite of this' (Ezra 10:2).

Having faced the gathering with that hope which comes through the faithful mercy of God, I underlined the human responsibility upon us as the people of God and the Church of Jesus Christ in this land. 'As we look at these situations of history, the prophets – and especially Jeremiah – called a spade a spade. They didn't cloak what the problem was or what the sin was. Yet I fear lest in the Church of Jesus Christ in this land or perhaps even in a great and sensitive gathering like this, we fail to realise that we have to repent of that which is our national sin. And our national sin is discrimination on the basis of race. I do not know the political solution but I do know that unless we repent of this sin and of this system, the judgments of history will become the judgments of God upon us.'

I wound up with a strong plea not only for repentance but for reconciliation between husband and wife, between race and race, tribe and tribe, denomination and denomination, nation and nation, friend and friend.

Other talks had been greeted with huge amounts of laughter, clapping and regularly interspersed eruptions of 'Hallelujah' and 'Praise the Lord'. Mine was received with quietness and silence.

Said Derek Crumpton later: 'The atmosphere of deep seriousness was not one for applause. Had people applauded it would have indicated they had not heard you.'

THE NIGHT THAT WAS

Back in my room that night I had a joyful and peaceful time of prayer with Michael Nuttall, then Bishop of Pretoria and now Bishop of Natal. He was a very old and treasured friend from Cambridge days. Our time of prayer over, we said goodnight and turned to the business of slumber.

But sleep would not come to me. Instead, quite out of the blue, the Spirit of praise came upon my soul. All seemed to be release. All seemed to be freedom. Hour after hour I praised my God in unrestrained and unrestrainable doxology and song. In words of men and angels I rejoiced. No fatigue visited me that night. All my senses were vibrantly alive to God. The Holy Spirit was blessing me. Wave upon wave, it seemed. Flow upon flow. He seemed to be bubbling up from within, surrounding from without, ascending from below and descending from above!

Somewhere in the early hours of the morning I said to myself: 'I don't know the correct biblical name for this, but this is the experience I've heard others talk of.' I wasn't quite sure of its exact name or nature. I would have to think about that later.

In the meantime I kept praising until my bishop's alarm clock went off at dawn. Then I told him of my night. And we kept praising some more till finally the insistent calls of bacon and eggs were allowed to intrude upon the delights of the soul. It had been a monumental night. I had never had one like it. Nor have I had a comparable one since.

A NEW DAY

The new day was new indeed. It was totally luminous with the love and light of God. In some ways the experience was not too dissimilar to the spiritual delights which had enthralled me at conversion. I remember shortly after my conversion at Cambridge in 1955 reading the testimony of Temple Gairdner of Cairo: 'That sense of newness is simply delicious. It makes new the Bible and friends and all mankind and love and spiritual things and Sunday and church and God himself. So I've found.'

It really was a bit like that. A Second Touch, if you like. My spiritual perceptions seemed strangely sharpened and I felt borne along on the wings of my Lord's love. The desire to praise and worship God was perhaps the most striking aspect of what the previous day and night had brought.

Next morning, on the platform, while waiting for the meeting to begin, I whispered to Derek Prince sitting next to me: 'How are you today?'

'Great,' he said, 'for the first time on this trip I slept all night.'

'I feel great too,' I chortled, 'for the first time in my life I praised God all night!' He looked suitably startled!

Yes, never had I had such a wonderfully sleepless night! When the singing and worship of the meeting began I almost took wings.

But one thought plagued me. What of the past and of all that had gone before? What of my life and ministry prior to this moment? Had I missed God's highest will? Had I been operating only on half-throttle – or on three cylinders? Had it all been second rate? Was this experience something which I should have received years ago?

At first that was how it seemed to me. However, my prayers on this received an unexpected answer the very next day – and from an unexpected quarter, although I knew that here again I would also have to get back to the Scriptures and think through from the biblical text itself. Anyway, in the meantime succour seemed to come from a very beautiful Zulu woman by the name of Elsie Buthelezi, who bounced up to me all full of the joys of life. Cousin to the Kwa-Zulu Prime Minister, Chief Gatsha Buthelezi, she has a royal look about her and invariably dresses in the most exotic African traditional garbs. This day was no exception. Her dress was a brilliant cascade of African colour and design. Her headgear was an intricate and fascinating mosaic of rural beadwork, while her arms and legs tinkled with the gentle sound of Zulu bangles.

I had known Elsie ever since the Durban Congress back in 1973. Now she greeted me with that unmatched warmth of the open African heart.

'Oh, Mike, my brother, I have been praying I would see you because the Lord has given me a message for you.'

'Really, Elsie,' I responded, a bit startled.

'Oh, *yes*, my brother,' she replied with emphasis, pulling me aside by the hand out of the hurly-burly of human traffic moving from the main auditorium to the seminar sessions.

'But first let me thank you for the other night. Oh, Mike, it was wonderful. We were all praying for you so much, especially the brothers and sisters from Soweto. We knew you would speak for us. Thank you, my brother, thank you. We are proud of you.'

At such moments one senses the deep privilege of being a white African bound in the love of Jesus Christ to black Africans.

'Now, Mike, I must give you a word. All yesterday the Lord impressed on my heart to tell you that all the past has been just right and in His will. Nothing has been wasted. This has been His plan and now, and not before now, is His timing of this blessing for you. Nothing is to be regretted. He has been leading you forward in His sovereign and perfect purposes.'

It was an astonishing and incredibly important word for me. In fact, if I remember correctly, I had exactly that question of the past all whirling round in my mind at the very moment Elsie came up to me. Strange and wonderful indeed are the ways of God to man. He was saying that my past was being beautifully interwoven into His sovereign plan for my future. We may seek new blessings, but the timing of reception is God's, not ours.

More theologically the point was punched home by Dr Godfrey Ashby, then Professor of Old Testament History at

Rhodes University in Grahamstown, and now Bishop of Transkei, in his address on 'Treasures Old and New'.

Reflecting on his own life prior to a fresh experience of the Holy Spirit, Ashby affirmed: 'I cannot and I must not say the Spirit has in any way been absent. At times He may well be denied, He may well be neglected, He may well be fought against, but He is always at work because His world is God's world. . . . If we deny the Spirit outside any special eruption like the baptism in the Spirit, we are playing into the hands of the Devil and selling our birthright. . . .'

He added: 'The Spirit is and was and always has been at work: praise God for that. . . . It is God in the beginning and God at the end. It is God at all points on the journey, even in the middle! There is not a series of sudden eruptions only. It is the Treasury of the Spirit, the ever present Spirit of Truth fulfilling all creation.'

This was helpful. None of the treasures of the past were to be renounced but to be embraced more fully and richly than ever before.

Accordingly I found myself experiencing a renewed commitment not only to biblical and evangelical truth, but also to ecumenical relationships, holistic evangelism and compassionate socio-political concern.

UNEXPECTED ENDING

The wind-up to that conference was a precious blur of happy and rewarding encounters, each of which enriched me in some way.

First came a momentous Communion Service on the final Sunday morning.

It was too long for many people, but the greatest experience ever of Holy Communion for me. My heart was locked in the heavenlies in worship and adoration. The Communion hymn said it all:

> When I survey the wondrous Cross
> On which the Prince of Glory died,

My richest gain I count but loss
And pour contempt on all my pride.

Were the whole realm of nature mine,
That were an offering far too small.
Love so amazing, so divine,
Demands my soul, my life, my all.

Then that night came the last evening meeting and in fact the final experience of the conference for me, because I had to fly out early next morning to Zimbabwe, thereby missing out on the closing session of the gathering.

However, the evening occasion was particularly memorable in my mind for two things – a prayer and a frolic.

First the prayer. In the latter part of the meeting someone gave me a slip of paper to pass on to conference coordinator Derek Crumpton. It said 'Please pray for Rhodesia' (now Zimbabwe).

'Why don't you lead us, Mike,' whispered Derek. 'After all you're going up there in the next day or so.'

'OK,' I agreed, stepping up to the microphone.

In praying that prayer I recollect a deep sense of being given the faith to believe for the ultimate healing and salvation of Zimbabwe. It was a strange experience. The sudden ability to believe God for a place. A seemingly hopeless place at that time. I felt God wanted to heal that land and would do it His way. My faith in the future of that great land still stands, having held firm since that prayer on Sunday evening, 4 September 1977, in the Milner Park Renewal Conference.

As to the frolic, this came a little later at the very end of the meeting.

'What shall we sing?' said Derek Crumpton to the crowd just before wind-up time.

'Let us sing, let us sing a song unto the Lord,' I called out, referring to that exuberant, rhythmic and joyful spiritual song. It was the closing song of the closing evening meeting. The place was ready for a burst-out. And it came.

The roof was almost lifted as the conferees erupted into

song. It was exhilarating. Liberating. Almost intoxicating. Tapping feet and waving arms became more vigorous.

Suddenly Francis MacNutt and Derek Prince burst into a sort of jig on the platform. 'Now this really is something different,' I thought. 'I don't know about this.' Scarcely had I formulated my reservation when I saw Derek Prince heading across the platform towards me like some sort of highland dancer-cum-toreador who has not quite made up his mind whether he is in a Scottish eightsome reel, a Yankee barn dance or a Spanish bullfight! His arm crooked against his side, he lunged towards me in invitation. There was nothing to do, short of being a cad and a spoilsport, and next minute I was jigging in figure of eight between Prince, MacNutt, Bishop Bruce Evans of Port Elizabeth and Sipho Bhengu of Soweto.

Down in the 'body of the kirk' as it were, my staggered colleagues, John Tooke, Ebenezer Sikakane, Bill Winter and David Peters, a great Indian evangelist, found their eyes popping, their sides convulsed and their minds boggled. 'There is Cassidy dancing for joy on a platform in front of three thousand South Africans. The ultimate de-tribalising of an inhibited conservative!'

The service over, I left the platform a little shame-faced – but full of joy. My heart was still praising God even though I realised that my spiritual burst in living it up would now have to be followed by living it down!

Chapter Thirteen

TODDLING IN THE SPIRIT

> However far the Christian has gone in the life of
> faith, he knows he is still only a child playing in the
> shallows and that there is far more to be discovered
> of the riches of the friendship of Christ.
>
> Bishop Stephen Neill

The day the Milner Park Conference ended I flew up to Zimbabwe to meet with some of my colleagues. In the plane I pondered the experience of the previous week and realised that the test of it all was now about to begin. How would this affect my personal walk with Christ, my relationships at home, my ministry, my social concern?

What came home to me with new force was St Paul's injunction to the Galatians to 'Walk by [or in] the Spirit' (Gal. 5:16). Having supposedly entered upon a deepened experience of the Spirit, I was now faced with the challenge of a deeper walk, yet one felt such a toddler. I saw that somehow I had to penetrate more seriously into what the Apostle highlights as his major theme in the book of Romans – namely 'the obedience of faith'. This pregnant little phrase, coming both at the beginning of the Roman epistle and at the end, underlines that *obedience* is what the life of faith is all about.

So in the opening paragraph Paul indicates that both the grace he had received and his very apostleship were granted in order to bring about *the obedience of faith*. In effect he is saying: 'This is what I am going to talk about in this letter.'

Then, like any good author, he summarises in the same terms at the end of the letter what he has been saying in the body of it – namely that the 'Gospel and preaching of Jesus Christ . . . according to the command of the eternal God' have one basic purpose which is 'to bring about the *obedience* of faith' (Rom. 16:25–6).

Was it not this, then, that my new experience was all about – the obedience of faith? Certainly this tied in with another passage which I noticed with new understanding during those few days in Zimbabwe – namely John 14:15 – where Jesus says: 'If you love me, you will keep my commandments. And I will pray the Father, and He will give you another Counsellor . . . even the Spirit of truth. . . .' The fourfold word stood out:

If you love –
You will keep –
I will pray –
He will give –

Here is the Second Person of the Trinity praying to the First Person of the Trinity for the giving of the Third Person of the Trinity to those who show Him their love by keeping and obeying His commandments.

Somehow or other the work of the Spirit and the obedience of faith were intimately tied together.

IN HIM

Flying back from Salisbury, I decided to reread Colossians and Ephesians. A number of things struck me afresh.

First of all, both in Ephesians and Colossians the little phrase '*In Him*' stood out with new meaning.* All our

---

* 1. *In Him* we are chosen before the foundation of the world (Eph. 1:4).

2. *In Him* we have redemption (Eph. 1:7).

3. *In Him* the mystery of His will is made known to us (Eph. 1:9).

4. *In Him* is a plan to unite all things (Eph. 1:10).

Footnote continues

blessings are in Him. Indeed we have been blessed 'in Christ with every spiritual blessing' (Eph. 1:3).

All this struck me afresh with tremendous force and I realised that much of the time our spiritual eyes are just not open to discovering and appreciating all that is *in Him* and all that we have *in Him* as believers.

Small wonder then that Paul's prayer for the Ephesians hit me like a thunderbolt: 'I do not cease to give thanks for you, remembering you in my prayers, that the God of our Lord Jesus Christ, the Father of glory, may give you a spirit of *wisdom* and of *revelation* in the knowledge of Him, having the eyes of your hearts enlightened that you may know . . .' the following three things:

> firstly, 'what is the *hope* to which He has called you'
> secondly 'what are the *riches of His glorious inheritance* in the saints' and
> thirdly, 'what is the *immeasurable greatness* of *His power* in us who believe. . . .' (Eph. 1:16–19).

I remember Johannesburg coming into view. The wing tipped and the plane turned in towards the runway. That's it, I thought. A Pauline prayer is being answered in me because in this whole experience I am receiving a new 'spirit of wisdom and of revelation' and the 'eyes of [my] heart' are being enlightened to grasp afresh these three things:

Footnote continued
  5. *In Him* we have been destined and appointed to live for the praise of His glory (Eph. 1:12).
  6. *In Him* all who have heard the word of truth and believed in Him have been sealed with the promised Holy Spirit (Eph. 1:13).
  7. *In Him* we sit in heavenly places (Eph. 2:6).
  8. *In Him* all things were created (Col. 1:16).
  9. *In Him* all things hold together (Col. 1:17).
  10. *In Him* the fullness of God was pleased to dwell (Col. 1:19).
  11. *In Him* we who were estranged and hostile are now reconciled (Col. 1:22).
  12. *In Him* are hid all the treasures of wisdom and knowledge (Col. 2:3).
  13. *In Him* we are to be rooted and built up (Col. 2:7).
  14. *In Him* the whole fullness of deity dwells bodily (Col. 2:9).
  15. *In Him* we *have* come to fullness of life (Col. 2:10).

1. The *hope* to which I have been called as a believer
2. The *riches* of the glorious inheritance that is mine as a believer
3. The immeasurable *greatness of His Spirit's power* in me as a believer.

In other words, I was starting anew to 'possess my possessions'.

HOMECOMING

When I got home all bright-eyed and bushy-tailed and ready to tell my precious Carol all about it, I was greeted with that look wives reserve for delinquent husbands when they seem to say 'And what, pray, have you been up to?' – the sort of look you get when you come in late from work, or have forgotten a chore!

I sensed she was concerned. Then it came out. Some eager beaver who had returned home from the Renewal Conference had phoned Carol. 'Oh, praise the Lord, He's worked mightily in Michael. We saw him dancing on the stage in front of the whole conference.'

Carol nearly had a cadenza, as the saying goes. What on earth had happened to her husband? Had he gone off his rocker? Had he made a total fool of himself?

How on earth could she understand and get the whole thing in perspective? This somewhat ill-advised advance word had queered the pitch and complicated for me the whole process of sharing the experience with the person closest to me in my life.

Anyway, we were fortunately scheduled to go away for some days of leave to the coast and this constituted a precious time of sharing, prayer and studying together. For hours Carol and I searched the Scriptures, listened to tapes and sought God in new ways.

LISTENING

I found myself waking very early every morning and wanting to pray and study the scriptures with fresh intensity. What began to come home to me was the importance of listening – listening, that is, for the whisper of the Spirit of God so that one might walk more obediently in the daily details of life. To walk obediently one had to get orders. To get orders one had to listen. Was God interested in the detailed unfolding of each day in the life of His children? I began to believe He was.

First of all, in the three consecutive chapters of the book of Acts, (Chapters 8, 9, 10) I saw three consecutive acts of listening plus the astonishing consequences flowing from each.

In Chapter 8 there was Philip in Samaria conducting mass rallies, and having a city-wide campaign even Billy Graham would have envied: 'The multitudes with one accord gave heed to what was said' (verse 6). Then comes the word from God: 'Rise and go . . . to Gaza' (verse 26). So 'he rose and went' (verse 27) 'And the Spirit said to Philip, "Go up and join this chariot"' (verse 29).

Philip then witnesses to the Ethiopian government official, wins him to Christ – and sends him on his way to *OPEN UP A CONTINENT*.

Then in Acts 9 there is the word to Ananias. Again it is 'Rise and go' (verse 11) and again there is prompt obedience. Ananias in fear and trembling goes to pray for the notorious Saul of Tarsus. That would be like you or me being sent to the Ayatollah Khomeini! Ananias prays for Saul, he is filled with the Holy Spirit, and the *world's greatest-ever missionary and evangelist* is galvanised into mission.

Finally, in Acts 10 it is the Jewish Peter being commissioned to go to the Gentile Cornelius – a tougher job for the Lord this time because Peter with all his cultural and religious hang-ups was a tougher character. Finally, after a few human refusals and a few divine visions, Peter goes on his way to Cornelius. Once more it is 'Rise and go' (verse 20) as a word from the Spirit. Once again there is obedience. 'And Peter went . . .' (verse 21). Peter now wins Cornelius to Christ. This time, it is the *whole mission to the Gentile world which is launched*.

Three words from God. Three men. Three acts of obedience. Three astounding sets of consequence. A continent is opened. The greatest-ever evangelist is empowered. The Gentile mission is launched.

Could the Holy Spirit not guide thus in our times? Obviously God had a plan for Philip, for Ananias and for Peter. Clearly in Acts 13 also the Holy Spirit has a will and He speaks it out: 'Set apart for me Barnabas and Saul for the work to which I have called them' (verse 2). Equally clearly the Holy Spirit had a detailed plan for Barnabas and Paul because after they had preached in Phrygia and Galatia, they were 'forbidden by the Holy Spirit to speak the word in Asia' (Acts 16:6). And again when they wanted to go into Bithynia, 'the Spirit of Jesus did not allow them' (verse 7). Then came the Macedonian call. That was where they were meant to go.

Obviously both in general and in detail these men walked in the Spirit in obedience to the whispered word of God to their spirits.

I began to long to know more of such a walk. I saw afresh that 'to obey is better than sacrifice, and to hearken than the fat of rams' (1 Sam. 15:22).

THREE WAVES

The morning after we arrived at the coast, I awoke particularly early. I felt almost as if I had been shaken awake and found myself with a strong compulsion within me to go down to the beach. It was about five o'clock and the sun was just peeping over the horizon in a glorious blaze of brilliant orange. I began to walk along the deserted beach in a spirit of prayer and rejoicing. When I had gone some distance I spotted a lone surfer out in the waves. I began to watch him with some fascination. A wave came along and he tried with much flurrying and paddling to catch it. He missed it and the wave flowed on leaving him becalmed in its wake. Then came a second wave. There was more flurrying and paddling and this time the surfer caught the wave, moved beautifully with it for a few yards, then twisted, turned and tumbled in a great surging mass of sea and board and surf and surfer! It was a spectacular tumble. I kept watching with fascination.

The young man, dogged as they come, retrieved his board, paddled way out into the sea again and waited patiently. A third wave came. This time he judged it perfectly. He moved quickly into its flow, was borne up on its surging power and began to ride it with perfect balance and control all the way in to the shore. It was an astonishing spectacle. He just seemed to keep going and going, moving sensitively with every ebb and flow of the wave's momentum until he was literally landed on the sand.

No sooner had all this happened than I suddenly became curiously aware of the Spirit of God seeming to say to me: 'This is why I brought you down here. It was to see this parable. Each wave represents the movement of my Spirit through the world at this time. The three experiences of the surfer represent three categories of people faced with this wave. Some miss the wave altogether and are left behind. A second group of people get into the wave but they do not ride it sensitively or with skill and they tumble and fall and they too are left behind. A third category moves into the flow of my Spirit and they are borne along by it and are landed safely on every shore to which I send them, and on that final Shore of a fulfilled ministry and a completed task. Do not be left behind by the wave of my Spirit. Do not stumble and fall. But ride the wave and know its power.'

This experience left me not only rejoicing afresh but reflective. I kept walking along the beach thinking about what it meant to ride the wave to all the shores and appointments of God. After a while I turned round and began to retrace my tracks. As I returned to where my friend, the surfer, was still enjoying himself, I saw another person standing right there on the beach, also all by himself and surveying the surfer. As I walked towards him our eyes met. Although I had never seen him before, he smiled a warm smile of recognition. 'Aren't you Michael Cassidy?' he asked. I couldn't deny it and we began to chat amicably after he had introduced himself. Suddenly I had the strong sense that this was part two of the lesson for the morning. It was a first little outworking of the principle of the parable. It was almost as if the Lord was saying to me: 'Here is your Ethiopian, here is your Saul, here is your Cornelius. Share with him what I have just shown you.'

So I began to tell my new-found friend of the experience with the surfer in the waves a few minutes previously. He was a Church member. In fact, it transpired I knew his minister and he seemed open and hungry for the word I was sharing with him. It seemed the Lord was eager to show me within minutes how the practice worked once I'd grasped the principle. He could indeed organise His appointments to be my appointments if I would listen to the whispers of His Spirit and be ready to obey.

MINISTRY ON THE WING

The chance to test this principle further came very soon when I had to leave for a time of overseas ministry. I was headed for California where my office had a pretty full schedule worked out for me. The only times which seemingly were not already structured were my flight times in the aeroplane! I accordingly said to the Lord that I would like to see how this principle worked as I put myself at His disposal on the different flights.

We took off from Jan Smuts Airport, Johannesburg, and headed, via Ilha do Sol off the western bulge of Africa, for New York. Also on the plane was my good friend Peter Eliastam, a brilliant Jewish commercial artist who had been led into Christian commitment through one of my colleagues, John Tooke.

Sitting together we had a wonderful time of fellowship. The first thing that happened was that one of the stewards spotted my Bible and came up and began to tell me that he, too, was a Christian. Then he brought another steward till finally we were quite a little cluster. Peter suggested in the early hours of the morning, when we were still two or three hours from New York, that we should have a little service together which we duly did, somewhat to the astonishment of an isolated passenger who ventured to the toilet during the night! However, the most interesting development took place a little while after this when a Chinese woman suddenly appeared right by my seat and knelt down in front of me in a posture of respectful enquiry.

'I heard you talking about Christ,' she said, 'and I want to hear more. I have great problems.' She was from the seat behind us so it was easy to move in next to her and hear her story. For the next hour or so I ministered to her, particularly in terms of her marriage which was in deep trouble. She said she had been praying for guidance and help and that what I had shared with her was just what she needed. I knew this was another of God's appointments.

After we reached New York, I headed for my connecting flight to California. 'Lord,' I prayed, 'that was a wonderful time of ministry, praise Your Name. Let me be available again.'

I was ushered to my seat on the next flight and duly began to settle down. However, I had not been seated more than two or three minutes when the steward descended on both me and the man next to me and said he wanted to move us and put a married couple in where we were. Locating the other man close by, he then took me all the way up the length of the plane, right out the other end of the economy-class section and into the first-class where he put me down next to a rather well-groomed young executive! I had never flown first class, so this was a new experience. If this was what toddling in the Spirit was all about then I was rather in favour of it! Every conceivable attention was lavished upon us, champagne was served, and the plane took off! 'A bit of all right,' as my father used to say.

Although the whole happening was in its way positively comical, I nevertheless felt that God was in this changing of seats. Before long I was chatting away happily to this young man and hearing his story. It transpired that he had been planning on going into a Catholic Order, but had begun to have doubts and problems with his faith, had turned aside from the procedure and had gone into the airline business. We had a simply tremendous Christ-centred talk.

'Listen, Peter,' I said, 'I really believe the Lord has something for me to share with you that is important for your life. In fact, I have been moved from economy class to first class to share it with you!' He seemed suitably impressed and in between the caviar and all that we covered considerable spiritual ground! I later had a wonderfully warm Christmas card from him.

ANOTHER DIVINE APPOINTMENT

The ministry on the Californian West Coast and in St Louis, Missouri, came and went and then I was on my way back East.

My excitement about the Lord's work on aeroplanes and what He was teaching me about His appointments knew no bounds. I took my seat in the centre section of a relatively empty aircraft bound for Newark, New Jersey. It seemed as if I would have the flight to myself, as there were no other passengers close by. In fact, the plane was almost empty. So I settled down to read. However, just before take-off, a young woman entered the centre block of seats and sat down one seat away from me. She was open and friendly and while settling into her seat she shivered and said: 'My, but this plane's freezing. There must be something wrong with the air conditioning.' I made some polite come-back, she bounced into further conversation, and we were off. Detecting my accent she asked me where I was from and what I did. Then she looked at me quizzically, 'Aren't you with African Enterprise? In fact, aren't you Michael Cassidy?'

'Well, Lord, you're on the job again,' I chortled inwardly. 'This is really fun!'

'Yes,' I replied to the young lady with my most astonished look, 'I am Michael Cassidy. How did you know?'

'Now, how about that!' said the girl. 'I come from the First Presbyterian Church of Salinas in California which supports your ministry. I know all about your work.'

I knew the Church well and had preached in it several times.

In no time she was sharing about herself and her situation. She told me she was in a very rough and difficult predicament in a relationship with her boyfriend. He wanted to marry her, but she wasn't sure and was terribly torn and in two minds. 'Anyway,' she went on, 'early this morning back in California my room-mate and I prayed earnestly that the Lord would give me some guidance quickly and clearly. I am on my way to meet him now in Newark and I desperately need clarity. I think you may be able to help me. I think this is part of the answer to my prayers.'

We chatted at length about the principles of guidance and clarification which the Lord can often use with us in the whole process of choosing a life-partner. Not knowing the details of the relationship I could only talk in generalities but I felt a great freedom in articulating to her certain insights which might be of relevance. In fact I felt I was sharing with her exactly what she needed. Later in the airport building she introduced me to her boyfriend and I waved them both a cheery goodbye. Six months later she sent me a letter saying that our conversation had been very important and that God had shown her very clearly during the following few weeks that it was not right for her to become engaged to that boyfriend. She had tremendous peace about this and knew in new ways that God had His hand upon her life. Then she added an interesting detail. 'You know, I quite often go on aeroplanes and whenever I do, I sit in a window seat. I never like sitting anywhere else. But that night as I went to check-in for my flight I heard a very clear voice within me saying: "Don't ask for a window seat. Allow the girl at the counter to assign your seat." The allocation, which put me next to you, was the first time in my life I had flown in the centre section of the plane!'

MUZOREWA

Leaving the East Coast I headed back via London to Africa. My last stop before heading into Johannesburg was Nairobi. By this time, every flight had taken on an excitement of its own. What would happen now? Having cleared Nairobi customs, all the passengers were herded aboard an airport bus to take us out to the plane. The little man pressed against me in the bus looked familiar.

'Aren't you Bishop Abel Muzorewa?' I asked.

'Yes,' replied the pocket-sized black bishop who was one of the main political leaders of Zimbabwe. The situation there was one that had been exercising my mind and heart for some time and I had had contact with many of the political leaders there in the different major political groupings. I had in the course of things met a number of Muzorewa's assistants, but not him. He was an important man and one who needed much prayer. Once again, I had the overpowering sense that God had ordered this encounter. The bishop happily agreed that we should sit together and for the next three hours we shared deeply on the Zimbabwean question. I was amazed that he opened his heart to me as freely as he did. Later on, back in Zimbabwe, about eight or nine months before he became prime minister of the interim government, we had fellowship once again and I, along with two friends, was able to pray with him and for him on the very day when he and his party had to make up their minds about whether to cooperate with the whites in seeking a political settlement.

Although Muzorewa later lost out to Robert Mugabe, I have always felt that in the mysterious economy of God, he played an important political role in the intermediate process which moved Zimbabwe towards majority rule. In any event, our encounter on the plane and our subsequent prayer together was, I believe, part of the Lord's plan and part of what He was teaching me about conscious surrender to the agenda of the Holy Spirit both in general and in detail.

The overseas trip had provided new insights and lessons in what ministry on the wing and life on the wave was all about.

FAILURE

However, not long after returning home, all full of the joys of my recent trip, I went away on holiday for our annual leave with the family.

As suddenly as I had been fired up a few months previously with new life in the Spirit, so just as suddenly it seemed as if I had run out of steam. All my victorious joyrides seemed to be over and instead I found myself down and depressed. Perhaps I was exhausted, but certainly I was not making it spiritually. I entered a spell of not wanting to pray or even read the Bible. I was irritable with everyone around me and impatient with myself. Where was all this new-found joy and power in the Holy Spirit? Poor Carol! To be sure she was no longer seeing her husband riding the crest of the wave. She must have wondered how authentic it all was. It was a depressing few weeks, especially as I knew I was badly failing my Lord in witness to Him and to the work of the Spirit. I wasn't walking in the Spirit. I wasn't even toddling. I was just stumbling and falling all over the place like the surfer on the second wave.

As high as the hill had been, so low now seemed the trough.

This really shook me as I had hoped this sort of spiritual fainting fit would be something of the past.

Rising early one morning, I went out for a walk. Sitting high on a sand dune I called on the Lord to show me what was wrong. Fiddling in the dry compressed sand with a stick I started a little slide of sand. It was like a mini-mini avalanche. And each time I moved any blockage to the sand it seemed to flow more freely down the dune. It was instructive.

I began to think. Had not some blockages come in my life in recent weeks? After all, I wasn't consciously appropriating the Spirit's presence. I wasn't, as it were, practising the presence of God. I wasn't keeping myself alert for spiritual opportunity. I wasn't being considerate of Carol and the children. I was being introspective and self-centred. Above all, I had allowed myself through fatigue and weariness to stop my regular devotions.

That was it. There were blocks. Remove these and the flow would start again. Go back down the road and see where I had taken a wrong turning. Reflect on words from the Lord which had been quickened to my heart and see where I was disobeying. That was the key. And I did it.

It seemed one had to maintain an almost constant state of appropriation along with up-to-the minute repentances for one's constant failures of love or care or discipline.

Some while later I met an African Christian outside the Nairobi Cathedral. I asked him how he was.

'Repenting and praising,' he beamed.

Yes, that was the key. If you kept repenting and kept removing the blocks of sin, your heart would keep praising.

In any event, it was salutary during that holiday at the coast to be reminded that failure, dryness and the work of the Spirit were not mutually exclusive. Climactic new experiences of the Spirit were no shortcut to spiritual growth and no guarantee of avoiding spiritual failure. In all this I grasped afresh that no one spiritual experience lands one safely in any Canaan of spiritual maturity. There remains the constant demand of walking, of appropriating, of practising, and of remembering that God has a will and a way and an agenda for the day. As I acted on all this by faith, it all seemed to work for me. When I forgot to act and live by faith, my floundering recurred. And in all honesty I have to admit that it has been a constant battle ever since that time. I haven't got it all licked. I am still a beginner. I am in motion. In odyssey. A pilgrim.

A further challenge in terms of seeking to walk in the Spirit came from David du Plessis' autobiography. He writes:

I began to be sensitive to the Lord's checking rather than relying only on those times when He said, 'Thou shalt do that'. . . . It became my practice to dedicate my mind to the Lord daily, often before I got out of bed in the morning, something like this: 'I am yours today, Lord, and whatever comes to my mind, every guidance I get, I'll just follow on. I will do what my hands find to do. I won't stop unless you stop me. Guide me hour by hour, and I don't want to know this morning what I am to do this afternoon. I have an idea of what duties there are, and I am going to do my duty. If there is any point in which I am losing the way or going where you don't want me to go, check me.'[48]

David testifies to the fact that he learnt to trust the 'checks' of the Holy Spirit. He adds:

> I just proceeded along the course that seemed right. And I learnt to recognise the checks. My mind might say one thing, but my heart felt something else. I began to pay attention to those feelings. If I developed a marvellous thought in my mind, but didn't feel comfortable down in my heart, then I knew that I was being checked. I stopped and waited.[49]

So then, while I knew I was still so very far away from a walk like this, I could say that I had caught something of a vision of what the Spirit wants from us. Perhaps it is summed up in the concept of yielding oneself consciously on a moment by moment basis to the indwelling Spirit. Was this what Paul was after when he said: 'Yield yourselves to God as men who have been brought from death to life and your members to God as instruments of righteousness' (Romans 6:13)?

I recollect a conversation in 1965 with John Pollock, the author, who was then busy on a biography of Billy Graham.

'What is Billy Graham's outstanding quality?' I asked Mr Pollock.

'There are two which go together,' the writer replied. 'First of all he is integrity personified. Secondly, he has the deepest sense of anyone I know of being an instrument of God.'

Perhaps such deep yielding to instrumentality explains such great fullness of the Spirit as is evident in the life and ministry of Billy Graham.

In any event, as far as I personally was concerned, it was good to work at walking in the Spirit, even if one ended up toddling much of the time.

Chapter Fourteen

A FILLING OR THE BAPTISM?

The church must lay down its norms for doctrine
and practice, but we should be as ready as the
Weather Forecaster to admit that however reliable
our calculations, most of the time we cannot
command the wind. And when the Spirit disobeys
our canons we should avoid the absurd sin of
rigidity.

Canon John Taylor

Of course, I could not for long delay the serious matter of putting on my theological thinking cap and reflecting on what seemed to have taken place in my life, both in terms of the new experience at Milner Park and in terms of the successes and especially failures in the period after it. Not that I had not reflected before on the theology of the Holy Spirit, but somehow all of this was adding new grist to the mill. What had happened? Was my Milner Park experience A filling of the Spirit, as one in a possible series of experiences? Or was it THE Baptism in the Spirit, as a once for all non-repeatable phenomenon?

I realised of course, as mentioned earlier, that neither I nor anyone else could or should build a theology on an experience.

Rather we build our theologies on the Word of God and fit our experience into the biblical picture which emerges. This point of procedure is important or we can land up in all kinds of confusion.

HUMILITY

Having said that, I would want to add the importance of approaching our theological formulations with humility, flexibility and grace – especially in so far as the Holy Spirit is concerned. In fact, brave, if not foolish, is the man who dares to present a final or definitive word on the Holy Spirit, because it seems to me that He is in a sense God, the surpriser – God, the unpredictable – God, the iconoclast – God the boxbreaker – God, the 'desystematiser' of systematic theologians!

I can't help feeling that much of the current confusion on the person and work of the Holy Spirit lies in just this – that we have tried to over-systematise One who is extraordinarily unsystematic and we have tried to confine in neat theological categories One who, like the wind, blows where He chooses, unfettered by the theological formulations in which we seek to contain Him, or the human predictables by which we hope to anticipate Him.

If I think of my own library, I have a host of books by authors not only orthodox, neo-orthodox and unorthodox, but also Pentecostal, neo-pentecostal and anti-pentecostal, all presenting equally dogmatically the last and definitive word on the Spirit's person and work! Every one, I suspect, has some of the truth. No one has all.

THREE DANGERS

What I see in most of these books highlights three dangers. Either we lock into talking a lot of theory about the Spirit without letting Him disturb our lives in any significant or creative way. Or we simply give up on the subject and say it's all too confusing and should therefore be pushed to the edge of our lives and thinking. Or we hungrily pursue an emotional experience of the Spirit on which we then build a theology regardless of the Bible's teaching and without struggling with the New Testament data.

Dangers one and two (academic theologising on the one hand and intellectual despairing on the other) threaten to leave our lives impoverished. Danger three (theologising on experience) threatens to leave our theology unbalanced.

In other words, neither the danger of dogmatising nor the impossibility of finalising our view of the Spirit's work must make us retreat from an honest attempt to understand the biblical data and apply it to our lives. After all we don't tolerate such retreats regarding the Bible's teaching on the atonement, or on conversion or on prayer. Nor can we tolerate such a retreat from the Bible's view of the Holy Spirit.

So, then, in coming to the matter of formulating our view we are to do so with both humility and flexibility, trying to distinguish between those areas where real clarity is possible and those areas where differences of viewpoint will remain and where a measure of agnosticism is almost inevitable.

PROCEDURE

Perhaps at this point it is also worth noting that evangelicals and Charismatics tend to have two slightly different approaches to the text of the Bible as they seek to determine their views.

In a nutshell evangelicals tend to build their theology of the Spirit from the distinctly theological sections of the New Testament (e.g. the Gospels and Epistles) while Charismatics and Pentecostals build theirs more on the historical sections of the New Testament (e.g. Acts). This is a slight over-simplification but perhaps a serviceable one in highlighting the approaches.

You see, many evangelicals believe it to be an important principle of interpretation (hermeneutics is the technical word) that theology is built on theological rather than historical sections of the text. History illustrates doctrine rather than constituting it, we say, at least not in any primary sense, though there is a recognised and obvious interplay. In other words, we start with theology and end with practice, not vice versa. Put differently, we could say we are to move from the general to the special, from the systematic to the historical, from doctrine, as found in the Gospels but especially the Epistles, to the historical outworking of it, as found in the book of Acts.

Pentecostals and Charismatics are less persuaded of this as a rigid principle of interpretation and therefore less squeamish about drawing theology from the book of Acts.

Perhaps a little give and take from each side would be useful.

So on the one hand we must ask evangelicals who press this so-called hermeneutical principle to avoid doing so too rigidly. After all, Paul asserts in 2 Tim. 3:16 that '*All* scripture – [i.e. ALL Scripture – not just doctrinal sections] is . . . profitable for teaching.'

It is also notable that in the Old Testament historical sections and prophetic sections are very much intertwined and interrelated, and in the New Testament history and teaching are certainly profoundly interrelated in the Gospels. So we must be careful not to push this principle too artificially.

On the other hand, Charismatics and Pentecostals need to exercise caution in their use of Acts, particularly if or when their handling of Acts lands them in doctrinal formulations which are hard to square with the systematic doctrinal statements of the Epistles. Nowhere is this more classically seen than in the controversy surrounding the phenomenon and term of 'the Baptism in the Holy Spirit'. The Epistles do not speak of any two-tier or double-staged process of initiation into the Christian life, but the book of Acts at points seems to suggest this.

Put differently and more personally, if I were to attach a label to my own experience at the Milner Park Conference, what would or should I call it?

There are basically only two terms which are used in the modern situation. One is 'the filling of the Spirit' and the other is 'the Baptism in the Spirit'. Which is correct?

Let's move one step at a time.

BE FILLED

First of all, the Bible commands us: 'Do not get drunk with wine . . . but be filled with the Spirit' (Eph. 5:18). So this is not a desirable spiritual option but a clear biblical command. What does it mean?

To me it can only mean one thing. If I received the Holy Spirit when I was born again, as I believe I did, and if He indwells me, as I believe He does, then Paul's exhortation must mean something like this: 'You have the Spirit, but does He have you? You have taken Him into your life, but you must now allow Him to fill you – in the sense of being released to occupy and control every area and every corner.'

I often think of it like the progression in the Second World War from the landings in Normandy on D-Day to the final conquest of Europe heralded on V-E-Day. When we are born again it is as if God by His Spirit lands on or in alien and occupied territory. Then He must be allowed to advance from that bridgehead, as it were, to occupy, conquer, capture and fill all the territory with His rule and His presence. This is the process of sanctification. This is the advance of the King and of His Kingdom or Kingship in our lives.

In many ways this must of necessity be a lifetime matter, but sometimes God may make extremely dramatic breakthroughs when all at once we allow Him by our surrender to capture and occupy massive and hitherto unsurrendered tracts of our lives. At such moments we may experience overwhelming joy, release, power and praise.

ALL BLESSINGS

Then we must recognise another great and important truth which is especially brought home in Paul's Epistles – and it is this: in Christ the believer has already been blessed with all spiritual blessings. It has already happened if we are *in Christ*.

Thus the Apostle can say in Eph. 1:3: 'Blessed be the God and Father of our Lord Jesus Christ, who HAS blessed us [this is an aorist tense in the Greek conveying a past happening] with every spiritual blessing in the heavenly places.'

In other words, if we are in Christ every spiritual blessing is already ours. It is all reckoned to our account. It is our possession. We '*have* come to fullness of life in Him' (Col. 2:10).

But, of course, we must possess our possessions, as the saying goes, and appropriate what is our heritage and our rightful inheritance. Rather sadly most of us do not do this and we impoverish ourselves most seriously in consequence. John Stott has put it in this way:

> For a healthy Christian life today it is of the utmost importance to follow Paul's example and keep christian praise and christian prayer together. Yet many do not manage to preserve this balance. Some Christians seem to do little but pray for new spiritual blessings, apparently oblivious of the fact that God has already blessed them in Christ with every spiritual blessing. Others lay such emphasis on the undoubted truth that everything is already theirs in Christ, that they become complacent and appear to have no appetite to know or experience their christian privileges more deeply. But these groups must be declared unbalanced. They have created a polarisation which scripture will not tolerate. What Paul does in Ephesians 1, and therefore encourages us to copy, is both to keep praising God that in Christ all spiritual blessings are ours and to keep praying that we may know the fullness of what He has given us. If we keep together praise and prayer, benediction and petition, we are unlikely to lose our spiritual equilibrium.[50]

Stott goes on to stress that in this great prayer for the Ephesians, Paul is not praying 'that they may receive the second blessing, but rather that they may appreciate to the fullest possible extent the implications of the blessing they have already received'.[51] Hence the Apostle's prayer that God may give them not only 'a spirit of wisdom and of revelation in the knowledge of Him', but also a set of enlightened eyes, the eyes of their hearts, to know and understand the immeasurable greatness of the power which is *already* in those who believe, and waiting presumably to be released as it is recognised and understood (see Eph. 1:19).

If this is the case, and if there are varying degrees of understanding and of surrender leading to various degrees of spiritual control and spiritual power, then we should not be surprised if Scripture recognises different types or levels of Christians. And that is exactly what we find with Paul's threefold categorising of human beings. He speaks firstly of 'natural' men, (those not possessing the Spirit at all), second-ly of 'carnal' men (those indwelt by the Spirit but governed by the flesh) and thirdly of 'spiritual' men (those both indwelt and controlled by the Spirit in fullness). This is set out in 1 Corinthians 2:14 and 3:1.

DEGREES OF SURRENDER

What this says to me at any rate is that our fullness in the Holy Spirit is in proportion to the degree of our surrender. We are as full of the Holy Spirit as our commitment permits. Disobedience therefore can both 'quench the Spirit' (1 Thess. 5:19) and 'grieve' Him (Eph. 4:30). This we do when we fail to allow Him to do in us that for which He has been given.

We can also say that the man who is filled with the Spirit is the man in whose life the *fruit* of the Spirit is evident (Gal. 5:22) and the *ministries* of the Spirit operative (1 Cor. 12:4–14). In this the key evidence of fullness is moral rather than overtly miraculous and it is something which is more evident to observers of someone's life and ministry than it usually is to the person himself. And so Luke can tell us how Peter, 'filled with the Holy Spirit', spoke to the rulers of the people and elders, (Acts 4:8) or how Stephen, 'full of grace and power, did great wonders and signs among the people' (Acts 6:8). Neither Peter nor Stephen seemed overly aware of their fullness, but others were. In fact to the best of my knowledge no one in Scripture ever claims to be filled with the Spirit and on the whole I suspect that most truly Spirit-filled men are largely unaware of what to others is quite evident. This has made me wonder whether the question – 'Are you filled with the Spirit?' – does not border on the illegitimate. The questioner ought to know. In fact I can think of numbers of people who if asked if they were filled with the Spirit would say 'No', while I would say of them, 'Yes'.

Could it also be a corollary of this that if or when we claim to be filled with the Spirit we become just a little less filled at that moment?

CRISIS INFILLING

However, I would not want by this to deny the validity of the crisis infilling when, sick of ourselves, our sin and our anaemia, we cast ourselves afresh on Christ with a cry for the infilling, anointing and visitation of His Spirit. Then God in His faithfulness will come upon us or be released in us in power, sometimes with and sometimes without the accompanying gift of tongues, but always with joy and release.

On all this, I suspect, most can unite. And would we not all want to agree with A. W. Tozer, that mighty twentieth-century prophet, when he makes the following observation:

Satan has opposed the doctrine of the Spirit-filled life about as bitterly as any doctrine there is. He has confused it, opposed it, surrounded it with false notions and fears. He has blocked every effort of the Church of Christ to receive from the Father her divine and blood-brought patrimony. The church has tragically neglected this great liberating truth – that there is now for the child of God a full and wonderful and completely satisfying anointing with the Holy Spirit. The Spirit-filled life is not a special deluxe edition of Christianity. It is part and parcel of the total plan of God for His people.[52]

Now it is unquestionable that multitudes of believers feel they have somewhere along the line entered some such experience, some in Charismatic or Pentecostal settings, and some not.

And inevitably there are varying understandings and different labels. Some call it a 'second blessing', but others protest at the term unless room is also made for a hundred and second blessing. Others call it 'crisis sanctification', or 'the filling with the Spirit' or 'the release of the Spirit' or the 'Baptism in the Spirit'.

What are we to say to all this? Certainly the term 'filled with the Spirit' (Eph. 5:18) or 'full of the Spirit' (Acts 6:3) is the one which regularly occurs and which seems best to describe the experience we are talking about. It is also the term the highest number of people can live with amicably and that is no mean commendation for it, especially if we place a high premium on fellowship and unity in the Body!

It is therefore for many, as well as for me, the preferred term, being also one which can fit either the once-for-all non-repeatable experience or the on-going experience of appropriation, rededication and, as it were, refilling – an understanding preferred by many, who have difficulties getting the New Testament data to support any rigid two-stage doctrine of Christian growth and experience.

And certainly those holding this view should not want to fight anyone who attaches a different label, for example 'Baptism in the Spirit', to the same reality.

However, if any of my readers do want to explore the term Baptism in the Spirit more fully, I'd like to refer you to my Appendix A where I have sought to set out in more theological terms and in more detail my own efforts to come to terms with exactly what the bible means when it speaks of being baptised in the Holy Spirit.

So at this point I set out only a few summary remarks about first the nature of the Baptism in the Spirit and secondly its timing. Details, as I say, in the Appendix.

NATURE OF THE BAPTISM

There is value first of all in noting that the terms 'baptism' or 'baptise' come from a rich Greek word (baptizo) which in secular Greek literature meant to plunge, sink, drown or overwhelm. And so a person could be drowned or sunk (literally baptised) by wine or 'overwhelmed' by sleep. Apparently Euripides, the Greek writer, used 'bapto' for when water was splashing into a ship, but 'baptizo' for when the ship was waterlogged.

One might therefore think of one Christian who seems to have been splashed by the Spirit and of another who has been waterlogged!

In the Old Testament the normal meaning of the word is overwhelm or immerse. So when John the Baptist, who in one sense links Old and New Testaments, says of Jesus that He will baptise with the 'Holy Spirit' (John 1:33) he means that Jesus is the one who can immerse us in the Holy Spirit or overwhelm us by the Spirit. He is the baptiser. He is the one who immerses us or overwhelms us in His Spirit.

The one image carries the idea of being pushed into or under the water and the other of having buckets of water poured over us. And curiously enough those who profess the Baptism in the Spirit in the Charismatic understanding probably divide pretty evenly in which of the two metaphors they find most useful to describe their experience – some saying they were baptised *in* or *into* the Spirit and others saying they felt the Spirit come *upon* them.

Perhaps it is worth noting that in the New Testament reference to being 'baptised in [or with] the Holy Spirit' occurs only seven times. It comes four times in the Gospels (Matt. 3:11, Mark 1:8, Luke 3:16, John 1:33) telling of John the Baptist's prophecy that as he had baptised or immersed or overwhelmed people with water, so Jesus would baptise, immerse or overwhelm them in the Spirit.

Then it comes only once in the Epistles at 1 Cor. 12:13 which tells of *all* being baptised by one Spirit into the one Body – so that *all* are made to drink of one Spirit. This is very strongly a concept of initiation into something which *all* Christians share.

Finally it comes twice in Acts, firstly, in 1:5 speaking expressly of the Day of Pentecost, and secondly, in 11:16 where Peter defends his Gentile activities to the critical 'circumcision party' (vs. 2) by telling them how he saw the Holy Spirit fall 'on them JUST AS ON US AT THE BEGINNING' (vs. 15). This, he says, reminds him of the Lord's pre-Pentecost word that 'John baptised with water, but you shall be baptised with the Holy Spirit' (vs. 16).

Reporting further on the Cornelius story, Luke also tells us of the dramatic evidence of the 'poured out' Spirit (Acts 10:45) in the shape of tongues and praise to God (vs. 46). Over and above that we learn that there was immediate or almost immediate and public (vs. 45) baptism in water for those who had 'received the Holy Spirit' (vs. 47). For a fuller study of the Cornelius case, see again Appendix A.

SEVERAL METAPHORS

So then we see in summary that the idea of being baptised in the Spirit brings together several metaphors – namely receiving the Spirit, being indwelt by the Spirit, being immersed in the Holy Spirit, being waterlogged or overwhelmed in the Spirit, having the Spirit poured out upon one, or even having the Holy Spirit fall upon one. More simply Peter can speak of being given the Holy Spirit (Acts 15:8) as when he reports to the Jerusalem Council on the conversion of the Gentiles.

Obviously, it is a very rich idea, not exhausted by any single one of the above metaphors and certainly not attached in any obvious or consistent way to some sort of second experience.

TIMING OF THE BAPTISM

This raises the matter of the timing of the Baptism in the Holy Spirit. When does it happen?

There are three basic views.

View One says that regeneration and Baptism in the Spirit synchronise and take place at the same time when a man is converted to Christ and indwelt by the Spirit.

View Two sees a two-stage initiation, the first being regeneration, when we are born again and indwelt by the Holy Spirit and the second being the Baptism in the Spirit, when we are anointed, filled, flooded and immersed in the Spirit and empowered for service. It is evidenced by the manifestation of the gifts of the Spirit – most notably tongues. Some would insist on the tongues evidence as normative. Others prefer to say of those baptised in the Spirit that not all do speak in tongues, but all may.

The *third view* is one which accepts the experience of the Baptism in the Spirit, but rejects the terminology. Thus David Watson can write: 'The term, baptism, is undoubtedly linked with Christian initiation, and in that sense, at least, every Christian is already baptised in the Spirit.'[53] David Watson accordingly comes out strongly for the alternative phrase of being 'filled with the Holy Spirit'.

My own view is a combination of one and three in so far as the term Baptism in the Spirit seems best to belong with initiatory Christian experience (e.g. Pentecost and Cornelius' household), and as such in those terms is non-repeatable. But new fillings, immersions, anointings and eruptions do obviously occur and these are real, vital and authentic, regardless of the label attached. Pentecostals and Charismatics call such experiences The Baptism in the Spirit. Others, myself among them, prefer to speak of a filling of the Spirit, and see it as repeatable.

SUMMARY

Let me try to summarise.

My own feeling is that the term 'filling' or 'infilling' of the Holy Spirit is the one which best fits both the exegetical data of the New Testament and the facts of Christian and especially Charismatic experience in the twentieth century. It also makes room for repeated experiences rather than simply one climactic second experience, although for some that seems to be the form it takes.

Apart from anything else, the idea and desirability of being filled with the Holy Spirit is shared by both so-called 'camps' and it is one both can embrace, even if understandings relating to timing and mechanics may vary somewhat. The term therefore has the advantage of being widely serviceable and of not being divisive.

However, if there are those on different sides of the fence who insist on using the term Baptism in the Spirit, the one lot applying it to the initial experience and the other to a subsequent second-stage experience, then some resolution can come from the dual meaning of the Greek word 'Baptizo' as both being 'initiated into something' (which would seemingly speak of a *status*) and of being 'overwhelmed by something' (which speaks of an *experience*).

Perhaps as David Watson has suggested, uncertainty and confusion come when either is over-stressed at the expense of the other. For example, he says:

> It is possible to think of the overwhelming of the Spirit as something entirely separate from Christian initiation, whereas the two, ideally and potentially, though not necessarily experientially, are one. On the other hand, it is possible so to stress that the Christian has 'got it all' by being baptised into Christ that the overwhelming of the Spirit is never experienced. This is a danger many evangelicals can fall into.[54]

Perhaps it is also valuable to recognise, as many are doing who are looking at this subject, that New Testament initiation, symbolised and sealed by water baptism, is basically a single work of God with many facets which together constitute what David Watson calls 'a cluster of overlapping spiritual realities'. This cluster would include:

(i) – the proclamation of the Gospel
(ii) – faith

(iii) – repentance
(iv) – forgiveness
(v) – justification
(vi) – adoption
(vii) – conversion
(viii) – regeneration and new birth
(ix) – Baptism in the Spirit
(x) – baptism in water
(xi) – new life in the Spirit

There is admittedly not always agreement in the Church on the relationship between these realities or how they should be proclaimed and taught in the evangelistic setting.

However, most could probably agree on two points. Firstly, even though these spiritual truths and experiences may have to be intellectually separated for teaching and learning purposes, they actually belong together theologically and spiritually since together they express the single and overall experience of the believer's incorporation into Christ which leads to sonship and power for living and serving in the Christian life.

Secondly, the initiatory cluster of experiences is grasped, apprehended, understood and to some extent 'entered' upon by different individuals in differing ways and in different time scales, often according to how they are taught or instructed by Christian pastors, evangelists and theologians.

In any event, we probably need to come back to the sovereignty of the Spirit who blows where He wills. John Taylor has said:

> The authenticity of the book of Acts is gloriously apparent in the inconsistency of the various incidents of the Spirit's intervention from the day of Pentecost onwards. The Holy Spirit does not appear to have read the rubrics. He will not and cannot be bound.[55]

This suggests that excessive rigidity is what must be avoided, for it is rigidity which divides God's people, not truth, because it is the nature of truth to set us free.

A LETTER

And new freedom was certainly what I felt had come my way back in 1977. Terminology was far less important than the sense that I had met my Lord in a new way through His Spirit.

About then I received a very helpful letter from a friend. 'Praise God for what has happened. It is He who is speaking to you. . . . But He has much more to say to you in every area of your life and for this reason I would strongly advise you not to describe your experience now but rather to live with it and let the Lord continue to work in you. Don't let it become a thing of the past, till it becomes a fossil and you are left high and dry. You can ride on a "high" for some time, but it might be in His plan that you walk in darkness through the valley *with Him*. This is not what others would have you do or be. But walk in your freedom with Him. Accept your own weakness, as He does, so that His strength will flow through you.'

Praise God, I thought, for friends and for the wisdom and perspectives which come through different members of His Body!

Chapter Fifteen

JUMPING-THE-MERRY-GO-ROUNDS

It is not easy to describe my religious development
during these years, for my heart and mind were a
battlefield of the most diverse influences.
W. A Visser't Hooft describing his late teens

The year after the Milner Park Renewal Conference, 1978,
was a very international and varied year for me. It opened
with attendance at a Full Gospel Business Men's Convention
in Washington D.C. in mid January, followed immediately
by a meeting in Bermuda of the Lausanne Committee for
World Evangelisation of which I was a member. Then came
three missions with Festo Kivengere in Panama, one in
Balboa (the Canal Zone), another in Colon at the Atlantic
end of the Canal and another in Panama City itself. In
March Festo and I and a large African Enterprise team were
in Egypt for a further three missions (Assuit, Cairo and
Alexandria). In May we were again together, this time for a
mission in Australia and finally in September to Nairobi, for
our second city-wide push, the first having been in 1969.

These international experiences and their demanding
ministry requirements not only created many challenges for
personal growth and for seeking to integrate the work of the
Spirit in a new way into my life and thinking, but they also
gave me a pretty rapid bird's-eye view of the state of things
between evangelicals and Charismatics in different parts of
the world. All this stood me in good stead for 1979 when we

sought to draw the whole South African Body of Christ together for the great South African Christian Leadership Assembly. But first back to January 1978 when I set off for Washington D.C., Bermuda and Panáma.

GREAT GULFS FIXED

It was Dan and Al Malachuk, then of Logos Books, who had asked me to attend the National Convention of the Full Gospel Business Men's Association. This is a group started a good many years ago by Demos Shakarian, an Armenian refugee who had come to the United States. His testimony was real and dramatic and his rise both as a businessman and as a lay leader had been meteoric. The movement he had started was already world-wide.

Graciously I was introduced to the leadership group and met with them behind the scenes. Fine, warm, and loving men, one and all. And the meetings were spectacular extravaganzas of bubbling life, dramatic testimony and exhilarating worship. When I shared my own modest testimony, I was given a rousing and caring reception.

Three things struck me about the experience. First of all, there was immense spiritual energy in the group. Secondly, it was light on theology. Thirdly, no one I knew from the so-called evangelical scene of the U.S.A. was there. Over the years, I had stumped the North American evangelical scene pretty thoroughly and knew most of its key leaders. But here I saw none of them. It seemed there was a great gulf fixed. On either side of the gulf were enormous merry-go-rounds of Christians. And ne'er the twain did meet.

Picking up *Logos Magazine* and *Christianity Today*, two national U.S. religious magazines edited respectively at that time by two personal friends, Dan Malachuk and Harold Lindsell – one might have concluded they were talking about the national Christian scene of two separate countries. There just seemed to be no overlaps. This struck me as not only sad and unhealthy, but unnecessary.

After sharing in my testimony that I was going on to

Bermuda for the Lausanne meetings they prayed for me, with the whole gathering holding out its arms in blessing towards me that I would be empowered in going and that I would be able to share something there which would encourage a greater evangelical openness to the Pentecostal world. There seemed to be a longing for meaningful contact, a yearning for greater fellowship.

In Bermuda for the Lausanne meetings, I was at once struck by the contrast, on the one hand negatively, and on the other positively. Negatively, the Spirit of worship seemed to me utterly impoverished by comparison with what I had just experienced in Washington D.C. But positively, there was a depth of theological perception which, even allowing for the lay status of the Full Gospel group, was almost wholly absent in the Washington experience. The one group seemed to have the theology, the other the vitality. Did not God want to bring the two together?

In my own Bible study one morning with the Lausanne Group I said as much. Curiously enough, the day of my new experience at Milner Park in August 1977, I had the distinct sense of the Spirit saying to me, 'Share this with South African evangelicals and with the Lausanne Group.' When I retorted in my heart that I could see no way I could suddenly stand up and talk about this to my Lausanne friends, the Lord seemed to say: 'I will make a way'.

So I sat back and waited. About two weeks before leaving for Bermuda a letter came from my dear friend Leighton Ford, Chairman of the Lausanne Committee. Would I give one of the morning devotional addresses? 'This is my way,' the Spirit seemed to say. 'Share your testimony.'

So there I was doing it. I spoke on 'Obedience and the Holy Spirit' and in the process challenged these two great constituencies of Christendom – the evangelical and the Pentecostal – to come together.

Afterwards, a number of the Lausanne members came up to me like secret C.I.A. or M.I.5 agents using a password, and whispered: 'We agree with that, but we have been scared to come out into the open and say so.'

Dear me, I thought, what have we done to Christ's Church?

Leaving Bermuda, Festo and I flew on to Panama. We were joined for a few days there by two LCWE colleagues – Orlando Costas of Costa Rica, a sort of ecumenical-cum-evangelical, and by the Bolivian, Bruno Frigoli, Director of Evangelism for the Assemblies of God in Latin America and one time bodyguard to Mussolini! He was, incidentally, the only one of Mussolini's bodyguards to escape public hanging. That was before he was converted out of gunrunning and diamond smuggling through a Pentecostal missionary in Bolivia! Now he has generated one of the fastest-growing Churches in the world through his work in that country.

In our hotel room Bruno asked me: 'Are the Pentecostals backing this mission? You know, there are thousands of Pentecostals here in Panama City.'

'I don't know. I have my doubts.'

'Let me find out,' said the volcanic Bruno with a vigorous look of resolution as he left the room.

He was back that evening.

'They weren't even asked,' he said with a defiant look. 'Can you believe it? They could have made all the difference in this mission.' Then his countenance fell. 'Anyway, it would not have made much difference,' he mumbled, 'they say they would have stayed out anyway because an Anglican bishop is taking part!'

Poor Festo! Pushing the Pentecostals out like that! Too bad they never stopped to hear him preach. Obviously, the gulf was even wider than I had thought.

Next afternoon I listened to Orlando Costas, with his passionate social concerns, locking horns in a truly Latin slanging-match with the passionately evangelistic Bruno. It was great stuff, like a sort of theological bullfight. They were miles apart, although congenially so. Yet each had much for the other.

I resolved to invite them BOTH as speakers to SACLA – the South African Christian Leadership Assembly which was set for July the following year (1979). Maybe battered old

South Africa could contribute to a rapprochement between Latin American evangelicals and Pentecostals!

GUIDANCE AND GIFTS

When the missions in Panama were over, three options faced me. One was to attend a healing seminar in British Honduras with Francis MacNutt. The other was to look over the Pentecostal ministries of Bob McAlister in Rio en route home, and the third was to respond to Doug Coe's invitation to me to attend the National Prayer Breakfast in Washington D.C.

Yet after praying about it, the strongest compulsion came over me to decline all three and hurry back to South Africa. I didn't know why. But I had to go.

Half an hour after reaching Johannesburg, I phoned my precious Carol who told me one of our dearest friends had just committed suicide in Cape Town. This was it. This was why I had to come back. Although longing to be together again, both Carol and I knew I had to go to the wife and children in Cape Town at once. Once there, I was assured there was no place in all the planet where I was meant to be more truly right then, than with that huddled, distraught and special family. It was a tiny bit like Philip rushing from the mass blessings of Samaria to the appointment with one needy Ethiopian down in Gaza.

Yes, I thought, on my flight home from Cape Town to Durban, the Spirit really does know where we are meant to be and when. So keep listening.

LAND OF THE PYRAMIDS

A month or so later Festo and I were in Egypt, the land of the pyramids. Here I did not have a successful experience of listening, but a failure. It happened like this:

One evening during an evangelistic series in Cairo, Festo and I decided to speak on the work of the Holy Spirit. During the course of my own contribution I noted that God was moving in new ways across the world and I spoke amongst other things of the Charismatic Renewal. I also alluded to the way the healing power of God was being manifested afresh and I quoted my eye-witness experiences in a couple of Kathryn Kuhlman services. Then Festo shared from his perspective. It seemed to me a good evening.

After the service, one engaging young Egyptian lad who couldn't quite credit our impossible inter-racial mix – a white South African and a black Ugandan – said to me through a wide, beaming smile: 'Michael you are the milk of the Gospel and Festo is the chocolate!'

But that was where the fun ended for the evening. I sensed several of the Egyptian clergy were quite upset. One came out in the open and said: 'Michael, if you ever want to preach in Egypt again, don't mention Charismatics or Kathryn Kuhlman.'

'Why?' I asked in bewildered astonishment.

'Well,' he replied, 'last year some Charismatics came through here and they tried to manipulate everyone to speak in tongues. They created chaos and left behind so many divisions and so much confusion. We don't want any more of that stuff here.'

I was dreadfully distressed. Obviously, the whole matter had touched some very raw nerves. Seemingly I had rushed in, like the proverbial fool, where angels feared to tread.

A couple of days later we were all in the train on the way up to Alexandria where our next series was to open that night.

A simply delightful and scintillating young Egyptian pastor came over and sat with me.

'Brother,' he said with loving concern, 'we were very anxious about your reference the other night to healing and the other gifts of the Spirit. Don't you feel the gifts were just for the first century? After all, Mark 16:20 says: "They went forth and preached everywhere, while the Lord worked with them and confirmed the message by the signs which attended it." Now do you believe that the message was confirmed?'

'Yes, indeed,' I replied. 'Obviously.'

'Then why does it need further confirmation now? It was confirmed then and that has now happened. The miraculous gifts were just for that time to authenticate the message. This is what the great B. B. Warfield taught and in Egypt we evangelicals go along with that.'

'But what would you do if you had actually seen, let's say, the gift of healing in action?'

'I'm not sure,' he answered. 'I suppose I would have to question its authenticity.'

'Or else,' I suggested, 'you could question your interpretation.'

At which he smiled at me with a quizzical look. And changed the subject.

GIFTS

The point at issue was really whether all the gifts of the Spirit were still operative or not. We have thought about this already in this story, but here was an opportunity to think further and a little more thoroughly.

My dear friend on the train had articulated a view known as Dispensationalism with which I had become familiar in my seminary days in California. This view says that God has dealt with His people in different ways during different dispensations of redemptive history.

Commenting on this position in its more extravagant forms, Michael Griffiths, Principal of London Bible College, has said:

> There is a serious danger that extreme dispensationalists will adopt an attitude to Scripture little different from that of destructive Biblical criticism, attacking the Bible with a pair of dispensational scissors. Both 'Apostles and Prophets' are eliminated from Ephesians 4:11 as 'not for this age' while references to prophecy, miracles, healing and tongues must all be cavalierly cut out of 1 Cor. 12–14 as 'long since ceased'. If the Bible is indeed the 'only infallible rule of faith and practice' (Lausanne Covenant Clause II), then we must be faithful to what we believe about Scripture. According to Scripture, the gifts are given by the Holy Spirit to 'edify' the Body of Christ.[56]

Michael Harper adds his word on this in his book *This is the Day*.

> 'With the evangelical world thoroughly penetrated now by the charismatic experience, there are fewer and fewer who still subscribe to a dispensationalism that relegates spiritual gifts and miracles to the first century, or to the express views of B. B. Warfield, whose influence on evangelicalism in the first half of the twentieth century was profound, that the 'supernatural' gifts were so wholly associated with the apostles that when they had all died the gifts were buried with them. What we see now is a faith in the 'supernatural' breaking out from the narrow confines of Biblical fundamentalism, mechanical sacramentalism and traditional dispensationalism. The ghosts of Schofield and Warfield are being well and truly laid.'[57]

I would agree with this. In fact, even the great Karl Barth, who would not be catalogued in most minds as unduly weighted towards Charismatics, expressed a concern that when there is a lack in the Church of these 'supremely astonishing activities resting on an endowment with extraordinary capacities . . . there is reason to ask whether in pride or sloth the community as such has perhaps evaded this endowment, thus falsifying its relationship to its Lord.'[58]

These are strong words which, if accurate, suggest that we ignore the gifts of the Holy Spirit not only at the peril of our personal growth, but at the peril of the forward movement of the Church as a whole.

Not that this is to exalt any one of the gifts above another, and least of all to make one gift (e.g. tongues) the normative experience of every believer as the evidence of the fullness of the Holy Spirit, but only to assert that ignoring the spiritual gifts is neither wise nor biblical.

C. Peter Wagner, in his book *Your Spiritual Gifts* puts it this way:

> Ignorance of spiritual gifts may be a chief cause of retarded

church growth today. It also may be the root of much of the discouragement, insecurity, frustration and guilt that plagues many Christian individuals and curtails their total effectiveness for God.[59]

A catalogue of these gifts, as Wagner sees them, is to be found in Appendix Ci. Appendix Cii presents a different sort of cataloguing. I know for myself that a deeper reflection on the workings of the spiritual gifts generally and my own specifically has helped me in my life and ministry in these last years. I am in accord with Wagner when he says:

> People who know their gifts have a handle of their 'Spiritual job description', so to speak. They find their place in the church with more ease. . . . Christian people who know their Spiritual gifts tend to develop healthy self-esteem. This does not mean that 'They think more highly of themselves than they ought to think'. They learn that no matter what their gift is, they are important to God and to the Body. . . . Secondly, not only does knowing about Spiritual gifts help individual Christians, but it helps the Church as a whole. Ephesians 4 tells us that when Spiritual gifts are in operation, the whole Body matures. . . . When the Church matures, predictably it grows. When the Body is functioning well and 'each separate part works as it should, the whole body grows' (Eph. 4:16 TEV). There is clearly a Biblical relationship between Spiritual gifts and Church growth. The third and most important thing that knowing about Spiritual gifts does is that it glorifies God. 1 Peter 4:10–11 advises Christians to use their spiritual gifts, then adds the reason why: 'That God in all things may be glorified through Jesus Christ to whom be praise and dominion for ever and ever.' What could be better than glorifying God?[60]

Wagner adds:
> I believe so strongly in the universality of Spiritual gifts. Every Christian has them and every Church has them.

Many are still buried in the ground like the talent in Matthew 25, but they can be unearthed and used for the glory of God and the growth of the Church.[61]

This is not, of course, to affirm that the gifts are of the essence of the Spirit-filled life. Paul clearly indicates that they are marked by a certain transience because they will in time pass away, not having the same permanence as faith, hope and love. But to minimise them or deny them is, I believe, to frustrate both one's own growth and that of the Church.

This was my conclusion that afternoon in Alexandria. And I have had no cause to modify it since then.

POSTSCRIPT

Before leaving my Egyptian experience, I must add a postscript relating to the distress I had felt after my talk in Cairo when I was reprimanded so strongly for referring to the gifts of the Spirit generally and Kathryn Kuhlman and the healing-gift specifically.

What was I to make of this? Still in my Alexandrian hotel, I took this earnestly to God in prayer.

Then the Lord ministered to me from 1 Corinthians where Paul speaks about how he went among the Corinthians as 'a skilled master builder' (3:3). Here is the picture of an immensely careful, competent, trained craftsman who lays his foundation and his individual teaching bricks with consummate care and skill.

The Spirit seemed to say to me: 'Those people who came into Egypt last year and upset everyone by pushing tongues and so on did not come in as skilled master builders. They did not sensitively lay a foundation of understanding. They were not wise. So they complicated everything They were not skilled master builders.'

'Ah, yes, Lord – the people who came in last year – they were not skilled master builders.'

Then, ever so gently came the Spirit's further word to me:

'Nor were you.' Hard though this was to face, I saw it at once. I had blundered in insensitively without comprehending my context properly and without praying through thoroughly on what I should say. I had failed my Lord and the Holy Spirit. And I had further complicated the building processes of the Spirit in the Egyptian Church.

DOWN UNDER

Other experiences of moving between Christian constituencies and jumping Christendom's merry-go-rounds followed some months later in Australia.

When I arrived there, a local Baptist pastor who was one of the participating clergy in a mission Festo and I were doing in the suburbs of Sydney, told me he had received an advance letter on me from a conservative evangelical in South Africa. The letter told him not to have me in his Church. 'Cassidy is too political and too Pentecostal,' said this helpful expression of inter-continental Christian communication!

I roared with laughter. 'Goodness gracious,' I said, 'both my political and my Pentecostal friends in South Africa would have a mighty good giggle over that. The Pentecostals think I'm much too tame for them and the political crowd view me as way too conservative!'

However, the recipient of this letter, a dear and capable man, did tell me that in his area the Charismatic Renewal had often had divisive consequences in Churches and some people's so-called experiences of tongues had been in his judgment positively demonic. He played me a tape of an interview he had had with one aspiring Charismatic, and certainly what I heard suggested something counterfeit.

It was a good reminder that the powers of darkness can indeed masquerade as angels of light. One couldn't be too careful. All spirits had to be tested (1 John 4:1).

Quite so. But none of this could in my judgment excuse the gaping chasm I saw in Australia between Charismatics and evangelicals. I was convinced the gap was between brothers, not cousins, and certainly not between enemies.

How glad I was therefore when I was later invited to return to Australia (May 1981) to speak at the National Evangelical Anglican Congress on 'Christ and the Spirit' and share a word which would seek to bridge some of the chasm in that land between these two groups.

All these international experiences in 1978 were good preparation for the massive experience of both Christian togetherness and pain which devolved upon us in 1979 when leaders from virtually the whole South African Church got together in Pretoria for SACLA.

Basically it was an attempt to get all the merry-go-rounds to mesh and synchronise, as in a well-oiled gear box.

Even so, some in the South African Church seemed to prefer reverse to any of the forward gears, because they made forward movement together such a complicated exercise. More on that anon.

Chapter Sixteen

FORWARD THROUGH CROSS-FIRE

> I baptise you with water for repentance, but He who is coming after me is mightier than I, whose sandals I am not worthy to carry; He will baptise you with the Holy Spirit AND WITH FIRE.
>
> John the Baptist – Matt. 3:11

For me these two years (1977–8) made up an extended period of seeking to go forward in my Christian walk, but finding often that the growth came firstly in situations of pain and purging and secondly, as mentioned, when I was caught in the cross-fire while moving between evangelical and Charismatic merry-go-rounds.

In fact the twin concepts firstly of taking up one's cross and secondly of being baptised not only with the Spirit but with FIRE became the only spiritual framework through which I could interpret many of the difficult and sometimes painful things which happened to me. The Cross-AND-the-fire. Yes, the Cross-fire. One was being forced to grow and move forward through *CROSS-FIRE!*

HOLINESS AND FIRE

Since early in my Christian experience I have been aware that God is more interested in our characters than our happiness, knowing as He does that the more and the quicker our characters are conformed to the image of Christ, the happier we will be.

In the light of this Hebrews 12:11 has always meant much. 'For the moment all discipline seems painful rather than pleasant; later it yields the peaceful fruit of righteousness to those who have been trained by it.'

However, I had not ever before very clearly linked up in my mind the twin phenomena of the Baptism with the Spirit and the Baptism with fire. But I can't think why not. After all, they were integral and inseparable in John the Baptist's mind. This One who was to come, whose sandals he was unworthy to untie, would have the distinction of performing a twin work upon His disciples. He would baptise not only with the Spirit, but with FIRE. He would come to His disciples with 'His winnowing fork . . . in His hand', and He would 'clear his threshing floor and gather His wheat into the granary' but burn the chaff 'with unquenchable fire' (Matt. 3:12).

As these years unfolded this whole truth impressed itself on me afresh. To come to His Spirit more deeply and to release His Spirit more fully was also to come to the fire more resolutely and be yielded to its painful, purging work. To say: 'Lord, fill me with Your Spirit' is to say: 'Lord, step up the heat of the fire and burn the chaff in me more freely,' because the two baptisms, if we can so talk, belong together. Put differently, the one Baptism involves two elements – the Spirit and Fire. Curious that we have so many books on our shelves on the Baptism with the Holy Spirit and none on the Baptism with Fire! Seemingly we have a strong, though perhaps not unnatural, preference for power over pain!

In all likelihood this is because we forget that He is the HOLY Spirit. And He is described that way over ninety times in the Bible. As such, His main concern will be with our holiness.

Yet, even from the beginning there was failure in the Church to grasp this. Michael Green has observed:

The Corinthians, with all their claims to fullness and to having entered on their heavenly reign were distressingly defective in Christian behaviour. Party strife, litigiousness, immorality of a dimension unheard of in paganism, coupled with greed and disorder in the assemblies, marked their lives. No wonder Paul had to castigate them as carnal Christians and yet they were the very people who possessed these gifts of tongues, miracles, faith, healing and the like which convinced them that they were the favoured children of Heaven and had already become full. It is still an observable fact that those who speak most about being full of the Holy Spirit are often governed by other spirits such as arrogance, divisiveness and party spirit, disorder, lack of love and criticism. It is hard to see how a man can be full of the Spirit if these glaring failures of character persist.[62]

This is what Paul was on to when he wrote to the Corinthians, and it is often as relevant today in our Churches and organisations as it was with the Corinthians: 'I, brethren, could not address you as spiritual men, but as men of the flesh, as babes in Christ. . . . For while there is jealousy and strife among you, are you not of the flesh and behaving like ordinary men?' (1 Cor. 3:1, 3).

Seemingly Paul's concern was to get the Corinthians to behave not as ordinary men but as extraordinary men. This could only happen as the flesh or old nature in them was subordinate to the Spirit and brought under His control.

SPIRIT AND FLESH

If I had felt in previous years how much work God still had to do on me, I felt it and have continued to feel it even more acutely over these years since Milner Park. It is the challenge of being and becoming, and one is always a beginner. How hard it is therefore to yield to the discipling processes of the Spirit as Peter had to when Jesus said: 'You are Simon. You shall be called Peter [the Rock]'. Jesus was alerting Peter to the fact that there was a signal difference between what he then was and what he would become, though mercifully he left Peter ignorant as to how painful the process would be!

Likewise with Moses in his Midian and Paul in his Arabia, there was an 'unlearning' process which had to go on as each was led more deeply, and often with anguish, to learn the ways of God and to unlearn the ways of man. That *is* what I too was battling then and it is still where I feel I am personally battling right now.

In a sense it is the whole challenge of learning to have God's attitudes and perspectives, even in situations of pain, pressure, personal crisis or inter-personal alienation. It is learning to allow the Spirit and the new nature to predominate rather than the flesh or old nature. And the way it happens is the way of the Cross. It is the way of the Baptism with fire.

In fact, each of the years from 1977 onwards had its own peculiar furnace with its own particular lessons in the school of the Spirit.

THE PAIN OF BEREAVEMENT (1978)

The new awareness of the Spirit's love and power was a particular blessing in mid 1978 when my father, to whom I was particularly devoted, became seriously ill and we knew he was dying.

Facing death and sadness had come my way in terms of close friends and extended family, but never in terms of someone really intimate in my immediate family.

I had always been very close to my father and his influence on me had been enormous. In fact it was he who first pointed me to God in a way I can consciously remember. That in itself made him very special.

And now this illness had come out of the blue and I was face to face with the grim prospect of seeing him slowly slip into those clawing clutches of the Last Enemy. I knew these would be weeks when the Spirit's wisdom, strength and guidance would be specially needed.

One dilemma faced me. Several weeks before Dad fell ill I had had an argument with him about South African politics. Not the first, I might say. These were curious exchanges because much of what I knew of racial justice and fair play between peoples I had learned from him, yet here he was taking a reactionary stand against more progressive politics in South Africa. This reaction was the result of wounds and disillusionment during the independence process in Lesotho where Dad had served pretty thanklessly for over thirty years, but I in my obtuseness had refused to show any understanding.

I recollect his phoning me the same evening of our argument. I had the powerful sense of the Holy Spirit whispering: 'Apologise to him for all those stupid political discussions that got nowhere.' But my pride was too great and I didn't.

A few days later he was in hospital with the medical death sentence over him. Somehow I still felt I should apologise for my insensitivity in these discussions and my own heated attitudes but events swept us along and the opportunity seemed to slip away. Remorse and regret gripped me.

Then early one morning I woke with the sense of the Spirit's word: 'Say to him today what is in your heart.' By this time the end was very close. After breakfast my sister Olave Snelling, who had come out from the U.K. to be with us and who knew nothing of my feelings over the political discussions, came to me in my study and said: 'In my devotional time this morning the Spirit said to me that we should say everything to Dad today which is on our hearts and which we may need to say'. It was confirmation.

That afternoon I whispered my words of apology in Dad's ear, thanked him for all he had meant as a father and asked his forgiveness for where I had failed him as a son. He shook his head vigorously, as if to say: 'No, you haven't failed', smiled a treasured smile of understanding and reassurance and gripped my hand as if to say 'thank you'.

But what blessed me over and above Dad's reaction was the Spirit's gentle dealing with both of us in this detail and His gracious leading and enabling so that the decks could be cleared of this one bit of clutter which was spoiling.

Also in these days of anxiety and sadness something else of the Spirit's work came home afresh.

There was one nurse tending Dad called Athene. She was a Christian and week after week I observed her ability to give extra care to all her patients, and especially to Dad.

One day I spoke to her about this. 'Well,' she said, 'I believe the Lord Jesus would express His care through me to all these people, especially the dying ones. You know, it's the little things that mean much to them. For example few nurses will bother to help these old folk in the terminal ward to clean their teeth. I make it my business to help them to do their teeth. They feel better for it as they turn in. Other nurses say I'm silly to expend energy on things like that, but I feel the Spirit has led me to this.'

Now, I thought to myself, how about that for an evidence of the fullness of the Spirit? Not a lot of extravagant bravado and talk about tongues and so on, but helping dying people to clean their teeth.

Later that night I wrote in my diary: 'Thank you, Lord, for pressing upon my heart that the ultimate mark of your Spirit's work and will is the Spirit of care. Baptise me into that Spirit and annoint me to care for people as never before.'

I was learning new things in the midst of anguish and sadness. A little poem came back to me, penned by Robert Browning Hamilton:

> I walked a mile with Pleasure;
> She chatted all the way;
> But left me none the wiser
> For all she had to say.
>
> I walked a mile with Sorrow,
> And ne'er a word said she;
> But, oh! the things I learnt from her
> When Sorrow walked with me.

In one other detail the Spirit's guidance was so meaningful. I was due in these weeks to go up to Zimbabwe to speak at a huge inter-church conference called NACLA (National Christian Leadership Assembly). It was an overflow of PACLA – the 1976 Pan African Christian Leadership

Assembly already referred to earlier. Six hundred leaders from over fifty denominations were to be present.

The question was – how long would Dad linger? Could I slip away early next day, speak at the conference, and get back to be with Dad? Or should I cancel out? Or should I have my message delayed in the conference or what?

Assured of the wonderful and gracious ability of the Spirit to speak and guide in such situations, I went down to the bottom of the garden, sat on the children's swing, pored over my Bible, and asked the Spirit of God to guide me as to whether I should board the plane early next morning or not.

Somehow I was constrained towards Psalm 90. I came on verses 9–10: 'For all our days pass away under Thy wrath, our years come to an end like a sigh. The years of our life are threescore and ten, or even by reason of strength fourscore; yet their span is but toil and trouble; they are soon gone, and we fly away.' The words 'SOON GONE' literally leaped at me from the page, as if radiating with the Spirit's quickened life. Dad would very soon be gone. That was the Spirit's word.

I rose, went up to my study, phoned Zimbabwe and said I would not be on the plane the next day, but I believed I would be up there before the end of the conference. And that is how it ultimately worked out. I then took out my journal and noted: 'Lord, I feel you are showing your mind. It seems I should stay and walk a day at a time on Rhodesia. Perhaps I am meant to speak a word at the end. In any event I am on standby to do your bidding.'

Early next morning I was called from a prayer meeting at our Church to go to the hospital. A long, searing, but precious morning followed. As a family we were knit closer than ever before. At one point Dad whispered: 'I am sorry I am taking so long.' It was characteristic of his selfless nature to be worrying even then over our pain. He died at 1.11 p.m. Had I not heard the Spirit's word the day before, I would have been landing at Harare (formerly Salisbury) airport at that very time.

And how precious was the sense of Jesus's presence

throughout that experience and after it! I remembered Paul's words: 'For the law of the Spirit of life in Christ Jesus has set me free from the law of sin and death' (Rom. 8:2). Yes, the Spirit is the One who embodies the law of life in Christ Jesus and he frees us from those dreadful clutches of sin and death. I now knew this in a new way.

I also remembered the words of Elizabeth Barrett-Browning:

> When some beloved voice that was to you
> Both sound and sweetness, faileth suddenly,
> And silence, against which you dare not cry,
> Aches round you like a strong disease and new —
> What hope? What help? What music will undo
> That silence to your sense? Not friendship's sigh,
> Not reason's subtle count . . .
> Not songs of poets, nor of nightingales . . .
>   Nay, none of these,
> Speak Thou, availing Christ! — and fill this pause.

It had been a time of grief and pain. A calvary time. Yet how gloriously rich and real had been the Holy Spirit's ministry to us all!

A YEAR OF PRESSURE (1979)

Another growth and discovery point came in the immense pressures some of us faced in 1978 and especially 1979 as we sought to mount the South African Christian Leadership Assembly (SACLA). The idea was to assemble leaders from the whole South African Church 'in order to discover together what it means to be faithful and effective witnesses to Jesus Christ as Lord in South Africa today'.

But in order to bring the thing about, those of us in leadership had to walk an extraordinarily painful and trau- matic gauntlet of misunderstanding, criticism, opposition and obstructionism, all on top of a crushing work load. Many times we felt at the end of our tether as, caught between different flanks or wings of the Church, we took the flak from both sides. Anonymous documents, slander, political suspicion, character assassination, police investigations, Christian pamphleteering and a thousand deadly darts constantly made life difficult and occasionally almost unbearable. I finally opened a file in my filing cabinet under M for 'mudslingers'. It makes fascinating though unedifying reading, and constitutes a sad commentary on the Christian Church. But in all these pressures the gentle, guiding, controlling work of the Holy Spirit brought relief and an ability to cope.

Even so I couldn't help from time to time putting the question to myself: 'If I have sought the release of the Spirit in new ways, how come all this trauma?' Then I would turn afresh to this fire which John the Baptist stressed and it all made sense. God was allowing pressure and pain in order to purge. It was an age-old principle. Jesus seemed very preoccupied with chaff. I hadn't grasped before so clearly the place of the winnowing fork (Matt. 3:12) and the top priority He places on clearing His 'threshing floor'. It came to a head for me just before SACLA opened. I was in the office of one cabinet minister in whose mind much suspicion against SACLA and against me had been sown.

'If SACLA blows up and gets out of hand, the Government will move in to close it down and we'll hold you accountable.'

'It won't blow up, Mr Minister,' I said quietly, 'because God is in it.'

But by this time, after so many months of this sort of thing, my soul was pretty tattered. The whole thing had been almost too much and it had taken its toll on our spirits. I felt stricken. Last straws can do that. And I needed to hear a word of assurance from the Lord.

I drove over to the Pretoria show grounds and went to the great assembly hall to check out the public address and sound reinforcement system.

Sitting way back in the empty bleachers I called to our African Enterprise media team to let me hear the system work. They put on a tape.

Suddenly the whole auditorium simply exploded into

magnificent stereophonic sound. The words of 'Great is Thy Faithfulness' along with a thousand strings filled the air.

Then suddenly it was not just a hymn and a glorious cavalcade of sound, but a word from the Spirit of God. It just seemed as if Jesus by His Spirit, entered, owned and possessed the affirmations of that magnificent hymn: 'Great is Thy Faithfulness, O God my Father, There is no shadow of turning with Thee.' The tears began to flow and I was bathed in the warm and gracious assurance of the Spirit of God that all would be well. SACLA would not disintegrate in a racial explosion. God's faithfulness would once again be demonstrated.

In this I learned afresh not only how the Spirit ministers to us just when we need it most, but I discovered that He can take anything, a song, a hymn, a phone call, a word of Scripture, a touch or handclasp to bring His ministering and refreshing life to us.

SACLA

Then came the SACLA Assembly itself as 6,000 South African Christian leaders came together in probably the most historic ecumenical assembly ever to happen in South Africa.

Again for me it was both ecstasy and agony, both Spirit and fire. As I prepared for my own address on the Holy Spirit I was led into the most unusual pre-address experience I ever had. I was simply overcome for nearly three hours with the most unaccountable grief for South Africa. A great weeping seized my soul for nearly an entire morning as I sought God's face and final guidance for my message. Never had anything like this happened to me. Not surprisingly, much of my text ended up in a new form, especially as I was powerfully drawn to elucidate Isaiah 58:6–12:

> Is not this the fast that I choose:
> to loose the bonds of wickedness,
> to undo the thongs of the yoke,

> to let the oppressed go free,
>   and to break every yoke?
> Is it not to share your bread with the hungry,
>   and bring the homeless poor into your house;
> when you see the naked, to cover him,
>   and not to hide yourself from your own flesh?
>
> Then shall your light break forth like the dawn,
>   and your healing shall spring up speedily;
> your righteousness shall go before you,
>   the glory of the Lord shall be your rear guard.
>
> Then you shall call, and the Lord will answer;
>   you shall cry, and He will say, Here I am.

Curiously, I was to touch on this same Scripture the following year in the second South African Renewal Conference. Colin Urquhart, one of the overseas speakers, spoke on Isaiah 56 and 57. He had been planning to go into Chapter 58 on '*the FAST I choose*' when the Spirit whispered to him, 'No, leave that. A South African must speak on Isaiah 58!' Astonishing. The demanding lot was mine. Moreover, it was instructive that the Spirit was so deeply interested in this sort of FAST – the fast of justice.

My point in all this is that these were very hard and tough and sometimes Calvary experiences, which previously I had not really seen as so integral to a fresh work of the Spirit in one, yet all these happenings were slowly being revealed to me afresh as necessary both for God's work in the world and for His work in me.

EXCEPT THE GRAIN DIE

I suppose all this goes back to that verse so powerfully applied to my heart in the Milner Park experience, namely John 12:24 'Unless a grain of wheat falls into the earth and dies, it remains alone; but if it dies, it bears much fruit'.

It's that dying bit that is so hard. I remember some months before SACLA returning from one of my trips related to the conference. I had been gearing up even then to prepare my own paper on the work of the Holy Spirit. But that same Spirit about whom I would be speaking convinced me that there was another brother in a nearby neighbouring country who had something against me and I needed to try to reconcile with him before the conference.

'But, Lord, he has hurt me; I haven't hurt him,' I protested, 'why should I go?'

'What does My Word say?' seemed to be the response of the Spirit of God. Then I thought of Matt. 5:23-4. It was rather plain. 'If you are offering your gift at the altar [i.e. you are busy with your religious exercises] and there [i.e. at the place of religious service] remember that your brother has something against you, leave your gift there before the altar and go; first be reconciled to your brother, and then come and offer your gift.'

'But, Lord, that's far away. It will mean an air flight.'

'Go, first be reconciled, then preach at SACLA.'

'But, Lord, it will be expensive. Who will pay?'

'You have some savings, haven't you?' the Spirit seemed to say.

Jolly presumptuous of God to touch my savings, I thought secretly!

Anyway, next day I was on my way. A strange, beautiful, but again difficult journey in spirit. A partial healing of the relationship took place. Later it became gloriously complete. But it seemed just so much dying had to take place to get there.

In the closing meeting of SACLA I referred to this experience and challenged all to reconciliation. An English girl who had just arrived in South Africa from England to do Christian work felt convicted. She had left her family totally alienated when she went abroad for Christian service.

So a few days later she took herself to the Cross. Then she went to the bank, drew out all her savings, plucked up courage, humbled her proud heart and set off for England. Her astonished and shaken family, whom she had left only weeks previously, all thoroughly alienated as much from her Gospel as from herself, now stood on spiritual tiptoe as she came back to seek forgiveness and reconciliation. Suddenly her Gospel had credibility.

But it was purifying and painful for her. The work of the Spirit in her heart at SACLA was now being followed by a Baptism with purifying fire.

This same sort of process took place in many others while they were at SACLA. Each evening we broke the 6,000-member assembly into small groups where pietists faced activists, white heard from black, evangelical was confronted by non-evangelical and Charismatics and non-charismatics prayed and sometimes agonised with each other. Often there were tears. At times there was anger. Generally there was pain. And nearly always there was repentance, the Cross and growth. For many SACLA was a Baptism with fire. That is why I knew so truly that it was a work of the Holy Spirit.

CALVARY LOVE

In due time I had the opportunity to discuss this whole aspect of spiritual growth with Festo.

He underlined to me a truth which lay at the heart of his own ministry on the Holy Spirit. This was also at the centre of the East African Revival. Pentecost flowed from Calvary. Calvary was its context. The Holy Spirit is the Spirit of Jesus and Jesus is the Christ of Calvary. Unless, therefore, our teaching on the Holy Spirit is allied to the Cross and its self-sacrificing imperatives we can miss the fact that the Spirit is primarily concerned to conform us to the image of Christ in our characters and in the producing of His fruit, especially love, in the life of the believer. The man who is full of the Holy Spirit is the one who loves and who is like Christ. There is no other ultimate test.

What we have to do is to reason and preach from Calvary. We have to sustain the view from the Cross – not just as our place of conversion and salvation, but as our means of growth. As self is crucified, the Spirit is released more and more in fullness. This has been the key in the East African Revival.

In fact, in Festo's excellent little book *When God Moves*, the very first paragraph is as follows:

> The word REVIVAL has 7 letters: three on one side, R – E – V; and three on the other side, V – A – L. In the centre is the letter 'I'. Now how do we get to revival? Simply by crossing out the 'I'. Try writing the word carefully with a capital 'I' in the centre. Then put a line through the 'I' and it becomes a cross. Self-centredness is the greatest enemy of spiritual life. You are going to be involved in inward battle and conflict, as long as the centre of your personality is occupied by that little god. It's too little to be your god. It can't occupy the throne. The throne is for Him who died in love for you – I mean God in Jesus Christ. When self is on the throne, it is conspicuously out of place: too weak to meet your needs, too small to satisfy your hunger, too dry to quench your thirst. The Bible begins by putting a line through the 'I' which is at the centre and turning it into a cross.[63]

A PERSONAL CRISIS

In spite of starting to learn something more of this principle in 1979, I was scarcely prepared for the greater depths in which I was to face it during a deep personal crisis in 1980.

After SACLA I was worn out in more ways than one. In fact, the pressures of 1978 and '79 were simply the culmination of a decade of pressure. I was more than ready for a sabbatical break. Mercifully this had been granted me sometime previously by the Board of African Enterprise.

With my wife and three children I set off in January 1980 for three months in the U.S.A., two in ministry and one in rest, and then three months reading and study at Cambridge and Oxford.

They were not easy months. In the first place I had become deeply concerned about aspects of our ministry in African Enterprise. My concern related to whether we always took care to discern the mind and will of the Spirit before we

plunged into miscellaneous ministry opportunities or social
care projects. The load, both financial and personal, was
becoming crushing for many in the work, yet Jesus had said:
'My yoke is easy, and my burden is light' (Matt. 11:30).
What is one to say when the yoke is anything but easy and the
burden anything but light?

Moreover, I was becoming increasingly suspicious of those
times when we became involved in frenzied ministries which
seemed not only to destroy one's spiritual peace but threaten
one's health. I remembered again the Lord's word through
Jeremiah: 'I did not send the prophets, yet they ran; I did not
speak to them, yet they prophesied' (Jer. 23:21). Here was a
picture of wasted, fruitless and frenzied ministry which had
nothing to do with the will of God. Then the Lord adds His
commentary: 'But if they had stood in my council, then they
would have proclaimed my words to my people, and they
would have turned them from their evil way, and from the
evil of their doings' (Jer. 23:22).

GOD'S AGENDA

In a sense the issue was whether as a work we would really
seek in new ways to walk in the Spirit in terms of the agenda
of God for us, or whether we would just do our own thing in
our own energy. Could self-will be eliminated even in the
scheduling of an entire organisation?

It was no light matter because it clearly involved the whole
purpose of God for one's earthly walk and work. Imagine
getting to Heaven and facing the Lord Jesus and hearing
Him say: 'Well done, my son. You did pretty well. The only
problem is that too often you worked the rose garden of your
own choosing and not the cabbage patch of mine. You
poured out great and sincere energy, but often on the wrong
thing.'

The thought became a nightmare to me. It plagued me day
and night – literally. For months and months I woke at 4
a.m. or earlier. Were we functioning the right way? Was I
personally doing the right thing? Had not the time come in

my life for a change? Was evangelism still my work? Or should I enter the political process? Or return to teaching? Should I stay in South Africa? Or should I go to Zimbabwe or East Africa? Or should I even leave African Enterprise as the vehicle I had launched and let others run it as they saw fit?

Beyond that I saw with eyes of fire the dangers of hitting the big time. AE was now a big organisation, spanning a number of countries across the world. Our budget was very large and growing larger and the whole machine had to be kept on the road. Money was an endless anxiety, though I knew I should be more relaxed and trusting in the Lord over this than I was.

There was also the now obvious danger of the proverbial ego trip. One wanted to succeed, be well thought of, widely called on, written up in periodicals and all that clap-trap. Suddenly it all sickened me. The spirit of the manger and the carpenter's bench could vanish so easily from a work and the whole point of what Jesus was on about could be subtly, slowly and lethally lost.

I suppose what suddenly began to worry me as much about myself as about our ministry as a whole was that it seemed at certain points to be operating more in the flesh and in the ways of the world than in the Spirit and in the ways of God. NOT that we were being consciously disobedient. We were just functioning as 'ordinary men' and doing many things in man's ways, in man's energy and in man's wisdom – that is, at certain points we were not being spiritual. We were not full of the Spirit and were behaving 'as babes in Christ', not as 'spiritual men'.

These were hard thoughts to entertain of myself, or of the organisation I belonged to. They are equally hard to hear and receive for any individual or group or congregation, especially if habits of 'doing it my way' have become well set and established. In fact breaking out of old ways hurts. And it is difficult. It involves constant crucifixion and many moments of pain which God uses to try to bring us more fully under His control, so that where the Master is, there is the servant also, not vice versa. Unfortunately, we, His servants, are often scampering across the Christian landscape on our own self-inflating errands, which of course we want the Master to bless mightily, while He is off somewhere else on His own agenda, though wondering no doubt when His highpowered and ever so important servants will get where He is!

IN HIDING

About this time I was due to skip out of Oxford, where I was studying under the great and encyclopaedic Bishop Stephen Neill, and head off for several weeks to Thailand for the International Congress on World Evangelisation. I even had a paper to give and a study group to lead.

However, in prayer one morning the Spirit mightily convinced me that I was not to go. I was to stay where I was.

'Hide yourself,' God's word to Elijah in 1 Kings 17:2, gripped me firmly in its grasp.

Perhaps, had I known what the next three weeks were to bring forth, I would have opted for the long journey east, like Jonah heading for Tarshish! But Oxford was my Nineveh of divine appointment for those days.

The mechanics of how it all happened are of less consequence than the spiritual process itself. But in effect in those following weeks all my Isaacs were systematically taken up my Mount Moriah and forced to the altar of sacrifice. My desire to be a good evangelist, my continuing involvement in African Enterprise, my ministry of evangelism itself, my ongoing presence in South Africa, our beautiful home near Pietermaritzburg, all were taken by the Spirit of God, not theoretically but existentially and truly. It was all gone or almost gone. I was left living at Mount Moriah with the knife poised over my Isaacs, and not knowing whether there would be a ram caught in the thicket.

My Isaacs – all things which in and of themselves were good – were in danger, as I began to see it, of becoming idols. They were getting in the way of God. This was especially true of my relationship to AE which I saw, as Abraham with Isaac, as the means by which I would bless the world.

Not surprisingly, God went for that one hardest. Finally I let go. It was gone. I was leaving AE. I felt curiously light, as if a massive weight of baggage had been lifted.

On the morning of Monday 26 May 1980, after a week-end in London, I walked on the Wimbledon Common with Carol and talked about what our future held, now that the Lord had seemingly taken AE. Says my journal: 'It was a time of searing crisis when I basically faced up to leaving AE and all that would mean. It was not an easy time. I basically experienced the emotions of bereavement.'

SERVANTHOOD

Two days later came Philippians 2 while I was cycling through Oxford to a tutorial with Bishop Stephen Neill! My journal records: 'The word of Philippians 2 came home to me. He made himself of no reputation and *became obedient* – unto death – even death on a Cross. He also emptied Himself of all to which He was entitled. The challenge to me was obvious in terms of laying down everything on which in a sense my reputation rests, yet which is now a potential if not actual impediment to my own obedience.'

Next day came a new insight. My journal again captures where I was: 'I think I have cultivated a fairly healthy, or perhaps unhealthy, though certainly not uncommon, desire to succeed, and to be someone! That I saw too must go and if AE is an unconscious vehicle to that relatively unconscious desire, then the altar of sacrifice must have yet another offering upon it'.

The end of a long week finally came. I went to Church on Sunday. The message, from a layman, was on Nehemiah the leader, the rebuilder, the mourner, the lamenter for Israel. It was momentous for me. The Holy Spirit was in it. The word was to rebuild. The word was to keep courage. 'Should such a man as I flee?' asked Nehemiah (6:11). The word was to persevere. 'So the wall was finished' (6:15).

Drake's prayer came to mind: 'Lord, when thou givest to thy servants to endeavour any great matter, grant us also to know that it is not the beginning but the continuing of the same until it be thoroughly finished which yieldeth the true glory; through Him, who for the finishing of Thy work, laid down His life, our Redeemer Jesus Christ.'

I was out of the woods – re-commissioned, re-called, renewed. AE was handed back to me, though I now held it in freedom. It did not hold me, nor ever could again in the same way as before. South Africa came back to me. We could return to our precious home, Namirembe. Above all I could continue evangelising, which was my love, but more as God's servant than as one of AE's preachers!

It had been an incredible time. A scorching time. Yes, one was going forward through Cross-fire!

CALVARY ROAD

But, lest anyone imagine I was now soaring on some new height of sparkling spirituality, I must add that the Calvary process kept going and it still goes on. I'm convinced we never get it taped. We are never finally on top. We never arrive. Not until Glory!

This was underlined when I was setting off on leave that Christmas. It was December 1980. The car was packed and the family waiting. As I left my study the words *Calvary Road* popped into my mind. That made me anxious, because I remembered this as the title to a very powerful and challenging little book by Roy Hession. I remembered picking it up twenty years ago as a seminary student and finding it too hot to handle.

The prompting to take the book on leave scared me a bit. But I duly read it and was greatly blessed and challenged by it.

Commenting on this Cross experience, Hession writes:

Dying to self is not a thing we do once and for all. There may be an initial dying when God first shows these things, but ever after, it will be a constant dying, for only so can the Lord Jesus be revealed constantly through us. All day long the choice will be before us in a thousand ways.[64]

Returning some weeks later with all this beautiful Calvary theology, and admittedly somewhat apprehensive as to why I was being led further into this truth at this time, I was confronted almost immediately with the situation of a friend who had exercised my patience at several points. In fact, perhaps unconsciously, he had hurt me. I was mad at him.

Wanting to face him with his supposed affronts to my person, I set off to set him straight and sort him out. The words 'mote and beam' sizzled into my spiritual consciousness from Roy Hession's book.

'Lord, you mean, my mote and his beam.'

'No, my son, I mean your beam and his mote. You leave him to me to sort out and in the meantime ask his forgiveness for your attitude.'

Oh, my goodness! That meant such a mouthful of humble pie, indeed a kingsize helping.

But if my brother has a mote, or a speck, and I have a beam, what is that beam, I wondered.

Hession had the answer:

Now we all know what Jesus meant by the mote in the other person's eye. It is some fault which we fancy we can discern in him; it may be an act he has done against us, or some attitude he adopts towards us. But what did the Lord Jesus mean by the beam in our eye? I suggest that the beam in our eye is simply our unloving reaction to the other man's mote. Without doubt there is a wrong in the other person. But our reaction to that wrong is a wrong too! The mote in him has provoked in us resentment, or coldness, or criticism, or bitterness, or evil speaking, or illwill – all of them variants of the basic ill, unlove. And that, said the Lord Jesus, is far, far worse than the tiny wrong (sometimes quite unconscious) that provoked it. A beam means a rafter. And the Lord Jesus means by this comparison to tell us that our unloving reaction to the other's wrong is what a great rafter is to a little splinter![65]

Hession goes on:

But let us not think that a beam is of necessity some violent reaction on our part. The first beginning of resentment is a beam, as is also the first flicker of an unkind thought, or the first suggestion of unloving criticism. Where that is so, it only distorts our vision and we shall never see our brother as he really is, beloved of god. If we speak to our brother with that in our hearts, it will only provoke him to adopt the same attitude to us, for it is a law of human relationships that 'with what measure ye mete, it shall be measured to you again'.[66]

But does this mean that my brother is without fault and I who would judge the only one who is guilty?

Not at all, says the author of *Calvary Road*.

But as we take these simple steps of repentance, then we see clearly to cast the mote out of the other's eye, for the beam in our eye has gone. In that moment God will pour light in on us as to the other's need, that neither he nor we ever had before. We may see then that the mote we were so conscious of before, is virtually non-existent – it was but the projection of something that was in us. On the other hand, we may have revealed to us hidden underlying things, of which he himself was hardly conscious. Then as God leads us, we must lovingly and humbly challenge him, so that he may see them too, and bring them to the Fountain for sin and find deliverance. He will be more likely than ever to let us do it – indeed if he is a humble man, he will be grateful to us, for he will know now that there is no selfish motive in our heart, but only love and concern for him.[67]

And so with all these thoughts rushing through my mind, I

met my friend and confessed my fault. I won't deny it was hard. It was veritably a Calvary road for my pride, but it was good. He confessed that he had indeed failed me. And we went forward in light – and growing!

CROSS CENTRAL

To sum up, the Spirit of God over these years has seemed in so many and various ways to be pointing to the dangers in my own renewal personally and in the Church's renewal generally when triumphalism or fleshly responses enter with all their self-satisfaction and self-assertiveness. God seemed to be underlining that the true mark of the Spirit's working is self-sacrifice, humility, servanthood and finally forgiving love as the hallmark par excellence of the Spirit's presence. The Cross must remain central. It was a tough challenge, but an unavoidable one. For this was and is the way of love.

So if we are going to go forward in the faith, not only appropriating and exercising the gifts of the Spirit in ministry but also manifesting the fruit of the Spirit, especially love, in life and character, then it seems we cannot avoid walking first via the Cross, with its Calvary demands, and secondly via the fire of the Spirit with its painful and purging power.

Beyond that, there will be complicating cross-fire to cope with from the different Christian merry-go-rounds as we leap from one to the other. But not to worry. If we do it enough, we may all one day go round together. It could be fun.

Chapter Seventeen

THE JESUS WAY IN THE WORLD

> Too many evangelical Christians are irresponsible
> escapists: Fellowship with one another in the
> church is much more congenial than service in the
> world's hostile environment.
>
> John Stott

It was not more than a couple of weeks after the first Renewal Conference at Milner Park in August 1977 that a young black consciousness leader called Stephen Biko died by torture in a South African gaol. He had been arrested without charge, detained without trial and now he was dead without explanation. He was not the first young black to die in this manner. He was part of an epidemic. Against the backdrop of a deafening silence from most conservative South African Christians, the world and the rest of the South African Church lifted their voices yet again in grief and protest.

DETAINEE DEATHS

My own profound concern found expression in my newspaper column. Thus on 17 September 1977 my article, under the title of 'Detainee Deaths', appeared. It included the following remarks.

Perhaps the most shattering aspect of this is that having become accustomed to the neo-pagan practice of detentions without trial, we are now in danger of becoming accustomed to the deaths without adequate explanation of people detained without trial.

That justice in any country must be done goes without saying. It should also go without saying, especially in a professedly Christian country, that it must also be seen to be done. . . .

The end does not justify the means. Nothing therefore which is morally wrong can ever be politically right. Expediency is not justice.

The challenge then to our authorities is clear. It is a challenge left to us not only from Christian principle but even from the pagan Roman Empire where people knew they could say: 'If [they] have a complaint against any one, the courts are open, and there are proconsuls; let them bring charges' (Acts 19:38).

Is it too much to ask for this – not in pagan Rome but in Christian South Africa? Is it too much to request an independent inquiry into these detainee deaths so that a restive public may have its troubled mind set at rest?

If so, then we all must truly Cry for the Beloved Country.

REACTION

Not long after this article appeared a white local parishioner, very high on spiritual renewal, approached one of my colleagues.

'I thought Michael got sorted out at Milner Park and now here he writes in his column about Steve Biko.'

'Did you read what he said?' asked my colleague.

'No,' said the irate parishioner, 'I just saw he was writing on Steve Biko and that was enough for me. I'm not going to support African Enterprise any more.'

We in AE were no strangers to this sort of response, because whenever we have addressed any social issue in this avowedly Christian country (a breathtaking 87 per cent of South Africans profess to be Christians), we have met with the above response in varying degrees of intensity from white Christians, though never yet from any black Christian.

In fact, even when I shared this Biko story at the second South African Renewal Conference in January 1980 I was faced with a barrage of criticism from whites and I put the Conference Executive Committee into crisis. I had asked if a new desire to know the fullness of the Holy Spirit made one more – or less – interested in a man dying by torture in one of our prisons. I was told by one sincere person that even to mention Biko, let alone quote Martin Luther King with approval as I had done, was inappropriate in a South African religious gathering. Apart from anything else it created a psychological guilt complex and made reconciliation more difficult.

This is a sincerely held viewpoint amongst many white Christians in my country. Of course the fact that we may suffer from the psychological ravages of authentic corporate guilt, rather than simply a guilt complex, and that reconciliation is impossible until we have faced the true extent of our socio-political crimes, does not seem to have pressed itself too readily upon many of us in this complicated end of the world.

'South Africa hasn't got a guilt complex,' I commented to a friend, apropos of this reaction. 'South Africa is guilty!'

Was I right or wrong as a Christian to lend my voice in challenge, along with many others, to the brutal pattern of political happenings of which Biko's death was only one aspect?

Put differently, should Christians be involved in any form of socio-political action? Should they indulge in actions of social concern? Should they ever challenge the State? It is a vexed matter.

I remember my deep-seated anger and almost bitterness at the time of Biko's death when our then Minister of Justice, Mr Jimmy Kruger, came on television with excuses and hollow explanations for the black leader's demise, especially when he had already said publicly: 'Steve Biko's death leaves me cold'.

Midstream in my anger, I had to ask: 'What does it mean to love Jimmy Kruger? And how do I voice my Christian protest in a manner which does not betray the very Gospel whose priorities I am trying to protect?'

It was a tough one. Trying to find the Spirit's way had involved a fairly lengthy process, though basically there were only two steps in it. The first step involved being brought to an understanding of the implications simply of being a human being. It related really to the doctrine of CRE-ATION and seeing all men as valuable. The second step involved being brought to an understanding of the implications of Jesus's own way in the world. It related to the doctrine of CHRIST and seeing all men as recipients of His compassionate concern.

STEP ONE – BEING HUMAN

I mentioned in the last chapter the influence my father had on me. My earliest recollections of him, as we grew up in the little British Protectorate of Basutoland (as it then was – Lesotho as it now is) were of a man who treated all people fairly. He had both blacks and whites under him in his capacity as senior engineer in the territory and to him people were people, regardless of their colour.

I don't think this view was based on anything very self-consciously Christian. It was just a corollary of being a human being. It was basically related to the way God had created us. To treat people differently on the basis of race was in a sense to deny something of one's own humanity, not to mention theirs.

Another very important influence on me through childhood came in the person of Patrick Duncan, son of Sir Patrick Duncan who had been Governor General of South Africa under Smuts. Pat lived next door to us and he was an easy candidate for a child's hero worship. He had a sparkling personality, was constantly full of hilarious fun and could mimic anyone. More than that he shared my childhood passion for horses, he showed me how to raid a beehive, taught me about birds and butterflies, and scared my mother silly as he introduced me to the giant-size bow and arrow. He was positively the most stimulating and interesting person I ever knew.

But above all, he had passionate political commitments to justice and a fair shake for all. He abominated apartheid and all its ways, but he equally abominated anything to do with violence. Mahatma Ghandi and his philosophy of *Satyagraha* or passive resistance or soul force constituted his guiding star. I became a childhood convert. Discrimination was wrong. Justice was right. Apartheid would doom South Africa. I was glad and proud when Pat joined Peter Brown and Alan Paton in founding the South African Liberal Party.

But tragically, over the following twenty years a desperate and disillusioned Pat gradually turned to violence, and we parted political company. He was banned in South Africa and fled the country.

Years later I talked to him of Christ but never knew if I got through. Once in New York he said to my sister: 'In Michael's message lies the answer.' Perhaps he came full circle. In any event, the commitments of his early years, based like my father's on the common humanity of the human race under God, had made their mark on me.

On the other hand I was not allowed to become crudely anti-Afrikaner. My maternal grandfather and grandmother saw to that. Although grandfather had come out with the Royal Canadian Cavalry to fight in the Boer War in 1899 and Granny had come as a British nurse, they had both developed strongly sympathetic views of the Boer cause after the war. Granny, who had nursed both British and Boer soldiers and won from Lord Kitchener the Royal Red Cross in the process, the highest women's decoration for bravery, always taught me that there were wonderful qualities in the Afrikaner. She was right. Naturally therefore both she and Grandfather longed for a new South Africa in which all races would live happily. They accordingly held out the hand of fellowship and reconciliation, especially to Afrikaners. It was simply the right and human thing to do.

If step one involved learning about what being human meant, step two related to being CHRISTIAN.

STEP TWO – BEING CHRISTIAN

At High School these commitments took greater shape around a specifically Christian framework. At Michaelhouse I learned that one was concerned for the world because Jesus was concerned for the world.

This developing framework set me up for the mighty step forward which came with reading Alan Paton's *Cry the Beloved Country*. When he came to our school in 1952 I was moved by his words and warnings and especially the lament in the last words of his book that when the white man turns to loving the black man will have turned to hating. He was a good prophet.

Then came conversion at Cambridge in 1955. This crystallised my conviction that Jesus was the answer for South Africa and His Way the only Way.

Trevor Huddleston came to the University shortly after the publication of *Naught for Your Comfort*, which I had devoured, and was followed by Alexander Steward from South Africa House who had himself just put out a book entitled *You are Wrong Father Huddleston*. After Steward had given his lecture, during which my brave roommate Alasdair Macaulay tried his first hand at heckling, the famous South African historian Eric Walker was asked to pass a vote of thanks to the speaker. What stuck in my mind were Walker's words to the effect that the only thing Mr Steward had missed out was 'Jesus – and He was interested in blokes'. It was a shattering condemnation of the politics of apartness because in its stark terseness it went to the nub of the matter. People mattered. They shouldn't be treated differently.

I became quite militant and with other friends we wrote vigorous letters of protest about South African policies to the London *Times* and even picketed South Africa House, carrying a cross and wearing black arm bands!

The South African High Commissioner was overheard by one of my friends saying to an official: 'I can understand the picket, but why the Cross?' It was a good question.

I then reacted from my militant line and embraced the view that all that was needed was for men to be converted. Then society would come right. Imagine my horror as a very young Christian when I began to find converted people not just tolerating but actively supporting or propagating the South African *status quo*.

THE JESUS WAY

In 1969 our team was gearing up for a city-wide mission to Nairobi when we learned with excitement that the veteran missionary statesman, E. Stanley Jones, could join us. How much we learned from him!

He presented a clear picture of the Cosmic Christ and of His Way as THE Way in all things, moral, political, marital, personal. If the universe is His, then it bears His stamp and doing things His Way is to do them the way which works.

The heart of his teaching was as follows:

> If the Christian way is a way among ways, you can take it or leave it, and nothing much happens. It doesn't really matter. But if it is true – if it is THE Way – then nothing else matters. This is the one thing in life with which we must come to terms, or ruin life itself. If the Way is imposed upon life, then it is A Way, but if it is a revelation of life, of life itself, then it is THE Way. If it is written in the Scriptures only, then it is A Way. If it is written in the nature of reality and the Scriptures, then it is THE Way.[68]

THE MORAL NATURE OF THE UNIVERSE

Slowly it all began to come into clearer focus. Suddenly Colossians 1:16 made all the sense in the world – politically, I mean. Here Jesus is presented as the Agent and goal in Creation. All things were made through Him and for Him, says the Apostle. The great socio-political implications of this for the Christian become obvious. Because the universe has Jesus's stamp on it we must tell society, both governments and governed, that for life to work, whether private, marital, social or political, the game must be played Jesus's way.

Later on I tried to spell this out in a letter to a South African political leader. First of all, bearing in mind the politics of love, I felt constrained to come to him not in judgment, but in love. I wrote: 'I come to you as a brother, not to complicate, but to try to help. The challenge is to think through *more* deeply AS A CHRISTIAN on the *ethical* and *moral* factors involved in the policies of our country. Let me elaborate, first on the principle – and then on some precedents.'

PRINCIPLE

I then went on to try to spell out the consequences of the biblical teaching that Jesus is the agent in Creation. I saw the implications as five-fold and spelt them out as follows:

1. It means that the universe is His and His stamp is upon it at every level.
2. It means that His laws – scientific, social, personal, psychological and moral – are operative throughout.
3. It means that if we want life and the universe to cooperate with us we must play the game His way. If we do, life and the universe cooperate with us. Things work.
4. It means that if we do not go the Jesus way at every level of life – whether personal, marital or political – then life and the universe do not cooperate with us. We lose their backing and instead of producing that which is integrative we produce that which is disintegrative. Thus a teenager violating the laws of sex is not breaking the laws but illustrating them when he or she becomes fragmented. Likewise a politician who violates Jesus's corporate and social laws (e.g. 'Do unto others as you would have them do to you' – or 'Love your neighbour as yourself') will find not that they are breaking laws but that the laws are breaking them and the society

around them. Nor will anyone persuade me that apartheid laws are not violating those two principles round
every turn. Not one white South African, least of all any
member of the Cabinet, would want to be on the
RECEIVING end of apartheid legislation.

5. It does not mean that a thing is wrong simply because
   the Bible says so, (as if it were something arbitrary) but
   rather the Bible says a thing is wrong because it doesn't
   work. It is not in accord with the moral fabric of the
   universe. In other words, biblical morality (whether
   personal, social or political) is not an *imposed* morality
   but rather an *exposed* morality. The Bible simply *exposes*
   the morality which is there and says 'If you want life to
   work, then do it this way'. It is like finding the direction
   of grain on a piece of wood so that one may plane it
   correctly. The plane works when it follows the grain
   which is there. Likewise if by faulty policy we go against
   the moral grain of the universe, the political plane just
   will not work.

   This is very close to Plato's definition of the good as
   that which best relates function to purpose. Thus a
   good knife is one which cuts well because it functions
   according to its purpose. A good man is a man who
   functions as God purposed him to function. And a good
   government is one which functions according to the
   divine intent. From a biblical perspective this means as
   'God's servant' for the 'good' of *all* its peoples (Rom.
   13:4).

   This is why I have often said in South Africa that the
   fundamental issue facing us is whether we live in a
   moral universe or not. If we do not, then we can
   discriminate (whether in microcosm or in macrocosm)
   and get away with it. But if we do live in a moral
   universe, and if we discriminate, then we can't and
   won't get away with it. And the judgments of life, of
   history and of the universe will become the judgments
   of God – because He has made one sort of universe and
   not another – a universe in which we reap what we sow.

PRINCIPLE

After sharing several biblical and historical precedents I concluded my hopefully not too presumptuous homily to my political friend with these words. 'I realise that all of this is almost certainly familiar ethical territory to you, but you are a Christian brother and therefore these things are worth underlining to one another. Exactly how all this is to be worked out within the realities of the South African situation is for those of you who are Christian politicians and statesmen to decide. But of this I am sure – anything that breaks with Christian principle will not work. It will only produce the kind of mounting fury which is now threatening to engulf our whole society – if not right now, then within a few years. It is self-deceiving to see all this as the work of a few agitators. It is not. It is a reflex in the machine, as it were, to what happens when the rules are broken. It is the cogs in a watch grinding because of sand which should not be there.

'Put differently, it is life and the universe in RE-ACTION. This is not to discount agitating, exploitive or even Marxist elements. But Marxists are never foolish enough to *exploit* anything except JUST causes. The devil always has a sound eye for the genuine grievance! We can only head him off by cleaving to what is right – no matter how much the darkness may call us to the dictates of expediency.

'So my challenge is to encourage subordination of policy to principle, bearing in mind it is better in the eyes of both time and eternity to lose in the short term with what must ultimately win rather than win in the short term with that which will ultimately lose.'

There my letter concluded. I had discharged my soul to a key political figure and felt glad and relieved to have done so. I was of course trying to project into the future as to the dread consequences in my own land of violating the moral fabric of the universe.

Then I came across a reflection as to the tragedy in a past situation in someone else's land of having allowed just that sort of violation to happen. It related to Hitler's Germany.

HITLER'S GERMANY

To be sure Hitler was a fellow who thought he could break all the rules. Instead he graphically illustrated them. The way he did so was spelled out after the war by Dr Paul Schmidt, Hitler's official interpreter, in a letter to a friend:

> The basically Christian ethics which activated most European statesmen in the '20s and early '30s, however vigorously they represented the interest of their countries, resulted in the progress which I saw achieved year by year at successive conferences in those days.
>
> Thereafter I witnessed the mighty struggle between the eternal principles of Christianity and the exponents of a new attitude towards human rights contrary to all accepted ideas. I saw the apparent triumph of this new attitude. But, by being closely associated with events, I perceived with increasing clarity on which side strength essentially lay. The outbreak of war in 1939 was the beginning of the end for this new force, at first victorious, but whose accelerated decline, culminating in the greatest catastrophe of all times, I also followed closely in all its phases, year by year.[69]

All this underlines that no Christian who has grasped the principles of the moral nature of the universe, as I believe all need to do in our time, can stand aside and let governments and societies or even so-called liberation movements try to do their own thing without reference to Jesus and His guide book. It would be as criminal as letting a ten-year-old own and drive a car without learning the principles of driving and without reference to the guide book. It is just the fastest way to organise a crash!

THE DIGNITY AND VALUE OF MAN

Another principle which relates to the moral nature of the universe is that of the dignity and value of man. This too is an extension of the doctrine of creation.

Writing of William Wilberforce (1759–1833), who laboured so long for the abolition of slavery, E. M. Howse, a recent chronicler of the influences of the Clapham Sect, the group of people who got together around Wilberforce to support him, observes that this and other movements 'sprang out of a new doctrine of responsibility towards the underprivileged, a doctrine which received its chief impulse from the evangelical emphasis on the *value of the human soul* and hence of the individual.'[70]

In making us in His image, God has endowed each of us with immense value and sacrosanct dignity. Anything which undermines that, whether political or social or personal, is to be opposed in the name of Christ.

It is worth reminding ourselves that Father, Son and Holy Spirit all participated in the act of creating the universe. The Father was the Initiator of creation. It was, we might say, His idea!

Then, Jesus was the Agent. This we learn from St John: 'Without Him was not anything made that was made' (John 1:3).

And the Holy Spirit was in on it all too, for 'the Spirit of God was moving over the face of the waters' (Gen. 1:2).

With all three Persons of the Godhead involved, it is understandable that the divine resolve should be: 'Let *US* make man in Our image' (Gen. 1:26).

And so God created the universe, the world, and finally man, the great amphibian between nature and supernature.

Here is the world fitted out by the Holy Trinity Itself for man, and man fitted by the Holy Trinity for the world. To live in the world, man must cooperate with it. He must understand how the world is orchestrated and must fit his own music to harmonise with Heaven's.

NO DICHOTOMY

What was becoming clearer and clearer was the fact that one cannot really divide up life or people into secular or sacred compartments.

While my doctrines of the Fall and redemption told me all men needed saving, and this challenged me as an evangelist, my doctrine of creation told me that all men were worth saving, and this increasingly challenged me as a human being. It meant that man, although a sinner, needing salvation, was also immensely valuable because he was made in the image of God. This gave each person equality, dignity and value in the eyes of God. Anything which denied that equality or which threatened that dignity or which minimised that value was to be challenged in the name of the God of both Old and New Testaments.

There was also the fact, which thrusts in on one constantly in South Africa, that man is man in community. He is not a soul without a body (so that our only job is to evangelise him) or a body without a soul (so that our only job is to feed and clothe him). Nor is he a body-soul without a community (so that our only job is both to evangelise and feed him), but rather he is a body-soul-in-community so that our job is to evangelise him, to care for his physical being and to see that he is rightly related to others within his society.

After all, no man survives or grows in a vacuum. He develops within a complicated interweaving of relationships and these influence and shape him for good or ill. Society thus has immense power to shape and mould individuals and how it does so depends on the nature and characteristics of that society. A society can stunt, warp or shrivel its people, or it can stimulate and inspire their fullest growth into freedom, wholeness and happiness.

John Stott points the finger at any Church which has allowed a corrupt system of society to develop:

> When any community deteriorates, the blame should be attached where it belongs: not to the community which is going bad, but to the church which is failing in its responsibility as salt to stop it going bad. And the salt will be effective only if it permeates society, only if Christians learn again the wide diversity of divine callings, and if

many penetrate deeply into secular society to serve Christ there.[71]

And one performs such service, not out of a desire to be politically provocative but because alongside the Great Commission to evangelise the whole world stands the Great Commandment to love the whole world, as a fundamental adjunct of loving God with all our being.

Unfortunately some sincere Christians seem to act as if the Great Commission supersedes the Great Commandment. However, while New Testament love certainly obligates us to share with our neighbours the greatest good news in all the world, the story of salvation and forgiveness in Christ, it does not stop there. It goes on into any areas of activity or initiative which are demanded by plain, straightforward compassion. Yet so many of my evangelical and charismatic friends seemed to challenge or ignore this.

SOMETHING WRONG

Obviously something was terribly wrong somewhere. It seemed increasingly to me that those who were advising the stance that Christians keep their hands out of such unspiritual things as politics, economics and the problems of society, were often concerned not so much for the souls of men and the spirituality of religion as they were for their own freedom to do as they pleased in social, economic and political matters.

Is this not a problem with the Lordship of Christ and the Kingdom of God when He is propagated as the Lord of private matters such as food, drink, sex and entertainment, but not over public matters such as racism, voting, education or justice? Are we to call for repentance from adultery and drunkenness but not from racial prejudice, discriminatory practices or participation in unjust structures?

With hindsight everyone recognises that the Victorian factory system which worked children twelve to sixteen hours a day was evil. Yet child labour, like slavery, was legal. But legal or not, these things destroyed people by the millions.

Were those Christians right who abstained from challenging these things because they didn't believe in becoming 'involved in politics'? What of Idi Amin's Uganda? Should Ugandan Christians have remained silent because 'involvement in politics' is out for the evangelical or Pentecostal Christian? After all, the powers that be are ordained by God! As far as I could see it, Ron Sider was dead right in his view that neglect of the Biblical teaching on structural injustice and institutionalised evil must rank as one of the deadliest omissions in theologically conservative sections of the church today.

In fact, the structural question to me as a South African Christian was one which became a particular challenge. It seemed that South African structures were not only frustrating true social progress but also full human happiness and dignity. Should they not therefore be challenged? Especially when one saw a generation of young blacks slowly turning away from the Christian Gospel because it seemed to have no relevance to the issues and pains they were facing.

SOWETO

This came home powerfully to me in 1970 when our team conducted a major mission in Soweto. Young blacks were patently losing patience with the Christian Church and becoming suspicious of the Bible.

'Why do the authorities give us the Bible free but make us pay for our school books?' they demanded as we visited high schools. 'It must be the book of the status quo – something to keep us quiet.'

Clearly to us the place was simmering over the whole political dispensation in South Africa.

'Soweto is going to blow,' I told the mayor of Johannesburg. He was concerned, and said he would inform the high-ups. I don't know if he did.

We told white Christians too.

'Surely it can't be that bad,' they said. 'Things will come right.'

Six years later, as the whole world knows, Soweto did blow. Hundreds died as the army and police quelled the rioting.

Eventually the rioting stopped. But the alienation of thousands of teenagers from the Gospel did not and has not stopped. The result of Christian silence and lack of adequate political reform has therefore pushed multitudes of these young blacks towards the Marxist option. This is a huge challenge to evangelical and charismatic Christians.

After all, the British working class turned away from the Gospel in the mid nineteenth century and has never really returned to it. The trouble was that personal ethics and social ethics simply never came together. In spite of crowded Churches, the social injustices of the time went unchallenged. The Church, which had tremendous influence, failed to use it for the healing and transformation of the society around it. Then came disillusionment among the working classes which has continued to this day. They had seen rampant religion which had no challenge to the conscience of the nation. The lessons for our present time are self-evident, especially for those concerned with renewal in the Holy Spirit as the Spirit of love.

All this brings us back to the basic question as to the right way through this issue for the Christian. The answer surely is that it must be the way of love.

BACK TO THE LAW OF LOVE

Perhaps the most political chapter in the Bible is 1 Corinthians 13. Here is the ultimate call to care. Here is the expanded version of Jesus's words: 'Whatever you wish that men would do to you, do so to them' (Matt. 7:12). Put differently, 'Love your neighbour as yourself' (Matt. 22:39).

Beyond that, Jesus has identified with us incarnationally in all our lostness, sin and need and has said to His Church: 'As the Father has sent me, even so I send you' (John 20:21). In His incredible love, compassion and care, He has not only given us a message, but a model – incarnational evangelism and Christian social concern. There are only two options vis à vis the world – either to turn our backs on it in rejection, or to face it in compassion – to escape from it, or to become involved in it. We can ignore its brokenness or seek to heal its brokenness. The former represents a failure of love, the latter an expression of it.

This also answers the vexed question as to how the Christian opposes injustice in a way which is different from, let's say, how the opposition political party would do it.

The law of love again is a sure guide. Love requires that we hate sin but love the sinner. It requires that we abominate injustice but seek to help the perpetrators of it to see another way. Love demands that we rebuke discriminators but relate to them as precious humans for whom Christ also died.

In the South African set-up many of us in the English Churches have for far too long simply denounced Afrikaners and the Afrikaans government without seriously facing the demands of love to care for them, to relate to them, to pray for them and to seek to be of service to them.

LOVE AND THE LAWMAKERS

Both the governing and the governed need to recognise that the principles of equality and of justice are in fact only approximations of the law of love in the kind of imperfect world which we know. This sort of insight should slow us down a bit in terms of facile and crude judgments on everything our political leaders do. As the saying goes, it is easier to shoot a lark than sing its song.

Perhaps this is why Paul so strongly urges Christians to pray for political leaders (1 Tim. 2:1–2). The fact is that their task is almost impossible.

For myself I have found it both a challenge and a blessing to seek to pray regularly and sometimes daily for six or seven South African political leaders, including the prime minister – men who span the total spectrum from status quo to revolutionary zealot. My prayer is that each may find 'the mind of Christ'. If all seven converged on that 'mind', we'd have a solution for South Africa!

None of this of course absolves political leaders themselves from constantly seeking to work out the law of love in their policies.

Let their inspiration come from William Wilberforce who epitomised love at work in the heart of a lawmaker and politician as he laboured most of his public life (1759–1833) to abolish slavery.

'Before this great cause,' wrote Wilberforce early in 1796, 'all others dwindle in my eyes. . . . If it please God to honour me so far, may I be the instrument of stopping such a course of wickedness and cruelty as never before disgraced a Christian country.'[72]

ROMANS 13 AND OBEDIENCE

But what if love in the Spirit involves us in directly challenging, criticising or even disobeying the state? After all, are we not, according to Paul in Romans 13, to be subject to the powers that be, seeing that they 'have been instituted by God' (Rom. 13:1). This is not an easy passage.

When Paul wrote that chapter he knew of biblical examples of civil disobedience. He knew of Moses's challenging the legitimate authority of Pharaoh. He knew of Samuel rebuking King Saul. He knew of Daniel defying Nebuchadnezzar. So he must have seen his words in Romans 13 not as contradicting these biblical precedents, but as complementary and in harmony.

This being so we must not make Romans 13 too absolute and construe it to mean that any form of protest against a legitimate government is out of the question for a Christian. In any event it is particularly important to note that Romans 13 does not simply speak of the legitimate power of the State, but of the proper limits to the power of the State. These limits are two in number.

TWO LIMITS

The first limiting factor in Romans is that the State's authority is under God. The State is to be 'God's servant' (vs. 4). In other words the State has its true legitimacy only as it works according to what God expects it to do as His serving instrument functioning under Him. So Romans 13 has to be set alongside Revelation 13 which describes a State which has become inhuman and unjust. The Church must be able to distinguish in which category a given government falls.

The second limit on the State's authority is found in verse 4. The State is to be 'God's servant for YOUR GOOD'. In other words it exists for the good, not the harm, of those in it and under it. The State is not just God's servant. It is man's. It not only serves God, it serves man. Here then is the basis and criterion for protest. When the State ceases to serve God and man, it deserves the criticism if not the condemnation of Christians. Thus the same conscience which obeys the government may in some cases disobey it.

Special significance is also to be attached to 1 Tim. 2:1–2 where the supreme responsibility of the Church towards the State is seen as intercession and prayer. This is in some ways, as David Bosch has stressed, the most radical form of the Church's involvement in government:

> The government as such cannot pray for itself. It is dependent on the prayers of the church. Indeed, even in times of state persecution, the church will pray for the state and be its conscience. The church will pray even for the unjust state. The church will defend the state against the state and this will be its most radical means of saving and repairing the state.[73]

SUMMARY

Both our evangelism and our social action are integrally part of our caring for the world and both are grounded in five key doctrines.

First of all there is our doctrine of *God* as the Creator. He loves the whole world (John 3:16) and all people in it and is concerned for all aspects of their existence. So we cannot and will not compartmentalise life into the sacred and the secular, the spiritual or the social.

Then there is our doctrine of *man*. As Christians we see the immense value of all human beings as precious creatures made in God's own image. This will make us care about anything which hurts, dehumanises or brutalises any person.

Thirdly, comes our doctrine of *Christ*. Jesus enfleshed His ministry and identified with humans in all their needs. He also said: 'As the Father has sent me, even so I send you' (John 20:21). In other words, He set us an example we dare not ignore. The Church's ministry must be incarnational too.

Our doctrine of *salvation* is fourth. Obviously in preaching salvation we preach Jesus as both Saviour and Lord. And if He is Lord, then He would be Lord of all aspects of our personal and corporate lives. Moreover, as Saviour He wants to save people from anything and everything which spoils, whether it be the sin which condemns us or the grim socio-political conditions which may cripple us. So we go out both to evangelise and to care.

Lastly there is our doctrine of the *Church*. As salt arrests decay and as light dispels darkness, so the Church functions in the world by identifying with the world's need but not its sin.

The Jesus Way in the world cannot but commit us to the politics of love. What a challenge to allow the Spirit's fruit of love to send us out in care for the world, in prayer for political leaders, in work for better societies and in demonstration to both powerless and powerful that Jesus is the Way, the Truth and the Life.

Chapter Eighteen

WITNESS TO THE WORLD

You shall receive power when the Holy Spirit has
come upon you: and you shall be my witnesses.

Jesus – Acts 1:8

Back in 1955 when my dear friend Robert Footner led me
into personal discovery of Jesus Christ as Saviour and Lord, I
couldn't for the life of me have told you what the word
evangelism even meant. The concept of witness likewise was
totally foreign to me.

On the other hand I recollect, during a six-month spell of
prep-school teaching after leaving school and before going to
Cambridge, that I did want to influence all those eager little
boys towards Christianity. This, like motherhood and helping old ladies, I deemed a good thing.

But neither with those boys or with friends could I ever say
more than 'wouldn't you like to come to Church with me?' In
one particular fit of daring I read a section of Henry Drum-
mond's classic, *The Greatest Thing in the World* to the senior
dormitory of the school before putting their lights out. I
counted this as an act of enormous boldness.

Then along with my Latin and French classes I was landed
with *Scripture* for most of the school because no one else
wanted to do it. This flummoxed me completely and I have
no recollection whatsoever of what I taught them – except
that I had modestly benevolent Christian feelings towards
my young victims and hoped they would all end up respect-

able Anglican communicants. Alas! I did not give them the world's greatest head start.

Then came October 1955 and the glorious wonder of conversion to Christ. The Holy Spirit entered my heart as I received Christ as Lord and Saviour and from that very same day I began to witness to Christ.

In fact after the Sunday evening service of the Cambridge Inter-Collegiate Christian Union (CICCU), my commitment having taken place that evening, I jumped on my bicycle and roared round to the digs of an old school friend and told him of this incredible person, the Lord Jesus, Whom I had come to know that very day. He was staggered because he had known me at Michaelhouse only as the 'let's go to Communion together' sort of Christian. We were churchy. But now this was something different. I was before him as a witness to Jesus Christ and what He had done in my life that very day. He looked shaken.

In fact in a short time half my college knew me as a pretty firey fellow religiously – 'a Hot Prot', one friend labelled me. But I simply could not keep quiet as to what I had found. My unstoppable and irrepressible acts of witness were in retrospect often ill-advised, insensitive and tactless. I even appeared to terrify the Chaplain. Woe is me! On the other hand the discovery of new life, new love, new meaning, new purpose, new peace, new everything was hardly something to suppress. Wisdom and discretion in sharing about it would have to come later, though I've since learned one can be tactful and cautious unto death, so that one can easily become inhibited from exhuberant and buoyant witness. Alas when that happens!

However, what all that early enthusiasm taught me is that the presence of the Holy Spirit and both one's desire and ability to witness were integrally related. That is true in the individual life as well as in the corporate life of the Church. When the Spirit is most truly at work, there you will find new burdens and commitments to witness to the Person and work of Jesus. After all that is the Spirit's ministry, whether people call themselves Charismatics, or Pentecostals, or Ecumenicals, Reformed or that notorious passport epithet 'C. of E.' or whatever. To be a Christian at all is to be a Holy Spirit person and therefore to be a witness to Jesus.

That's why I agree with my good friend Wolfgang Heiner, of Germany, a prominent youth evangelist, who once said to me: 'It's a pity the Charismatics don't call themselves a "Jesus Movement". That would solve a lot of problems because all Christians want to elevate Jesus and it is also the ministry of the Holy Spirit to do so. Why elevate the word "charismatic"? After all, every truly born-again believer who has the Holy Spirit is strictly speaking a Charismatic.'

This is a good point and one I fully embrace. The Holy Spirit, according to Jesus, would have one major characteristic in His ministry. 'He will bear witness to me,' said Jesus in John 15:26, and 'He will glorify me, for He will take what is mine and declare it to you' (John 16:14).

As the one bearing witness to Jesus and glorifying Jesus, the Holy Spirit is the Spirit of Mission. The acid test therefore of supposedly renewed individuals and of Renewal as a whole is whether it produces new impulses of evangelism and missionary outreach to a lost world. The Spirit was given not so that we might have lovely spiritual experiences and beautiful fellowship in the Church, but so that we might be equipped to be witnesses to Jesus in Jerusalem, Judaea, Samaria and to the uttermost parts of the earth.

THE SPIRIT OF MISSION

Not surprisingly, the work of the Spirit therefore in the book of Acts is a missionary work. It is the story of people being mightily motivated and activated to evangelism. It is the story of a Church which only gathers in worship and fellowship in order to disperse in evangelism and witness. It is the story of people moving out in mission, mightily energised by the Holy Spirit.

In fact, the book of Acts reveals the Holy Spirit as the great Commander-in-Chief of the whole missionary enterprise as it

spread more and more widely throughout the Mediterranean
world.

Thus it is the Spirit who comes upon those first believers at
Pentecost and galvanises the previously timid Peter into his
dynamic Pentecostal address which won 3,000 souls to
Christ (Acts 2). It was only as he was 'filled with the Holy
Spirit' (Acts 4:8) that Peter was able to make his telling
defence before the Sanhedrin after he had healed the lame
man at the 'Gate Beautiful'. It was the Holy Spirit who
inspired the Apostolic group to speak 'the word of God with
boldness' (Acts 4:31). It was the Holy Spirit who guided
Phillip in his word to the Ethiopian eunuch (Acts 8:29), who
in turn would go and penetrate the missionary frontiers of
Africa for the cause of Christ. It was the Holy Spirit who
comforted the Church 'throughout all Judea, Galilee and
Samaria', so that it had peace, was built up and was multi-
plied (Acts 9:31).

Most spectacular of all perhaps is the Spirit's word to
Peter: 'Rise and go' (Acts 10:20), which sent him to evangel-
ise Cornelius and his family, thereby opening up the whole
Christian mission to the Gentile world.

Then, almost as dramatically, it is the Holy Spirit who
interrupts a beautiful time of worship, fasting and fellowship
in the Antioch Church and says: 'Set apart for me Barnabas
and Saul for the work to which I have called them' (Acts
13:2). Maybe they had planned to settle down there for a
while, but no! '*Being SENT OUT by the HOLY SPIRIT*, they
went down to Seleucia and from there they sailed to Cyprus'
(Acts 13:4).

Thereafter we see the Holy Spirit, like a sort of project
director cum travel supervisor, directing the whole work of
missionary expansion, forbidding them to speak in Asia, not
allowing them to go into Bithynia (Acts 16:7) but directing
them by vision to Macedonia (Acts 16:10).

And so it went as the Apostles and others criss-crossed
their world sharing the Good News of Jesus. And always it
was the Holy Spirit initiating and inspiring. More than that,
He was always elevating Jesus. Nowhere do we see a stress on

the Holy Spirit per se with Jesus being squeezed out, as if allegiance to Him somehow reveals a lower-level walk of Christian experience.

Bishop John Taylor well summarises the role of the Spirit as the inspirer of mission:

> The very mandate to engage in this world-wide mission could only be given simultaneously with the gift of the Holy Spirit. This is made quite specific in the 4th Gospel. Jesus repeated 'Peace be with you' and said 'As the Father sent me, so send I you.' Then He breathed on them, saying, 'Receive the Holy Spirit' (John 20:21–22). Luke makes the same point succinctly in the 2nd verse of the book of Acts where he calls the Apostolic mandate 'instructions through the Holy Spirit'. The marching orders and the gift of the Spirit came in the same package. How could it have been otherwise, seeing that Jesus Himself received His mandate and His sense of mission only by being caught up into the operation of the Holy Spirit and dominated by him?[74]

This begins publicly with His baptism when the Spirit descends upon Him (Matt. 3:16), it continues as the Spirit leads Him into the testings of the Wilderness (Matt. 4:1) and it bursts upon the world with the opening of Jesus's public ministry as He returns 'in the power of the Spirit into Galilee' (Luke 4:14) and then announces in the Nazareth synagogue that the Spirit of the Lord is upon Him in anointing power for the mission at hand.

And it was the same with those early Christians. Once they were on their way nothing could stop them. They were, as one might say, an overwhelming minority. Not the opposition of Jewish religious orthodoxy, nor Roman political might, nor Greek intellectual sophistication, nor Mediterranean moral decadence could hold them back.

Bishop Taylor adds a question: 'If for Jesus Himself both Messiahship and Mission are derived from His self-immersion in that flood-tide of the Holy Spirit, how could His followers possibly be involved in the same mission except through the same immersion?'[75]

And what an immersion they had! It made them nothing less than firebrands, even under persecution. When attacked, persecuted and scattered, they just 'went about preaching the Word' (Acts 8:4). The late Canon Max Warren in his book *I Believe in the Great Commission* comments on this wider scattering or diaspora of Jewish believers as 'no panic measure'. What is quite certain is that these people on their way home told the Good News of Jesus wherever they went. Quite clearly here was the beginning of a movement which was creating very serious anxiety among the Jewish leaders. After all, one reason for the crucifixion of Jesus, the one which had satisfied the Roman authorities, was precisely that He was a centre of disaffection. It wasn't long before we find a mob in one Roman colony protesting that these followers of Jesus were advocating 'customs which it is not lawful for us Romans to accept or practise' (Acts 16:21).

> Within weeks, another mob in another city was complaining that these men 'who have made trouble all over the world have now come here. . . . They all flout the Emperor's laws and assert that there is a rival king, Jesus' (Acts 17:6–7). Something like a forest fire had started. Luke, on his frescoe, can almost be seen etching in the flames just to show the link between what was happening everywhere and what had happened in Jerusalem on the day of Pentecost. And it all centered upon Jesus. Those commissioned had indeed begun in Jerusalem as instructed, and as instructed, they had not stopped there.[76]

Certainly the early Church, in the power of the Holy Spirit, faced the missionary task of their world with incredible dedication, faithfulness, courage and effectiveness.

And what of us?

TESTIMONY

For myself the vision of witness to the world first became real when Billy Graham came to Cambridge not long after my own conversion. It was a momentous experience for me. For I saw evangelism in action for the first time – though not without opposition and reservation from both within the Church and out of it.

Apart from the more than spirited correspondence in the London *Times* when British Christians poured out their views pro and con an evangelist being let loose in the supposedly rarefied intellectual atmosphere of Cambridge, there was also vigorous opposition in Cambridge itself. Students threatening to kidnap the evangelist were deliciously foiled, I thought, as Billy Graham was smuggled into Cambridge by some ingenious back door.

Then in his first Bible Study to the CICCU, fireworks were lobbed into the Union Debating Chamber and I recollect the startled knee-jerks and uncharacteristically British jumping of the praying brethren as the vicious little explosives detonated at their feet. It's amazing what a good thunder-cracker can do for the prayer life! That was when I first began to see that evangelism and witness often produce opposition. No wonder the early Church had to pray to often for 'boldness' (Acts 4:29) through the Holy Spirit.

But it was also when I first saw the real spiritual need and hunger of the human heart because, in spite of all the resistance and turmoil elicited by Graham's presence, the majority of the university turned out in force to hear the Gospel preached and hundreds responded to the claims and call of our Lord Jesus. In spite of full heads and lots of academic learning, the hearts of students were yearning for reality, for peace, for purpose. And to find it they had to respond to the Gospel of our Lord Jesus preached in the power of the Spirit.

Nor has that need changed with the passage of nearly three decades since that time.

THE CONTEMPORARY CHALLENGE

In fact the spiritual need of the world has escalated spectacu-
larly with the population explosion of these last decades.
Christian statisticians tell us now that there are somewhere
in the region of three billion people who have yet to hear the
message of Christ. And most of those have not even heard the
name of Christ, let alone had an intelligible presentation of
the Gospel made to them. In fact, one Jewish girl in New
York, when asked, confessed that she had never heard the
name Jesus Christ. A friend of mine in the Orient asked a
young student if he had heard of Jesus Christ and his
incredible reply was: 'Is that a new species of soap?'

Certainly the task before us is daunting. It has been said
that if we were to herd 50,000 people a day, from among this
number of unreached, into a great stadium so that Billy
Graham could preach to them, and to a different crowd each
day, it would still take more than 165 years to let all those
billions hear the Gospel clearly just one time. In the meantime, billions more would be born. That is the measure of the
immense challenge facing the Church of Christ at this time.

But the task is made even more daunting by the fact that so
many Christians in our time have lost their vision for
evangelism and especially for world missions. In fact, in 1975
a group of British Christian leaders were surveyed on their
thoughts regarding world missions. Apparently 23 per cent
of them thought missions were optional and only for those
who have the time; 21 per cent saw it as a duty, though a
nuisance; 16 per cent no longer thought it concerned the
Western Church. The rest were positive.

This is an extraordinary state of affairs. We must therefore
ring it out that if the renewing work of the Holy Spirit around
the world has a unique and special contribution to bring for
our time, it should be right at this point in inspiring God's
people the world over with the evangelistic and missionary
enterprise.

Speaking at the Lausanne International Congress on
World Evangelisation in 1974, Billy Graham made this
observation: 'Many sincere Christians around the world are

concerned for evangelism. They are delighted at evangelising in their own communities and even in their own countries. But they do not see God's big picture of "world need" and the "global responsibility" that He has put upon the Church in His world. The Christians in Nigeria are not just to evangelise Nigeria, nor the Christians in Peru just the people in Peru. God's heartbeat is for the world.'

This is true and we have to understand in our time that God has given a global mission to His Church which we at this moment in history must fulfil.

In a challenging volume entitled *In the Gap*, David Bryant, an American missionary thinker, powerfully challenges the Church to step out of our pea-sized Christianity to stand in the immense gap between God's world-wide purpose and the fulfilment of it.[77]

Bryant believes that a new breed of what he calls 'World Christians' should step into the gap:

> World Christians are day to day disciples for whom Christ's global cause has become the integrating, over-riding priority for all that He is for them. As disciples should, they actively investigate all that their Master's Great Commission means. Then they act on what they learn. . . . World Christians are Christians whose life directions have been solidly transformed by a world vision.
>
> Some World Christians are missionaries who stand in the Gap by physically crossing major human barriers (Cultural, political, etc.) to bring the Gospel to those who can hear no other way. But every Christian is meant to be a World Christian, whether you physically go or stay at home to provide the sacrificial love, prayers, training, money and quality of corporate life that backs the witness of those that go.

Bryant goes on to quote the great missionary leader, John R. Mott, who founded the Student Volunteer Movement which sent out 20,000 new missionaries in the early part of this century. Mott called for a particular breed of person to face the task, and Renewal leaders in our time must do no less.

An enterprise which aims at the evangelisation of the whole world in a generation, and contemplates the ultimate establishment of the Kingdom of Christ, requires that its leaders be Christian Statesmen – men with farseeing views, with comprehensive plans, with power of initiative, and with victorious faith.[78]

But, many might ask, why bother?

WHY BOTHER?

Indeed. Why bother? Does it matter? Will it make any difference, either now or after people die? After all, aren't people managing pretty well and isn't their religion a private and personal matter with which we have no right to interfere? Moreover, 'Pie in the sky when we die by and by' seems to have almost no appeal to 'live-it-up-now' twentieth-century men and women. By the same token divine condemnation or eternal separation from God is a concept which is counted antediluvian by most moderns – that is until they stare death in the face. At that moment minds and hearts can become most wonderfully concentrated.

In any event, the question 'why bother' is a good and important one.

The issue first came deeply before my mind in Madison Square Garden in New York during Billy Graham's Crusade there in 1957.

The fact that I was there at all involved, I believe, the Lord's own special workings in terms of His plan for my life.

In early '57 I heard of some student charter flights from London to New York for the princely sum of £87 return. Ah yes, those were the days! I duly booked and although the plane had no fewer than three false starts trying to get away from London, thanks to the precarious state of its mechanical innards, we finally made it on a wing and a prayer.

Gracious relatives in New York kindly received me and I had my first exhilarating taste of the New World.

By this time I was beginning to think of theological

training. Not being a candidate for the ordained Anglican ministry, I could not secure a scholarship to an English theological college. This led me to think of the U.S.A.

But who could advise me as to seminaries? I knew no Christians in the States at all. But there was that distant hero, Billy Graham. I heard he had a crusade on in New York. I would write to him.

My letter, along with thousands of others filling multiple bags of mail, went into the Crusade office. I naïvely believed he might get it! That was not to be. God had other plans.

Amongst the teams of people helping to sort mail was an American-Japanese student from Fuller Seminary called Harry Kawahara. The mail bag with my letter landed on his desk. He opened my letter, read it and phoned me. I was mad with excitement when I was called to the phone for a call from the Crusade Office. 'Billy Graham is phoning me,' I exulted.

My disappointment that it was a mere seminary student from who knows where was scarcely concealed, I suspect, in my flat response to the voice on the other end.

'You want to know about seminaries?' asked Harry.

'Indeed', I replied.

'Well, why not come down to the Garden? Come to a Crusade meeting and we can talk about it.'

I went. It was probably one of the most momentous things I ever did. Indeed, I can say my whole life and future destiny turned on that phone call and that visit to Madison Square Garden. More accurately I could say it turned on the way one little letter found its way into one particular mail bag which landed on one particular desk in front of one particular person. That puts some Calvinism into one, doesn't it!

The fact is that through Harry's phone call I went to Madison Square Garden where I both received my call to evangelism and also set my face towards Fuller Seminary and all which that would mean for my later life, ministry and the founding of AE with Dr Charles Fuller's help. Just where one letter landed. That's all. A tiny, tiny thread. But it was God's.

It was also while listening many evenings to the preaching of the Gospel in Madison Square Garden that I began to come to terms with three basic reasons why I ought personally to bother about world evangelisation:

They were as follows:

(i) because Christ commands us to bother. He urges us to take the Gospel to all the world.
(ii) because men and women without Christ are lost.
(iii) because the deep and desperate needs of human beings can only be fully met through the transforming, reconciling, and saving power of Jesus Christ.

Let's take these in turn.

CHRIST'S COMMAND

Almost imperceptibly it became clear to me that to come to Christ is to come to His Great Commission to go out into all the world and take the Gospel to every creature. I couldn't get round the Great Commission without getting round Jesus altogether. Reaching out into all the world in His name became a matter of obedience.

The Great Commission comes to us in different forms. For example, in the 'longer ending' of Mark's Gospel, which many scholars admittedly feel was added later by a hand other than Mark's, we find Jesus's words: 'Go into all the world and preach the Gospel to the whole creation' (Mark 16:15). On the other hand Matthew's version reinforces this command with Jesus's words to 'go . . . and make disciples of all nations, baptising them in the name of the Father and of the Son and of the Holy Spirit, teaching them to observe all that I have commanded you; and lo, I am with you always, to the close of the age' (Matt. 28:19–20).

Luke, for his part, states Jesus's affirmation that 'The Christ should suffer and on the third day rise from the dead, and that repentance and forgiveness of sins should be preached in His name to all nations, beginning from Jerusalem' (Luke 24:46–7). And, of course, in Acts Luke also has Jesus's great word to which we have already made reference: 'You shall receive power when the Holy Spirit has come upon you; and you shall be my witnesses in Jerusalem and in all Judaea and Samaria and to the end of the earth' (Acts 1:8).

John, on the other hand, records the Great Commission in even more pressing and costly categories when he tells first of Jesus's prayer to the Father, saying: 'As Thou didst send me into the world, so I have sent them into the world' (John 17:18), and then of His direct Commission to the disciples saying: 'As the Father has sent me, even so I send you' (John 20:21).

In both this prayer and this Commission Jesus is making His mission the model of ours and telling us that the Church's mission must be grasped and understood in the light of that carried out by the Son of God. And in this respect we note that not only was Jesus's mission costly, compassionate and humble, but it was a mission which went right out in deep penetration of the world. He did not remain in any ivory tower but moved right out into the nitty-gritty needs of the lost and broken humanity around him.

It is noteworthy that most of those who are interested in or profess to be part of the current renewal in the Church are people who take Jesus and the Bible very seriously. This being the case they must face up to the imperatives of the Great Commission in new ways and gird their loins for the missionary and evangelistic task. Apart from the manifestation of love, one of the clearest evidences of the fullness of the Holy Spirit is a major concern to see others won to Christ. Says Jesus in effect: When the power of the Holy Spirit is come upon you, you will be witnesses, and not only locally and not only with your Samaritans (i.e. the people with whom you normally have no dealings) but also to the uttermost parts of the earth (Acts 1:8).

To be witnesses, missionaries and evangelists is a reflex of obedience to Christ. Nothing more, nothing less.

THE LOSTNESS OF MAN

The meetings in Madison Square Garden which went on for some three months underlined to my heart not only the spiritual hunger of people but their lostness and their longing to find their way home.

The incredible individual stories and testimonies night after night revealed that people basically felt like sheep without a shepherd and when they heard a clear and uncompromising preaching of the Gospel they responded to it as a drowning man to a lifebelt.

Now after twenty years of ministry myself the settled conviction has developed and deepened that there is nothing in time or eternity men and women need more than the salvation which is in Christ. Otherwise they are lost both in time and in eternity.

I knew, even in the sixties, that this would put me at odds with theological liberalism (a view which opts for a rather loose interpretation of the Bible) and which taught, in Reinhold Niebuhr's pithy phrase, that a god without wrath brought men without sin into a kingdom without judgment and to a Christ without a cross!

Later on I saw that this sort of stance, which had been quite popular in the latter part of the last century and in the early part of this century, had lingered on, often almost subconsciously, in much of our contemporary Christian thinking. Most believers in times before us could accept that men without Christ were lost. But early twentieth-century liberalism collapsed this saved–lost division of humanity. All men were simply seen as part of a general brotherhood of man under the benign and harmless general fatherhood of God.

At seminary the history of all this filled out a little for me when I read of the famous ecumenical conference in Jerusalem in 1928. Almost for the first time in such a gathering, I learned, there was no clear-cut biblical simplicity, but rather a religious syncretism, which basically said that all religions were part of the way of God. In other words an inclusive approach to non-Christian religions became evident in ecumenical circles. Commenting on this, Bishop Stephen Neill once remarked: 'This was the moment at which liberal theology exercised its most fatal influence on missionary thinking, the lowest valley out of which the missionary movement has ever since been trying to make its way.'

Not long after that (1932) a book appeared by a man called W. B. Hocking, called *Rethinking Missions*. Hocking, a Harvard philosophy professor and a prominent layman, stressed his view that the time had come to set the educational and other philanthropic aspects of mission work free from the work of conscious and direct evangelism. He saw the missionary as working to find the most harmonious coexistence with non-Christian religions so that each could stimulate the other in growth towards the ultimate goal of unity in the completest religious truth.[79]

A response to this came in a volume called: *Christian Message in a Non-Christian World* by Hendrik Kraemer (1938). The author warned of the dangers of this sort of thinking because it 'blurs and relativises the question of truth. . . . It constitutes a perennial threat to the distinct character of the truth of the Christian message.'[80]

In other words, if we are saying, like the queen in *Alice in Wonderland* who had refereed the race, that 'everyone has won', then we are really simply placing Jesus alongside the general pantheon of religious leaders and prophets. There is nothing distinctive about Him. We are in fact challenging His deity, His distinctiveness and the exclusiveness of His claims.

We are also denying very specifically Jesus's assertion that mankind is 'lost', and that at the very heart of His coming into the world is the intention to 'seek and to save the lost' (Luke 19:10). On the other hand if the lost will turn to Him and repent they will not perish (Luke 13:3) but will have 'eternal life' (John 3:16). Otherwise there is no other way of salvation (John 14:6; Acts 4:12).

I remember in 1973 being thrown out of Uganda by Idi Amin and his merry men. My crime was that my passport announced me as a missionary. 'Missionaries are no longer welcome,' I was told. Anyway, after men from Amin's

Security Squad had tracked me down I was ordered to report to an official at the Foreign Affairs Department.

While this gentleman was out of the room collecting a form to declare me 'undesirable', John Wilson, one of my African colleagues from Uganda, said to me: 'This fellow's name is very interesting. It means "without Him (i.e. Jesus) I will not get there (i.e. Heaven)"!'

When the official returned to the room I commented on his interesting name.

'I'm told it means "without Him I will not get there". Do you believe that?'

'Oh no!' he snorted. 'My parents believed that, but not I.'

'Well, I believe it,' I said, 'and I hope you come to believe it too, because this is what the Bible says.'

And I believe that still. Without Him we will not get there. In both time and eternity we are lost without Him. That is the Bad News. But, praise God, there is Good News.

Therefore, although we know from Luke 15 for example, that men are lost by circumstances like the coin, by nature like the sheep, and by choice like the son, nevertheless, we also know most gloriously that over and above this lostness is the unbelievable and matchless biblical assurance that 'God sent the Son into the world, NOT to condemn the world, but that the world might be saved through Him' (John 3:17). And of course Luke 15 also gives us that glorious picture of the waiting Father Whose joyful compassion overflows as the Prodigal returns.

All this is the Good News. Forgiveness and eternal salvation through Christ. Is it not worth heralding and telling to the ends of the earth? No wonder Jesus's commission is called the GREAT Commission. And it can only be carried out in the power of the Holy Spirit.

HUMAN NEEDS

As compelling as any other reason for getting out to the world is just the immense extent of human need on all sides. One's experience in a thousand situations down the years has brought this home.

And this need is felt and experienced in so many ways.

One of these is emptiness. Many psychiatrists feel that this is the chief neurosis and central problem of modern man. It is not even that many people do not know what they want, they often do not even have any clear idea of what they feel. A little girl once said to her father: 'I want something, Daddy, but I don't know what.' Many twentieth-century people are like that. And they can identify with what T. S. Elliot wrote way back in 1925 when he said: 'We are the hollow men, we are the stuffed men, leaning together, headpiece filled with straw.'

Nor is this problem new. Pascal spoke and wrote about 'the God-shaped Vacuum in the Human Heart'.

Another way the problem is experienced is in a loss of purpose and meaning. I remember a student friend saying to me once: 'Oh, for peace and purpose.'

Gloriously, peace is one ingredient of the Spirit's 'fruit' (Gal. 5:22).

LONELINESS, BOREDOM AND ANXIETY

Yet another way the problem is experienced is in terms of loneliness. Oh! How many lonely people one has encountered. Small wonder that one modern author, David Riesman, could write a book called *The Lonely Crowd*. In fact many people, even when surrounded by swarms of other people, still feel totally lonely and isolated. It's a strange thing, but many people really fear finding themselves alone and so they don't find themselves at all. In fact, it has even been said that all man's history is a struggle to shatter and break out of his loneliness. People need real fellowship and companionship and this is never richer than when it is in and through Christ and amongst Christians. What a glorious reason for getting out to the world with the Gospel!

The problem of man's lostness is also experienced simply in chronic boredom and in a sense of futility. I heard the story, which I don't believe is apocryphal, of a New York bus driver, who one day simply drove away in his empty bus to Florida. He explained that he had become tired of driving the same route every day and had decided to go away on a trip. His venture produced both publicity and hilarity. More than that, by the time he was back in New York he was a hero and huge crowds were on hand to welcome him and give him a ticker-tape parade!

When it was announced that the company had decided not to turn him over for legal punishment, but to give him his job back if he would promise not to take any more jaunts, the whole of New York was cheering! He had protested against boredom.

Perhaps harder to bear is that particularly twentieth-century pain of anxiety. Being hollow and lonely would be relatively manageable if it did not make us prey to that peculiar psychological pain and turmoil which we call anxiety.

No one who reads the morning newspaper needs to be persuaded that we live in an age of anxiety. Wars, crime, accidents, divorce, suicide, economic collapse, racial tension, international build-up of armaments and many other things all stare out at us from our morning newspapers or our television sets and combine to give twentieth-century man an overpowering sense of anxiety. Many psychiatrists feel anxiety is the greatest destroyer in modern times of human health and well-being.

Yet Jesus said repeatedly: 'Do not be anxious' (Matthew 6:25, 34, 24:6). And St Paul can write: 'Have no anxiety about anything' (Phil. 4:6). This is impossible outside of Christ and His Spirit.

Possessing a prescription for peace of mind and freedom from anxiety, how can the Church refrain from taking its Gospel to a lonely, bored and anxiety-stricken world?

ALIENATION AND ESCAPE

But perhaps the greatest crusher of our times is alienation. Blacks are alienated from whites, husbands from wives, children from parents, business colleagues from one another, and old from young. One way and another people are chronically at odds with each other. This perhaps produces more distress of spirit than anything else. Especially is this true in the breakdown of the modern home. The average modern marriage is only lasting seven or eight years and often it is much less. The result is that even the very institution of marriage is coming into question. It seems to be an unworkable relationship.

And so with all these chronic and desperate needs, and not knowing the astonishing and glorious way that Jesus Christ can meet these needs, and enable these relationships to work, multitudes of people take the escapist routes of illicit sex, extravagant drink or enslaving drugs. Alas, all are cul-de-sacs. But in Jesus is a way out. Should we not tell the world? Dare we keep such glorious news to ourselves?

The interesting thing is that in spite of all the many and different ways which people use to try to find answers to life, basically they sense that there must be some answers deep down, hence the desperate nature of their search. Whether they articulate it or not, they can feel with the great poet Robert Browning that 'Life has meaning and to find its meaning is man's meat and drink'. Likewise Will Durant in his *Story of Philosophy* can say:

> So much of our lives is meaningless – a self-cancelling vacillation and futility. But we strive with the chaos about us and within: and we want to believe all the while that there is something vital and significant in us, could we but decipher our souls. We want to understand. We want to seize the value and perspective of passing things and so pull ourselves up out of the maelstrom of daily circumstances.[81]

NEW INITIATIVES OF EVANGELISM

In the light of this fact and in view of the massive and monumental needs of modern man, dare the Christian who has the great and ultimate answer in Jesus Christ remain silent? Dare he spend his life looking inwards? Dare he be part of a Church which never looks beyond its own doors? Dare he embrace a Christian fellowship which is introverted and self-preoccupied with Charismatic kicks at the expense of the chronic and pressing spiritual and physical needs of the outside world?

Believers who do this fail their Lord, their Church, their society, their world, their neighbours and themselves.

With the tremendous spiritual energy which has been released into the Church by the renewing activity of the Holy Spirit in modern times, we will quench that same Spirit, we will hinder that same working and we will shackle, stunt and misdirect that splendid energy unless we look from the Church to the world with massive new initiatives in evangelism, missionary enterprise, socio-political concern and Christian witness. All of this is required by the Great Commission, by the command of Christ, by the reality of human lostness and by the urgent, poignant and desperate nature of human need in our times.

But how are we to do it?

BUT HOW?

I have several replies. First of all, we must explore the work of the Holy Spirit, not less but more. We are only touching the hem of His garment. As He is released more in us so He will make us not only shine more brightly with the character of Jesus Christ but burn more fully with a zeal to make Him known and let His caring love be felt across the globe.

Nor will we bog down in the problems of vocabulary, semantics and terminology but will press on to appropriate the Spirit's power to energise us for the task. Three billion people are waiting to hear the Gospel, multitudes are oppressed, millions are hungry, countless relationships are daily shattered and if we are only busy singing and clapping in our little religious ghettos then we can be quite sure that those untold millions will remain untold and a myriad others will never know the compassionate and practical care of our blessed Lord. And the reason would be that we have permitted ourselves the most tragic amnesia in forgetting that the Holy Spirit of God is the Dynamic Spirit of mission.

In the second place, we will need to repent of what I call SIWs. This is a military term which refers to Self-Inflicted Wounds. This is what happens when a soldier, instead of throwing the grenade at the enemy, allows it to explode in his own hand. He wounds and immobilises himself. This is militarily catastrophic and almost criminal. It is also spiritually so. Nothing is more tragic than when the Church participates in all sorts of acts by which it wounds itself and tears itself down. I don't believe in our own ministry that we have ever had any of our projects or enterprises torn down or immobilised by Marxists, by pagans, by free lovers, by atheists or by Moslems. The only people who have ever torn down any Christian initiatives in which we have personally been involved have been other Christians. And what makes it worse is that when Christians knock each other down they hardly ever do it via frontal assault. It is almost always via the arrow from behind. This is a destructive killer in the Church. It is inexcusable. Over and above that it will incur and does incur the judgment of God.

My plea therefore is that Christians should cooperate in the great task that is before us of holistic, incarnational witness to the world in our time. Particularly is this true of all those who share a high view of the Bible, an exactly identical understanding of the deity of our Lord Jesus Christ and who believe in the importance of the Spirit's work, even if their vocabularies and terminologies are different.

However, this is not to be construed as a call for Evangelical-cum-Charismatic-cum-Pentecostal solidarity at the expense of a total solidarity in the total Church. I believe that all sections of the Church need each other. No one has twenty-twenty vision on the truth of God and in some ways it takes the full-orbed nature of the whole Church of Christ to reflect the full-orbed truth of the whole Gospel of Christ. We do not have to agree in every detail. But we can make dramatic progress at this great moment of history if we can see every other Christian, not only as our brother, but also as our teacher, and if he will see us in the same light as well.

The new wine is there. But the old wineskins of rigidity, of inflexible denominationalism, of hide-bound traditionalism and of Christian factionalism are often blocking the flow with lethal corks. The new wine being created by the work of the Spirit within the old wineskins must be poured out and released, thereby allowing God to bring fresh wineskins into being. But first the old wineskins must burst. Only this way will a thirsty world be able to drink.

It is for this, I believe, that God the Father, God the Son and God the Holy Spirit are waiting. The world is waiting too.

Let us therefore arise and go.

Chapter Nineteen

SO WHAT'S THE DIFFERENCE?

> Does the road wind uphill all the way?
> Yes, to the very end.
> Will the day's journey take the whole long day?
> From morn to night, my friend.
> Christina Rossetti

At a temperance meeting in London a Cockney got to his feet to share how he had been delivered from alcoholism.

'Lydies and jentlemen,' he thundered, 'three years ago, oi' was a fisical wreck – 'orible to behold. Now oi' want to tell yew wot 'as brought about this wonderful change.'

'Wot change, Guvnor?' called an impudent voice from the back of the room.

In this closing chapter I want to summarise, draw threads together and try to delineate the difference and some of the changes this lengthy quest into the Spirit's work has brought in my life and ministry.

This is a slightly unnerving assignment of postscript because those who know me best, such as my wife and children and colleagues, would probably retort 'wot change, guvnor?' if I were to launch into an extravagant affirmation of personal transformation!

This humbling realisation alerts me to the fact that I must at this point be both realistic and honest, neither overstating nor understating what this has all meant to me.

UPHILL

Perhaps the first thing to say is that for me the road continues to wind uphill all the way and I suspect it will be like this to the very end. The day's journey of my spiritual odyssey will take the whole long day. As Christina Rossetti has said: 'From morn to night, my friend.' A deeper appropriation of the Spirit's work has not provided any shortcut to spiritual maturity. Beyond that a number of my old anxieties, insecurities and irrational fears are still with me, though less pronounced.

Nor dare I affirm that I am now the model husband or father or colleague. I seem to have almost as many failures as before.

This may disappoint some pilgrims who have followed me through these pages hoping for some more dramatic and encouraging word that I had now found the way to live a peerless Christian life. But that would be to depart from the facts. In fact, if anything, a deeper insight into the Spirit's ways has brought me to a deeper sense of just how far I still have to go and just how drastically my old nature still needs dealing with. It's that old problem of trying to walk in the Spirit and finding that one is still only toddling. But perhaps the long-term interests of true encouragement for the pilgrim are best served by realism.

On the other hand, the yearning to do better for the Lord and to strive upwards for His purpose and will is undoubtedly greater. In spite of both failures and lapses one presses on with genuinely renewed determination. Especially is this so in terms of my desire to be a better husband to Carol and a better father to Catherine, Debbie and Marty.

However, I suppose, if I must be quite frank, I have been disappointed that the change in me has been as modest as it has been, because back in late 1977 right after the Milner Park Conference, I thought I had left behind all my previous ups and downs. But this, it seems, was not to be. Am I more incorrigible than others, even for the Holy Spirit of God? I don't know.

That's why I like the badge some people wear with the letters 'PDGUOMBGNFWMY'. The enigmatic hotchpotch, as explained to any bewildered enquirer, stands for 'Please Don't Give Up On Me Because God's Not Finished With Me Yet'!

That's the first thing to say. The battle for holiness of character, for charity of heart and for consistency of life goes on.

But then I should have known, because this is Scripture's word from cover to cover. I quote just three references from three consecutive books in the Bible. Thus Hebrews 12: 'For the Lord disciplines him whom He loves, and chastises every son whom He receives (vs. 6). . . . For the moment all discipline seems painful rather than pleasant: later it yields the peaceful fruit of righteousness to those who have been trained by it.' (Vs. 11.)

Then there is James Chapter 1:2–3: 'Count it all joy, my brethren, WHEN [not if!!] you meet various trials, for you know that the testing of your faith produces steadfastness. And let steadfastness have its full effect, that you may be perfect and complete, lacking in nothing.'

Finally Peter gives a highly salutary exhortation: 'Beloved, do not be surprised at the fiery ordeal which comes upon you to prove you, as though something strange were happening to you' (1 Peter 4:12). Then he adds: 'For the time has come for judgment to begin with the household of God' (vs. 17). To round it off he speaks of the righteous man as being 'scarcely saved' (vs. 18). Indeed, he sees suffering being 'required' of believers so that God may ultimately 'restore, establish and strengthen' His children. (1 Peter 5:9–10).

All these Scriptures indicate that God is going to be working on our characters all our days. The Spirit's work is an integral aspect and dimension of the process, but in my experience it offers no magical shortcuts.

HEADWAY

Having said that, I do want to testify, the Cockney temperance testimony notwithstanding, to certain positive changes!

One has, praise God, made *some* headway!

First of all, the renewing work of the Spirit has truly changed both my attitude to and my experience of Christian worship. That has been lasting and real and ever deepening. In my pre-Milner Park days I enjoyed Christian singing, but the yearning of the heart to worship the Living God and really connect with God in praise was not there in the same way.

For example I could never quite come to terms with the endless fixation of the Psalmist on praising God, not only with all voices, but with the most unconservative range of musical instruments, including if you please the trumpet, lute and harp, the timbrel and dance (goodness gracious!), the strings and harp, and – jiminy cricket! – even 'with loud clashing cymbals'!! (Ps. 150:3–5).

This made me put question marks over the Psalmist's sense of decorum! After all, were not God's holy instruments the organ, the piano and the violin in that order? And was not human doxology an act to be entered upon with both social and classical restraint?

But now the desire in me to praise God with freedom of expression and with every musical means at man's disposal is real and deep. Worship, which meant little before, means a great deal now. In this I have been freed from many previous inhibitions. I can even, on rare occasions where it is not ruled out as shockingly inappropriate, dance a little jig before the Lord and not feel that lightning will strike! This has been exhilarating.

MINISTRY

Another plus in the realm of ministry lies in a deeper ability to trust the sovereignty of the Holy Spirit in bringing results from evangelistic preaching. 'No one can say "Jesus is Lord" except by the Holy Spirit' (1 Cor. 12:3). It is His prerogative to bring results. A deeper grasp of this prevents inflation when one sees results and deflation when one does not. We can therefore relax into His purposes and plans as we preach the Gospel.

In ministry there is also the fact that I no longer fear praying for the healing of people at the end of an evangelistic meeting or whenever called on to do so. Whereas previously I felt paralysed in this exercise, because I knew of excesses on the Christian lunatic fringe and because I feared seeming to fail if nothing happened, I am now willing, particularly in the concept of shared ministry with others in the Body of Christ, to pray for those who need healing. And how wonderful it has been to see numbers of people authentically healed in such times of prayer. Not usually anything wildly dramatic, as some can report, but generally a quiet but real work of healing grace, perhaps that night or next day or over a period.

In this whole dimension I hope to grow and develop as my confidence and understanding deepen. But the point is that I am more open to the miraculous intervention of God in this way than I was before.

GUIDANCE

Another exciting new dimension which has opened up relates to the different ways God may guide and reveal His will.

Earlier teaching and conditioning introduced me to ortho- dox principles of guidance through God's Word, through the counsel of friends, through the peace of God ruling in one's heart, through the inner whisper of the Spirit and through the circumstantial opening and closing of doors.

But by opening up to the wider possibilities of the Spirit I have come to see that His guidance can come through '*vision*', as when Paul received the Macedonian call in Acts 16:9, through *angelic testimony*, as when Paul got the word in Acts 27:23 that none on the ship to Rome would be lost as a result of the storm, or through *prophetic utterance*, as when Agabus was thus used to alert the Antioch Church to imminent famine and the need to send relief to the brethren in Judaea (Acts 11:28–9).

There is also the extraordinary place in the Scriptures given to dreams. Not that one dare ascribe every dream to the

Spirit of God because the Scriptures clearly warn against 'lying dreams' (Jeremiah 23:32).

But from Genesis 20:3, where God 'came to Abimelech in a dream,' through to the New Testament where 'an angel of the Lord appeared to him [Joseph] in a dream' (Matthew 1:20), this divine use of the subconscious dream life to communicate God's mind has been in use.

Why should it stop? In fact, since 1977 I have had several meaningful experiences of being guided during my sleep. Maybe that's the only time the Lord can get me when I'm quite still and not answering back!

In this connection it will be remembered from the early chapters of this book that it was a series of dreams about my alienated freinds, Jim and Mary, which finally led me to be reconciled to them just before the Milner Park Renewal Conference in 1977.

Anyway let me mention a couple of other instances. As programme chairman for the South African Christian Leadership Assembly (SACLA), I had the job of devising the programme. People kept saying to me: 'When are you going to come up with the programme?'

'The Lord hasn't given it to me yet,' I replied time and again, admittedly with a sense of developing anxiety as the preparatory months slipped away.

Then early one morning, just before I woke, there it was as clear as could be in my mind. Witness, as drawn from the first three chapters of Acts, was to be the theme. The outline rolled on to my fingers as I rushed through to my study to write it down. Over SACLA's seven days the theme was to subdivide as The Focus of Witness (The Person of Jesus), the Community of Witness (Fellowship), the Message of Witness (The Kingdom of God), the Dynamic of Witness (The Holy Spirit), the Scope of Witness (The Great Commission), the Bearers of Witness (Incarnational Ministry), the Acts of Witness (Worship and Evangelism).

When I shared this with the different SACLA committees, they all said 'Yes that's it!' And so it happened. But the outline was given in a sleeping not a waking moment!

At another moment in 1979, when the pre-SACLA press-ures and problems and the poison darts of verbal assault were coming thick and fast, I heard a very distinct voice in my sleep say: 'Early in Ezekiel – the short chapter.'

I was not then, nor am I now a great student of Ezekiel. So I knew little if anything of the shape of the book.

However on waking and opening up to Ezekiel I found that Chapter 2 has only ten verses, as compared with Chapter 1 which has twenty-eight and Chapter 3 which has twenty-seven. It is indeed 'the short chapter'.

The whole chapter ministered mightily to my spirit as I read it, especially verses 6–7: 'And you, son of man, be not afraid of them, nor be afraid of their words, though briers and thorns are with you and you sit upon scorpions; be not afraid of their words, nor be dismayed at their looks, for they are a rebellious house. And you shall speak my words to them, whether they hear or refuse to hear; for they are a rebellious house.'

It was an extraordinary affirmation and encouragement, And it enabled me to press on with vigour.

Another incident from that SACLA period: because of all the opposition to SACLA, we found ourselves some eleven weeks from the event with only 800 people registered. We had been hoping for five to seven thousand.

'The SACLA vision is unsellable,' our Chairman David Bosch had said in one committee meeting not long before this moment.

Then yet again the Spirit's word came during sleep. It was virtually audible. It was very simple. It was just one word: 'Jethro.'

I rose, went to my study and reread the story of Moses's father-in-law, Jethro, coming to him and telling him he should share more of the load and delegate more responsi-bility to others.

Clearly a few of us were doing too much. We needed more help in recruiting people. The thought came that this could be done by drawing in perhaps forty other recruiters, as it were, to help break the log jam.

I at once wrote out a list of 'able men from all the people, such as fear God, men who are trustworthy' (Exodus 18:21). Then I spoke my concerns and guidance into a tape, had forty copies made and sent them out urging these forty friends with all vigour to bend their backs in the Lord's strength to the task of breaking the log jam in recruitment.

Shortly thereafter the results of this and other initiatives were dramatically evident. People began to register in their hundreds. And SACLA opened on 5 July 1979 with 6,000 registrations. There were 7,000 in the closing meeting.

Interestingly enough, Richard Foster in his little classic *The Celebration of Discipline* affirms that 'for fifteen centuries Christians overwhelmingly considered dreams as a natural way in which the spiritual world broke into our lives'.[82]

He then quotes Morton Kelsey's assertion that 'every major Father of the Early Church, from Justin Martyr to Irenaeus, from Clement and Tertullian to Origen and Cyprian, believed that dreams were a means of revelation'.[83]

Foster bemoans the fact that with the rationalism of the Renaissance came a certain scepticism about dreams. But if in the Scriptures God used dreams to speak to His people, why should He not do so now?

Is it not in fact just a matter of opening up to all the Scriptural options and evidence of a supernatural God? This is something the Spirit seems to do. He reworks our presuppositional world, as it were, thus preventing us from screening out by some naturalistic presupposition those miraculous workings of God which are evident in both Old and New Testaments.

READING ALL SCRIPTURE

This brings us to another bonus – the Spirit's way of getting us to read the whole Bible without prejudice. In the last years I have found myself facing the Spirit-inspired Scriptures with a greater degree of openness to everything they say. Not that I am referring to any doubt ever as to Scripture's inspiration and authority, nor am I wanting to deny interpretational or hermeneutical problems which do, I know, exist. But I also know that like Martin Luther who judged the Epistle of James 'a right strawy epistle', because it didn't seem to speak of justification by faith, so we all tend to filter Scripture through our own limited experience. We ride high on our purple passages, on our strong points, and what our theological background or conditioning has decreed as normative. We then ignore or subconsciously discard what is either outside our experience, our tradition or the theologically acceptable framework and practice of our denomination, circle, or group.

As already indicated, social activists will thus often ignore the Scriptures on new-birth, salvation, human lostness and evangelism, while many evangelicals overlook prophecy or tongues or dreams or visions or healing. For their part, charismatics and pentecostals will in many instances ignore Jesus's injunctions in Matthew 25 about clothing the naked, feeding the hungry, visiting the prisoner, or taking in the stranger. And so on.

We thus all tend to live in spiritually selective categories based on our selective reading of Scripture.

While I still do this to some degree, I can testify that I do it much less than before. In short I have become more open to all Scripture. This has been exciting.

WORKING WITH GOD

Another area where a deepening grasp of the Spirit's work has been helpful lies in a developing aversion to working *for* God on my own agenda as distinct from working *with* God on His! No longer do I want to dash with quite the same impetuosity into my own plans and then drag God in to bless them, if He has nothing else on His mind. What a joy now to relax into the Spirit's agenda as one finds it and seek to cooperate with the Father's plans rather than my own.

In this connection the beautiful picture in Isaiah 40:30–31 has come to mean so much. There the prophet notes that 'even youths shall faint and be weary, and young men shall fall exhausted; but they who wait for the Lord shall renew their strength, they shall mount up with wings like eagles, they shall run and not be weary, they shall walk and not faint.'

This glorious promise explodes into new life and meaning when it is realised that the eagle is a bird of distinctive flight habits. One of these is to wait for the thermals or updrafts of air by which he can mount to incredible altitudes. The eagle doesn't waste its precious energy by attempting such feats in its own strength. It mounts on the power of the thermal. And for this power it waits.

A friend of mine who was taken gliding told me recently how the art of gliding lies in the pilot's ability to spot where the thermals are. As the glider is steered into the thermal, it will suddenly mount hundreds of feet in the most exhilarating climb. Then it glides on in relaxation till the pilot can find the next thermal. Then whoosh! – up it goes again, all the time mounting on a power not its own.

This is what the eagle also does. No wonder therefore that the text does not say: 'They shall mount up with wings like pelicans!' Poor pelicans! They flap, and flub and puff and pant and in a furious feathery flurry of flying energy manage an embarrassingly modest lift-off! Not the eagle. He waits for the thermal. Then he sets his wings and mounts effortlessly on a power not his own and to a place of the thermal's choosing.

More and more in recent years this image has become meaningful. We are not to try to mount like the pelican, but to wait on the thermals or updrafts of what God is doing and where He is going by His Spirit. Then we simply get in on the thermal of His agenda and in the Spirit we mount up with wings like eagles, we run and are not weary, we walk and do not faint. We are no longer working for God, but with Him.

Yes, there's the ideal. And it's a thrilling one to aim for. So the question for the evangelist who contemplates where to go now or what to do next is simply: 'Where are God's thermals?'

BUILDING THE BODY

It will not surprise anyone who has followed me through these pages that my own quest to know more of the Spirit's working should have resulted in an ever deepening commitment to the building up of the Body of Christ. In one sense that is what this book has been all about, so I must re-declare this as a parting shot.

We need one another. Therefore the lines of estrangement within the Body of Christ must be dissolved by a balancing understanding of the Spirit's way in assigning to each of us different gifts and insights. There seems to me no reason why we cannot find a Christian life-style of integrating spirituality which can move between the different poles of Christian insight without insecurity, threat or fear. How else can we grow to full stature?

By this commitment we can all develop into the ideal, once verbalised as *ecclesia reformata semper reformanda* – a reformed Church always reforming! Ghetto syle living prevents this.

Nor will such reformation happen through facile judgments of supposedly renewed believers that all denominations or groups or individuals who do not think or act or respond as they do are 'dead or dying' and therefore to be forsaken for pastures new, as if those new pastures will forever avoid the same problems.

If we are giving up on each other, or separate from each other on these grounds, we betray that patience of God which has not yet given up on us! Imagine if the Corinthian Church had been abandoned by St Paul or given up as a lost cause by the Lord Himself. And what of all those defective Churches in the book of Revelation which received the Spirit's letters of admonition? What if all the 'true-blue', renewed believers had left those fellowships for some promised land of ecclesiastical purity and perfected spiritual power!

One can of course sympathise with people who despair of 'stick-in-the-mud' congregations or denominations which won't move into the new day of greater life in the Spirit. Beyond that the hiving off into separatist fellowships or isolated house-churches of those who have thus lost hope is

up to a point understandable. Nevertheless I remain personally persuaded that while this may bring short-term gains it
is more likely, if Church history is anything to go by, to bring
long-term losses to the Body of Christ as a whole.

Richard Lovelace, the New England historian of spiritual
renewal, brings his judgment:

> Revival and division are ultimately antithetical . . . the
> hope of renewal is ultimately bound up with church
> unity. . . . Dividing the church in the interest of renewing
> it is no more feasible than severing the parts of a body to
> improve its health. Even if the severed parts survive, they
> suffer loss and they will never function properly until they
> are re-united in fellowship. Leaders who secede from
> imperfect denominations and denominations which eject
> imperfect leadership simply lose the values of the group
> they reject while they ensure the unrestrained growth of its
> defects in a body of future converts.[84]

In one sense one could even say that the separatist mentality
is a form of religious flesh and spiritual pride. It says: 'We're
better than you or spiritually purer than you.'

Writing on the eighteenth-century Revival in New England, Jonathan Edwards notes that 'the spiritually proud
person is apt to find fault with other saints, that they are low
in grace; and to be much in observance of how cold and dead
they are'.[85]

Pursuing this line Richard Lovelace comments:

> Under the guise of prophetic righteousness, pride can
> move awakened believers to censorious attacks on other
> Christians, a lack of meekness in rebuking those who really
> need it and a hair-trigger readiness to separate from those
> less holy or less orthodox. It can do things to Christians
> which make their religion grate painfully on the sensibili-
> ties of fellow-Christians.[86]

The inimitable Jonathan Edwards once again puts it in a

nutshell when he speaks from the renewal experiences of nearly two centuries ago.

> Spiritual pride commonly occasions a certain stiffness and inflexibility in persons, in their own judgement and their own way: whereas the eminently humble person, though he be inflexible in his duty, and in those things wherein God's honour is concerned . . . yet in other things he is of a pliable disposition . . . ready to pay deference to others' opinions. He loves to comply with their inclinations and has a heart that is tender and flexible, like a little child.
>
> And though he will not be a companion with one that is visibly Christ's enemy . . . yet he does not love the appearance of an open separation from visible Christians . . . and will as much as possible shun all appearances of a superiority, or distinguishing himself as better than others.[87]

In these last years this spirit has become more and more beautiful to me and ever more worthy as an ideal. In other words my own ongoing pilgrimage in the Spirit is committing me more deeply in mercy to the whole Church of Christ, knowing that it is also the mercy of both God and others that I must count on for myself and for my own progress in the Body.

WORKING ON THE WRAP-UP

To conclude. If I were to try to put in a nutshell what these last years have done for me I would say they have pressed me more and more to work on the wrap-up of the Gospel.

That this is both worthwhile and possible has been underlined in a thousand ways both in Africa and overseas. For example this conviction was confirmed during the two Spring Harvest conferences in North Wales where I was privileged to minister in April 1982. These were great experiences.

What encouraged me there was to find my own quest and purpose reflected in thousands of people, many of them quite young, who were also working on a wrap-up of the Gospel embracing zealous evangelism, sane and gentle renewal, profound social concern, deep marital commitments and solid biblical theology. Thus they were as concerned to see the 'Siberian Seven' freed (Seven Russian Christians who have sought asylum in the U.S.A. Embassy in Moscow but whom the authorities will not allow to emigrate) and to see a peaceful way through the Falklands crisis which was then looming, as they were for the proposed evangelistic visits to Britain of Billy Graham and Luis Palau. On top of that they were allowing the Holy Spirit to be released in renewing power, in breathtaking worship and in motivation of believers to deepened intercession and fasting.

I thought that was just great. The fact is that when the mix truly comes together it is almost intoxicating in its exhilaration, power and appeal.

To embrace this wrap-up is to embrace the whole word of God, within the fellowship of the whole Church of Christ, and exercise the whole range of the Spirit's gifts in love and humility as He enables.

Not that this comprehensive, inclusive, holistic concern excludes or ignores the reality of specialised callings. We know 'there are varieties of gifts, but the same Spirit; and there are varieties of service, but the same Lord; and there are varieties of workings, but it is the same God who inspires them all in every one' (1 Cor. 12:4–6).

Therefore, we need those who major in evangelism, or in social care, or in political protest, or in healing, or in renewal, or in pastoring, or in teaching or in helping, or in administration.

But the point is to make real room for one another and to take into one's heart the full range of the Spirit's concerns, even if one is not called oneself to give major or equal expression to each of those concerns.

For me the best statement of faith in the Holy Spirit is still Clause 4 of the Lausanne Covenant because it so clearly sets the full range of the Spirit's work in the context of the mission of the Church in the world.

Mission and evangelism and reaching the world for Jesus Christ is still what it's basically all about.

Surely then all of us who know and love our Lord Jesus Christ can take the Lausanne Covenant's affirmation of faith and purpose and unite around it, not only for our own sake, but for God's and for the world's:

We believe in the power of the Holy Spirit. The Father sent His Spirit to bear witness to His Son; without His witness ours is futile. Conviction of sin, faith in Christ, new birth and Christian growth are all His work. Further, the Holy Spirit is a missionary Spirit; thus evangelism should arise spontaneously from a Spirit-filled church. A church that is not a missionary church is contradicting itself and quenching the Spirit. Worldwide evangelisation will become a realistic possibility only when the Spirit renews the Church in truth and wisdom, faith, holiness, love and power. We therefore call upon all Christians to pray for such a visitation of the sovereign Spirit of God that all His fruit may appear in all His people and that all His gifts may enrich the Body of Christ. Only then will the whole Church become a fit instrument in His hands, that the whole earth may hear His voice.

Amen. Even so, Lord, let it be.

Appendix A

WHAT IS THE BAPTISM IN THE HOLY SPIRIT?

In this appendix, I want by way of introduction to kick off with a brief résumé of what is clear in terms of the person and work of the Holy Spirit, and then move to that which is less clear.

I. INTRODUCTION

1. The Clear Things

(i) The Holy Spirit is a person

He is not an 'it', not an impersonal influence. The fact that Jesus uses the masculine pronoun 'He' (e.g. John 14:26, 15:26, 16:8, 13, 14.) when referring to the Holy Spirit makes this clear. Moreover Scripture assigns personal attributes to Him in speaking of His *mind*, as when He 'will teach you all things' (John 14:26), His *emotion*, as when He may 'grieve' (Eph. 4:30) and His *will*, as when He forbids (Acts 16:6–7).

(ii) The Holy Spirit is also God

He is coequal with the Father and the Son and proceeds from both Father and Son as the Nicene Creed affirms. Article V of the Anglican Church's 'Thirty-Nine Articles' speaks of Him as 'of one substance, majesty and glory with the Father and the Son'. Small wonder then that Jesus can send His servants out to make disciples and baptise them in the ONE name of The Father and of the Son and of the Holy Spirit, while the

Apostle can commend people to 'the grace of the Lord Jesus Christ and the love of God and the fellowship of the Holy Spirit' (2 Cor. 13:14).

In this connection we note that the doctrine of the Trinity, a word not used in Scripture, arose not from metaphysical speculation but from Scriptural evidence and early Church experience. The early followers of Jesus had in their pre-Christian experience known God ABOVE them, as they walked the hills of Galilee and surveyed the majestic middle-eastern skies at night. Then they had known God WITH them as Jesus shared three breathtaking years of their lives. Then they had known God IN them as the blessed Holy Spirit entered their lives and hearts following Pentecost. So they had experienced God as Trinity and could therefore speak of Him in no other way.

(iii) The Holy Spirit is the Spirit of Jesus

Throughout the New Testament, and certainly most clearly from Acts to Revelation, the Holy Spirit is the Spirit of Jesus. Jesus said: 'I tell you the truth: it is to your advantage that I go away, for if I do not go away, the Counsellor will not come to you; but if I go, *I* will send Him to you' (John 16:7). As the Father had sent Jesus into the world, so Jesus would send the Spirit. In this sending the Father too would share, but the Spirit would be sent in the *Name of Jesus*. Thus John reports Jesus's words: 'But the Counsellor, the Holy Spirit, Whom the Father will send *in My Name*, He will teach you all things' (John 14:26).

In other words the Holy Spirit would universalise the presence of Jesus. The disciples had perhaps unwittingly known the Spirit *with* them during the earthly ministry of Jesus, but now they would know Him IN them. Said Jesus to the disciples as He spoke of the Counsellor: 'The Spirit of Truth . . . you know Him, for He dwells with you, and *will be IN you*' (John 14:17). The Spirit makes it possible for the presence of Jesus to be everywhere in the hearts of His disciples. He cannot be localised as Jesus had to be in His earthly ministry.

The implication of this is that He is not there to glorify Himself but to glorify Christ. 'He will be a witness to me', said Jesus simply (John 16:15). He is, as it were, the man behind the projector. He is not there just to give us an experience and knowledge of Himself, but of Christ. This gives a certain objectivity and identity to the Spirit's work in an age which hankers for subjective experiences of any spirit and any type of spirit. The point is we are not after experiences of experience, which makes for dangerous sentimentality or emotionalism, but for that knowledge and experience of the Spirit of Jesus which will build us into a greater likeness of Him. Indeed any 'spiritual' experience which does *not* result in greater likeness to Christ is to be considered suspect, because the *Spirit* whom we should be seeking or releasing is the Spirit of *Jesus*. There is therefore only one evidence that we have received the Holy Spirit of the Bible and that is if we are gradually becoming like Jesus, (Gal. 5:22) and are desiring to bring people to Jesus (Acts 1:8).

All of this says to us that the doctrine of Christ (theologians call it Christology) is a doctrine about God, because the God with Whom we have to do is the God and Father of our Lord Jesus Christ, and the doctrine of the Holy Spirit (theologians call it pneumatology – from the Greek *pneuma* = spirit) is a doctrine about Jesus, because the Spirit is the Spirit of Jesus. As Michael Green has succinctly said of the Spirit: 'You cannot get Him except through Jesus or get to Jesus except through Him.'[1]

All this means then that if we ask how far God will go with us, Christology answers 'All the way'. And if we ask how much Jesus wants to fill us and possess us, pneumatology answers 'Completely'.

A statement of Christian theology could therefore well and appropriately follow the outline of the Grace – thus:

Volume One: The grace of our Lord Jesus Christ
Volume Two: And the love of God
Volume Three: And the fellowship of the Holy Spirit
Volume Four: Be with you always!

(iv) Threefold Ministry

The next item of clarity, as I see it, is that the Holy Spirit, as we observed in Chapters 2 and 3, has a threefold ministry in the life of any who become the followers of Jesus. This takes place as the person *seeks*, *believes* and then *follows*.

So we can reiterate that the Holy Spirit works in us:

a. *before conversion* – when He illumines the mind of the *seeker* (1 Cor. 12:3) and convinces him of his sin and need of a Saviour (John 16:8).

b. *at conversion* – when He regenerates (John 3:5–6) and then indwells the life of the *believer* (1 Cor. 3:16, Romans 8:9–10, 2 Cor. 1:22), and finally seals him as a purchased possession (Eph. 1:13).

c. *after conversion* – when He sanctifies the disciple (1 Thess. 4:7–8, 1 Cor. 6:19–20), guides him (John 16:13), helps him to pray (Rom. 8:26–27), strengthens him (Eph. 3:16), brings forth His fruit (Gal. 5:19–20), and equips for service through His gifts (1 Cor. 12:4–11).

2. The Less Clear

All the above seems to me to be pretty clear and straight-forward. What is not so clear is the matter of how being filled with the Holy Spirit does or does not relate to being 'baptised in the Holy Spirit' (See Chapter 14) and how both terms or experiences relate to being regenerated or born again.

More specifically we must pursue further whether being filled with the Holy Spirit is the same as or different from the Baptism in the Spirit. Are different terms being used to describe the same experience? Moreover, when does the Baptism in the Spirit happen? And does it happen once or many times? In other words, what is the exact nature and timing of the Baptism in the Holy Spirit? And where, if anywhere, does the gift of tongues fit?

It is at these points that all the tensions and confusions come, so the matter deserves more thorough discussion.

II. THE NATURE AND TIMING OF THE BAPTISM IN THE HOLY SPIRIT

1. The Term Defined

At this point, to keep one flow of thought clear, we repeat what we said in Chapter 14 so that the different strands of thought are kept together.

We noted there that the terms 'baptism' or 'baptise' come from a rich word (Greek *baptizo*) which in secular Greek literature meant to plunge, sink, drown or over-whelm. And so a person could be drowned or sunk (literally baptised) by wine or 'overwhelmed' by sleep. Euripides, the Greek writer, used *bapto* for when water was splashing into a ship, but *baptizo* for when the ship is water-logged.

In the Old Testament the normal meaning of the word is overwhelm or immerse. So when John the Baptist, who in one sense links Old and New Testaments, says that Jesus 'baptises with the Holy Spirit' (John 1:33) he means that Jesus is the one who can *immerse* us in the Holy Spirit or *overwhelm* us by the Spirit. The one image carries the idea of being pushed into or under the water and the other of having buckets of water poured over us.

Acts Chapter 1, for its part, brings both ideas together, verse 5 speaking of an imminent baptism in (Gr. *en*) the Holy Spirit and verse 8 promising power to witness when the Holy Spirit had 'come *upon*' them.

We also noted that the phrase 'to be baptised with the Spirit' is not very common in Scripture. It comes four times in the Gospels (Matt. 3:11, Mk. 1:8, Luke 3:16, John 1:33) telling of John the Baptist's prophecy that as he had baptised or immersed or overwhelmed people with water, so Jesus would baptise, immerse or overwhelm them with the Spirit.

Then it comes once in the Epistles at 1 Cor. 12:13 which tells of *all* being baptised by one Spirit into the one Body – so that *all* are made to drink of one Spirit. Finally, it comes twice in Acts, firstly, at 1:5 speaking expressly of the Day of

Pentecost, and secondly, in Chapter 11 where Peter defends his Gentile activities to the critical 'circumcision party' (vs. 2) by telling them how he saw that the Holy Spirit 'fell on them JUST AS ON US AT THE BEGINNING' (vs. 15) and this reminds him of the Lord's pre-Pentecost word that 'John baptised with water, but you shall be baptised with the Holy Spirit' (vs. 16).

2. Light from the Cornelius story (Acts Chapter 10)

Cornelius, I feel, is worth special note because he perhaps has the clues we need for the way forward.

What is especially interesting and significant is that in Cornelius's story several concepts relating to the Holy Spirit are drawn together in one package.

Thus, while Peter was speaking to Cornelius's household 'the Holy Spirit FELL ON [Idea One] all who heard the word' (Acts 10:44). Reporting this Luke says the believers were 'amazed because the gift of the Holy Spirit had been POURED OUT [Idea Two] even on the Gentiles' (Acts 10:45). The evidence of this, apparently, was that 'they heard them SPEAKING IN TONGUES [Idea Three] and extolling God' (Acts 10:46). Peter then asks how water-baptism can be denied to 'these people who have RECEIVED [Idea Four] the Holy Spirit' (Acts 10:47).

Back in Jerusalem, Peter reports how the 'Holy Spirit fell on them *just* as on us at the beginning' (Acts 11:15) and this reminds him of Jesus saying: 'John baptised with water, but you shall be BAPTISED WITH THE HOLY SPIRIT' (Idea Five – Acts 11:16).

Then in the very next breath Peter says: 'If then God GAVE [Idea Six] the same gift to them as He gave to us when we believed in the Lord Jesus Christ, [N.B. – at the START of their Christian experience] who was I that I could withstand God?' (Acts 11:17).

Then the assembled group of 'apostles and brethren' (Acts 11:1) who heard this story jumped immediately to the irrevocable conclusion on the basis of the data received that 'to the

Gentiles also God has granted REPENTANCE UNTO
LIFE' (Acts 11:18, Idea Seven).

When this whole happening is next reported (i.e. at the
Jerusalem Council (Acts 15), Peter simply summarises the
whole Cornelius happening as God 'GIVING THEM the
Holy Spirit just as He did to us' (vs. 8) (*cf.* Idea Six).

In the story then, seven ideas are concurrently brought
together, (i) The Spirit *falling*, (ii) The Spirit being *poured out*,
(iii) the recipients speaking in tongues, (iv) the Spirit being
received, (v) the people being *baptised* with the Spirit, (vi) the
Spirit being *given*, (vii) the people *repenting*.

Five of the terms used (falling, being poured out, being
received, being baptised and being given) seem to refer to the
SAME happening. This would suggest that they are inter-
changeable.

So we note that, here at least, 'falling upon', 'being
immersed in' and 'receiving or being given the gift of the
Spirit' at the time of faith and conversion are all powerfully
and persuasively brought together, along, of course, with
immediate water baptism as Acts 10:47–8 tell us. Here then
is the whole package in this early situation of New Testament
evangelism (Acts 10). We could itemise it slightly differently
and observe:

(i) There was the Spirit working to prepare Cornelius
(10:22, 31) and his household. (*Illumination*)

(ii) There was proclamation from a Spirit-directed
preacher (10:20, 34). (*Evangelism*)

(iii) There was the reflex of conversion (15:3) repentance
(11:18) and presumably faith because God doesn't
pour out His Spirit without these. (*Repentance*)

(iv) There must have been the divine response of
justification and regeneration because no true
Christian life can begin without these blessings.
(*New Birth*)

(v) There was the falling of the Holy Spirit (10:44) on all
who heard, identified by Peter at 11:15 as similar to
if not identical with what happened to the first group
on the Day of Pentecost. (*Baptism in the Spirit*)

(vi) There was the dramatic evidence of the 'poured out' Spirit (10:45) in the shape of tongues and praise to God (10:46). (*Signs*)

(vii) There was immediate or almost immediate and public (10:45) baptism in water (10:47) for those who had 'received the Holy Spirit'. (*Incorporation*)

(viii) There was follow-up as Peter and the believers with him remained 'for some days' (10:48). (*Consolidation*)

Of course some argue that this first preaching to the Gentiles was inevitably unique and special, but I wonder if that has not been pushed too far. Maybe there is more of a norm here than we find easy to admit.

Certainly neither Peter nor Cornelius nor God had to contend with the hearers having been told by the minister that they had received the Spirit at the font in infant baptism and were accordingly regenerate, by the bishop at high school that they were getting the Spirit at confirmation, by the evangelist at the town hall that they had missed the Spirit at the font and the confirmation but would find Him either at conversion or in lesson five of the follow-up series, or by the Pentecostal preacher that they'd missed the Spirit at the font, confirmation, town hall and in the follow-up series but could receive Him plus tongues no less, at the altar rail of the tabernacle at Fifth and Lily Streets where revival would be taking place at 7.30 p.m. each night next week. Cornelius, the listener, was a lucky man to have been spared all that. So was Peter the preacher.

Maybe some of our inordinate problems in this whole matter are the legacy of the exceeding great theological tangle and confusion that is our context in a semi-Christianised Western world.

Peter and Cornelius were fortunate because the slate was clean and uncomplicated and the proclamation, human response, divine initiative and public incorporation could all take place AT ONCE in a situation void of theological and ecclesiastical clutter.

All this would suggest that we need to look afresh in our

preaching and teaching at bringing all these happenings together in one package so that spiritual experiences which belong together in both teaching and experience are not separated.

We shall have cause to return to this later. In the meantime, we must look in more detail at current views as to the *timing* of the Baptism in the Spirit.

3. The Timing of the Baptism in the Spirit

When this happens, and how, is unfortunately a major point at issue between Pentecostals and non-pentecostals and between Charismatic and non-charismatics. We repeat the three prominent views itemised in Chapter 14.

(i) *View One*

Regeneration and Baptism in the Spirit synchronise and take place at the same time when a man is converted to Christ and indwelt by the Spirit.

This view is based broadly speaking on 1 Cor. 12:13: 'For by one Spirit we were *all* baptised into one Body . . . and *all* were made to drink of one Spirit'. In other words, at conversion all believers are baptised in the Spirit and what Charismatics call being baptised in the Spirit belongs strictly to what it means to be a Christian at all.

In this view, tongues is one possible gift, given in the sovereignty of the Spirit (1 Cor. 12:11) but not a normative expectation or requirement for every believer.

As to the fullness of the Spirit, this comes through moral and spiritual surrender to His leading and Will. It happens as we keep coming and keep drinking of the Spirit. The fullness is to be continuously appropriated.

In this view 'water baptism is the initiatory Christian rite, because Spirit baptism is the initiatory Christian experience'.[2] So says John Stott in his lucid booklet *The Baptism and Fullness of the Holy Spirit*. He adds: 'The Baptism in the Spirit is not a second or subsequent experience,

enjoyed by some Christians, but the initial experience enjoyed by all.'[3] The initiatory rite follows the initiatory experience.

(ii) View Two

*This view sees a two-stage initiation – the first being regeneration,
when we are born again and indwelt by the Spirit and the second
being the Baptism in the Spirit, when we are anointed, filled, flooded,
immersed in the Spirit and empowered for service.* This is evidenced by the manifestation of the gifts of the Spirit –
most notably tongues. Some would insist on the tongues
evidence as normative. Others prefer to say of those baptised in the Spirit that not all do speak in tongues, but all
may.

This position is based on four Scriptures primarily. The
first is the *Acts 2* experience of the disciples at Pentecost. It is
assumed in this view that they received the Spirit after
Jesus's resurrection, as referred to in John 20 when He
breathed on them and said: 'Receive the Holy Spirit' (vs. 22)
and they were then baptised in the Spirit in a second
experience on the day of Pentecost itself.

Acts 8 is the second passage. Here we read of the Samaritans who firstly 'believed Phillip as he preached Good News
about the Kingdom of God and the name of Jesus Christ' (vs.
12). Secondly, they 'received the word of God' (vs. 14).
Thirdly, they were baptised (vss. 13, 16) in the name of the
Lord Jesus but *without* receiving the Holy Spirit (vs. 15) or
having Him fall on them. (vs. 16). At least, observes Luke, it
had '*NOT YET* fallen', the implication being that this would
happen before long. Finally, the Samaritans did receive the
Holy Spirit (vs. 15) but only after being specially prayed for
by Peter and John who had been sent down from Jerusalem
(vss. 14–15) by the apostolic band.

It is perhaps worth noting in passing that 'baptism with
the Holy Spirit' is not referred to as such in this passage, but
only *the receiving of the Spirit*.

The third much-used passage to sustain View Two is *Acts 9*

where there is, it would seem, a three-day gap between Saul's 'conversion' on the Damascus road (vss. 1–9) and his filling with the Spirit (vs. 17). But we again note that the term used is filling with the Spirit, not baptism with the Spirit.

The fourth passage is *Acts 19* which tells of 'some disciples' at Ephesus (vs. 1), 'about twelve of them in all' (vs. 7), who had been followers of John the Baptist but who declared that they had neither 'heard' of the Holy Spirit nor 'received' Him when they 'believed' (vs. 2). However, they had only believed 'in the one who was to come' (vs. 4) after John the Baptist. But when they heard of 'Jesus' (vs. 4) they were baptised in His name, after which Paul laid hands on them, 'the Holy Spirit came *ON* them; and they spoke with tongues and prophesied' (vs. 6).

Yet again we observe no reference to the 'Baptism in the Spirit' but only to the now oft-noted phenomena of receiving 'the Holy Spirit' (vs. 2) and having the Holy Spirit come 'on' one (vs. 6). We also note that tongues is referred to in this Ephesian experience, this being the second instance (the other is Pentecost), while there is no indication of tongues in either the Samaritan situation or in Saul's Damascus infilling (Acts 9:17).

(iii) View Three

The third view is one which accepts the experience of the Baptism in the Spirit but rejects the terminology. Thus someone like David Watson can write: 'The term, baptism, is undoubtedly linked with Christian initiation, and in that sense, at least, every Christian is already baptised in the Spirit.' Watson accordingly comes out strongly for the alternative phrase of being 'filled with the Holy Spirit'.[4]

Likewise Cardinal Suenens of Belgium in his book *A New Pentecost* rejects the terminology 'baptism in the Spirit' but encourages the pursuit of the experience. He feels it would be better to look for another expression.[5]

Michael Green also follows this line, accepting, approving and promoting the experience of Charismatics, but en-

couraging them 'to call the rose by some other name' and
giving them the assurance that 'it will smell just as sweet'.[6]

Many of those holding this view would not want to draw
swords or break fellowship over the terminology issue, but
they would observe its exegetical problems and caution
about its pastoral problems if it leads to arrogance in those
who are supposedly stage-two Christians and depression in
those who feel locked into stage one. The idea of first- and
second-class Christians is considered both unfortunate and
inaccurate, especially on this basis. Imagine landing Billy
Graham, Mother Theresa and John Wesley in the second
class because they neither claim a Baptism in the Spirit
subsequent to conversion nor speak in tongues!

4. Pros and Cons

So there are the three views. The first says regeneration and
Baptism in the Spirit synchronise and are simultaneous. The
second says there are two stages in Christian initiation – the
first by regeneration and the second by Baptism in the Spirit
to equip for life and service. The third accepts the Charismatic experience, but rejects the label 'Baptism in the Spirit',
choosing rather to speak of a filling with the Spirit as a
desired experience and goal following on the reception and
Baptism in the Spirit at conversion.

So what then of the pros and cons of each view and what is
the way through?

(i) View One (Regeneration and Baptism in the Spirit Synchronise)

View One in its basic idea of the synchronisation of the two
experiences has the backing of some twenty centuries of
Christian thinking, a two-stage initiation in these exact
categories not ever having been part of the Church's
teaching, to the best of my knowledge, until the rise of
twentieth-century pentecostalism.

The view is also sustained by a very considerable weight of
exegetical data. Four presentations of this in varying degrees

of detail are John Stott's *The Baptism and Fullness of the Spirit*, Michael Green's *I Believe in the Holy Spirit* (noting especially Chapter 8), James Dunn's elaborate treatise *The Baptism in the Holy Spirit*, and Billy Graham's more popular study *The Holy Spirit* (noting especially Chapter 5). All of these repay careful scrutiny.

However, while the case for retaining the term 'Baptism in the Spirit' as an initiatory spiritual happening is well argued in all these volumes, perhaps only Michael Green does full justice to the astonishing evidence of the twentieth-century Charismatic renewal which has received its major impetus and perhaps its spiritual power and effectiveness from the sustained preaching of the Baptism in the Spirit as a second experience.

It is noteworthy that Derek Crumpton sees 1 Cor. 12:13 – 'For by one Spirit we were all baptised into one body . . . and all were made to drink of one Spirit' – as referring not to the Baptism in the Spirit, as traditional Evangelicalism has it, but to a Baptism into the Body of Christ by the Spirit. This is seen as something different.

Says Derek:

> There is a baptism by the Spirit into the Body of Christ and a drink of the Spirit. The Spirit is the agent, we are the subjects of the baptism, the element is the Body of Christ and He gives us to 'drink' of Himself. He becomes thereby the 'indwelling' Spirit, the Spirit of Christ of whose fullness we have all received. So I would see the Baptism into the Body of Christ. Then the Baptism in the Spirit has JESUS as the agent, we are still the subjects and the Spirit is the element in which we are baptised.[7]

This kind of line presses us either to re-examine our traditional exegesis, or if we remain sure of it, to re-examine *what* exactly it is which the Renewal Movement is preaching and teaching which has brought such life and blessing across the world. Says Crumpton:

Evangelicals may argue about the terminology. But the
evidence is that where this teaching is given, the resultant
response is undeniable. . . . I have also observed that
wherever this emphasis (i.e. on Baptism in the Spirit as a
second clear experience) is lacking, the renewing move of
the Spirit loses impact, momentum and meaning. . . . For
myself I would be very happy to testify anywhere to my
being baptised in the Spirit by Jesus. I would be very
reluctant to claim, even with my dearest brother, that I am
filled with the Spirit. That is my daily longing. The
evidence, I fear, indicates that there is so much more to
gain.[8]

Alternatively, while retaining the traditional evangelical
view of Baptism in the Spirit as initiatory and belonging with
the gift of the Spirit at conversion, one could conclude more
generally that what God is honouring is not so much the use
of the term (Baptism in the Spirit as a second experience), as
the much neglected emphasis on *the work of the Spirit AS A
WHOLE*. Maybe the Holy Spirit has indeed been the step-
child of theology and the neglected person of the Trinity in
much Church life. Perhaps the Pentecostals and Charismatics have stumbled on to the heart of Christian reality and
power for life and ministry and so the Lord is honouring them
with His great blessing, even if some of the vocabulary used
may in the judgment of many lack theological precision. The
Renewal Movement thus becomes a bell or gong sounded in
the ears of the Church saying: 'Hey, everyone, here's what
it's all about. Here's an emphasis you've forgotten!'

(ii) View Two (Two stages in Christian initiation – Regeneration, then Baptism in the Spirit)

If evangelicals and others must look deeper at what the
Renewal Movement is all about and why it is producing
dramatic new life and vitality across the world, then Pentecostals and Charismatics must likewise pause to hear what

evangelicals and the Church down the ages have to say about the terminology in use in the Movement, especially about whether the Baptism in the Spirit is indeed the correct term to describe the new release or fullness of the Spirit which has come to so many through their ministrations.

There is little value in simply or even simplistically writing off what Church history or exceedingly able biblical exegetes of our own time are saying. In other words some humble give and take on both sides is in order so that the truth they are looking at from different perspectives may become clearer to all. The two groups, evangelicals and Charismatics, are not simply cousins, they are brothers. They are certainly not opponents and if they relate as such, then the only laughter will be in Hell.

I must admit for myself that the term 'Baptism in the Spirit' is problematic to describe my own Milner Park experience. As I said earlier in this appendix, in none of the seemingly two-stage situations – the Samaritans (Acts 8), Saul (Acts 9) or the Ephesians (Acts 19) does the term 'Baptism in the Spirit' come. Where it IS used is with Cornelius's household, which reflects an initiatory situation par excellence, with all the ingredients of human and divine initiative, as mentioned earlier, all coming together in one package. This makes the Cornelius story an unconvincing basis for any two-stage idea.

This means then that the case for View Two (the two-stage idea) and for some Charismatic vocabulary, does begin to rest rather fully on the disciples' experience at Pentecost. In this, much depends on the understanding of John 20 where the risen Jesus breathes on them and says 'Receive the Holy Spirit' (vs. 22). Were they born again then, as David du Plessis believes? Or was this a promise of something still to come as John Wesley believed? Or is the 'one-volume John', who will not be doing a second volume like Luke, conflating the post-Resurrection and Pentecost teachings into one climactic account?

Discussion on this will undoubtedly continue, as indeed it should, but in doing so we will all have to be careful not to erect our castles on one text. Castles can only stand on converging conglomerates of exegetical data, and I am not persuaded myself we can claim such a convergence for the two-stage concept in the way we can for the idea of the 'infilling of the Spirit', which, as I see it, does cover the data of both Charismatic experience and pentecostal phenomena as we see them in our time.

Besides, as far as Acts 1 is concerned, we do have to recognise that when Jesus told them to 'wait for the promise of the Father' (vs. 4) which he seems to equate with 'being baptised in the Holy Spirit' (vs. 5) and with the power of the Holy Spirit coming UPON them (vs. 8), He was surely alluding to the Old Testament promise that the Spirit would not simply come UPON the few big shots like Moses, Gideon, Samson, Isaiah, Jeremiah and Ezekiel, but would actually be available to INDWELL ALL. And so the Lord can speak through Ezekiel: 'A new heart I will give you, and a new spirit I will put *within* you. . . . I will put my Spirit *within* you, and cause you to walk in my statutes' (Ezek. 36:26–7). Likewise the promise through Jeremiah of the new covenant has as its heart the Lord's promise that 'I will put my law *within* them' (Jer. 31:33), while the Joel prophecy, which Peter sees fulfilled in the Day of Pentecost, focuses on the pouring out of the Spirit 'ON ALL FLESH' (Joel 2:28).

In other words, Pentecost (especially Acts 1:4–8) seems to bring together the two ideas of the Spirit coming INTO the believer (which all would agree is initiatory) and the Spirit being poured out UPON the believer which many Charismatics press as a second experience. But in Acts 1 the Spirit UPON is in fact either equated with the Spirit being received INTO the believer (or else extremely closely associated with it) IN THE INITIATORY PROCESS.

Perhaps therefore, Pentecost, like the situation in Cornelius's household, again reflects a package happening first for the disciples, who had been the beneficiaries of Jesus's own teaching, and for the hearers of the disciples who like Cornelius's household had the package teaching correctly presented to them.

This package, if you take your Bible and look at it in Acts 2, consisted of:

(i) The Good News of Jesus (vss. 23, 32), His death (vs. 23), His resurrection (vs. 32) and His exaltation (vs. 33).

(ii) the promise from the Father of the Holy Spirit (vs. 33).

(iii) the challenge to repent (vs. 38).

(iv) the dual offer of forgiveness, dealing with the past (vs. 38) and the gift of the Holy Spirit, empowering for the future (vs. 38).

Then follows reception of the word and immediate public baptism (vs. 41), plus effective follow-up with teaching, fellowship, sacraments and prayer (v. 42).

All of this to my mind points further to the conclusion intimated earlier, that many of our problems come from mistaken processes of preaching, teaching and instruction which separate in presentation and in time biblical concepts, theological ideas and spiritual experiences, which really BELONG TOGETHER.

Just conceivably Philip made the same sort of mistake in Samaria. Or alternatively, we could follow the view that God was preventing a spill-over into the Church of the Jewish/Samaritan split by withholding the Holy Spirit from the Samaritan believers until senior *Jewish* leaders from Jerusalem (people from whom they might have been tempted to disassociate) had come in love and solidarity and been instrumental in God bringing them the Holy Spirit. What witness could there have been to the world of that time if one of the most scandalous and long-standing divides of all had not been healed or if believers from the Jews and believers from the Samaritans had found a common blessing but not found each other? Perhaps Acts 8 is there not to show a norm, but first to prevent a catastrophe and secondly to warn against an eccentricity – namely *believing without receiving* the Holy Spirit.

If we reject both these alternatives we must either land in

the exegetically precarious position of building a two-stage theology on what is clearly an exception rather than a rule, and thereby also stepping out of line with the teaching of the Epistles, – or of ascribing the Acts 8 happenings to the mystery of the Spirit doing His own thing, as it were, and baffling all our attempts to categorise them!

At which point, regardless of the stance to which our spirits are finally drawn, we can perhaps embrace the conviction of John Taylor that:

> the whole weight of New Testament evidence endorses the central affirmation of the Pentecostalists that the gift of the Holy Spirit transforms and intensifies the quality of human life and that this is a fact of experience in the lives of Christians. The longing of thousands of Christians to recover what they feel instinctively their faith promises them is what underlies the whole movement.[9]

A similar conviction comes from Michael Harper.

> The basic theological position of the charismatic renewal, with some variations, is that the God who invaded our world in the person of Jesus Christ nearly two thousand years ago, and will come again 'in like manner' sometime in the future, still actively moves amongst his people, and the effects of that real presence are to be expected and experienced in our own lives.[10]

These two affirmations about the centrality of the Holy Spirit in Christian experience and life seem to me to be the heart of the Pentecostal emphasis and as such can hardly be argued with.

(iii) View Three (Acceptance of Charismatic experience but questioning of Charismatic terminology)

Given my line on the two previous views it will by now be guessed that my own inclination is in the direction of the third view which accepts the Charismatic experience of the so-called Baptism in the Holy Spirit but queries the terminology. My own feeling is that the term 'filling' or 'infilling' of the Holy Spirit is the one which best fits both the exegetical data of the New Testament and the facts of Christian and especially Charismatic experience in the twentieth century.

Apart from anything else, as stressed in Chapter 14, the idea and desirability of being filled with the Holy Spirit is shared by both so-called 'camps' and it is one both can embrace, even if the understanding relating to timing and mechanics may vary somewhat. The term therefore has the advantage of being widely serviceable and of not being divisive.

However, if there are those on different sides of the fence who insist on using the term Baptism in the Spirit, the one lot applying it to the initial experience and the other to a subsequent second-stage experience, then perhaps (see Ch. 4) some resolution can come from the dual meaning of the Greek word *baptizo* as both being 'initiated into something' (which would seemingly speak of a *status*) and of being 'overwhelmed by something' (which speaks of an *experience*).

Perhaps, as David Watson has suggested, uncertainty and confusion come when either is overstressed at the expense of the other. For example, he says:

> It is possible to think of the overwhelming of the Spirit as something entirely separate from Christian initiation, whereas the two, ideally and potentially, though not necessarily experientially, are one. On the other hand, it is possible so to stress that the Christian has 'got it all' by being baptised into Christ that the overwhelming of the Spirit is never experienced. This is a danger many evangelicals can fall into.[11]

It is also valuable to recognise, as many are doing who are looking at this subject, that New Testament initiation, symbolised and sealed by water baptism, is basically a single work of God with many facets which together constitute what

David Watson calls 'a cluster of overlapping spiritual realities'. This cluster would include:

- the proclamation of the Gospel
- faith
- repentance
- forgiveness
- justification
- adoption
- conversion
- regeneration and new birth
- baptism in the spirit
- baptism in water
- new life in the spirit

There is admittedly not always agreement in the Church on the relationship between these realities or how they should be proclaimed and taught in the evangelistic setting. However, most could probably agree on two points. Firstly, even though these spiritual truths and experiences may have to be intellectually separated for teaching and learning purposes, they actually belong together theologically and spiritually since together they express the single full reality of the believer's incorporation into Christ which leads to sonship and power for living and serving in the Christian life.

Secondly, the initiatory cluster of experiences is grasped, apprehended, understood and to some extent 'entered' upon by different individuals in differing ways and in different time scales often according as to how they are taught or instructed by Christian pastors, evangelists and theologians.

This is where I believe more work and reflection is needed by all who preach the Gospel or teach young disciples. The Pentecost and Cornelius stories seem to call us to bring together the whole didactic package so that we not only preach repentance and faith in the evangelistic setting, but reception of and Baptism in the Spirit as well. People should leave our evangelistic meetings not only knowing new theological truths and having new spiritual commitments but aware of the Spirit of God by whom they have been indwelt and in whom they have been baptised, by Jesus, the Baptiser in the Spirit.

Having said all that, intellectual honesty also requires one to record one's own recognition that there are immensely capable scholars, exegetes and men and women of deep piety and spirituality who in full integrity argue for different positions very convincingly. Perhaps part of the problem comes from the fact that we are all seeking to systematise the work of the Holy Spirit Who, because He blows where He wills, is very unsystematic and unpredictable, and therefore the bugbear of systematic theologians!

The fact is that in Acts there are no really tidy theological schemes of Christian initiation. Sometimes reception of the Holy Spirit *follows* baptism, as in the Pentecostal proclamation of Acts 2:38. Sometimes it precedes baptism, as in the experience of Cornelius and his household (Acts 10:44–8). And sometimes a man like Simon is baptised who has no part or lot in the Christian thing and whose heart is still 'not right before God' (Acts 8:21).

So too in modern times. The Spirit is blowing where He wills. He is falling on little old ladies and filling theologically untutored businessmen. He is coming on bishops and archbishops at the most odd moments. He is invading high schools and meeting with countless housewives as they study the Scriptures in their living rooms and pray.

And He is sending this one out to preach renewal. He is sending that one out to evangelise. He is sending the next one to bring justice in society. And He is sending a few eccentrics out to do all three!

All of this creates frantic problems of predictability for our tidy theological minds! But it underlines, I believe, the hazards of trying to stereotype or straight-jacket the work of the Holy Spirit or the experience of individual Christians.

As John Taylor has said:

The authenticity of the book of Acts is gloriously apparent in the inconsistency of the various incidents of the Spirit's intervention from the day of Pentecost onwards. The Holy

Spirit does not appear to have read the rubrics. He will not
and cannot be bound.[12]

Even such a lucid and precise brain as that of Michael Green
has to affirm: 'There is no tidy doctrine of the Spirit to be
found in Acts or for that matter in the whole New
Testament.'[13]

All of this would suggest that excessive rigidity is what
must be avoided, for it is rigidity which divides God's people,
not truth, because it is the nature of truth to set us free.

5. Gospel and Spirit

Perhaps we can allow a summary word to come from a
remarkable little document called 'Gospel and Spirit' which
emerged from a dialogue in England between the Charismatically oriented Fountain Trust, which was closed down
in 1980, and the more traditional Church of England Evangelical Council. Their debate in the spirit of love and openness produced the following affirmation which is an extract
out of the whole statement.

> We are agreed that every Christian is indwelt by the Holy
> Spirit (Rom. 8:9). It is impossible for anyone to acknowl-
> edge sin, confess Christ, experience new birth, enjoy the
> Saviour's fellowship, be assured of sonship, grow in holi-
> ness, and fulfil any true service or ministry without the
> Spirit. The Christian life is life in the Spirit. We all thank
> God for this gift.
>
> In recent years there has been a fresh enrichment in
> many Christians' Spirit-given experience of Christ and in
> many cases they have called it 'baptism in the Holy Spirit'.
> Some of these people have seen their experience as similar
> to that of the disciples on the day of Pentecost and other
> comparable events in Acts. Despite the observable par-
> allels, however, there are problems attaching to the use of
> this term to describe an experience separated often by a
> long period of time from the person's initial conversion to
> Christ.

In the first place this usage suggests that what is sub-normal in the New Testament should be regarded as normal today; namely that a long interval should elapse between new birth and any conscious realisation or reception of the Spirit's power.

In the second place, the New Testament use of the words 'baptise' and especially 'baptise into' stresses their initiatory content and context and therefore refers to Christian initiation, rather than to a later enrichment of Christian experience.

However, we see that it may be hard to change a usage which has become very wide-spread, although we all agree in recognising its dangers. We would all emphasise that it must not be employed in a way which would question the reality of the work of the Spirit in regeneration and the real difference that this brings in experience from the outset. On that we are unanimous. Some who speak of a post-conversion 'Baptism in the Holy Spirit' think of it mainly in terms of an empowering for service similar to the disciples' experience at Pentecost, though all are agreed that we should not isolate this side of the Spirit's work from His other ministries to and in the believer.

Some, stressing the experiential content of the term 'baptism in the Spirit' value it as having played a unique part in awakening Christians out of spiritual lethargy and bondage and regard it as still having such a role in the future. Others concentrating rather upon its initiatory implications, prefer to use it only to describe one aspect of new birth.

None of us wishes to deny the possibility or reality of subsequent experiences of the grace of God which have deep and transforming significance. We all affirm that a constant hunger and thirst after God should characterise every Christian rather than any complacent claim to have arrived. We urge one another and all our fellow Christians to press on to know the Lord better, and thus to enter into the fullness of our inheritance in Christ.[14]

To me that about says it all.

Appendix B

PROPHECY IN THE NEW TESTAMENT

The word 'prophecy' is used basically in three ways in the New Testament.

Firstly, it is used to announce something as a revelation from God.

This would seem to be the usage in Acts 19:6 where the Holy Spirit 'came on' the Ephesian disciples who then 'spoke with tongues and prophesied' (*cf.* Acts 21:9).

Also in Peter's sermon on the day of Pentecost we find him affirming that Joel's prophecy was being fulfilled in that moment, because had not God said: 'On my menservants and my maidservants in those days I will pour out my Spirit; and they shall *prophesy*' (Acts 2:18).

However, alongside these references we must set 1 Corinthians 14:3 where Paul says that 'He who prophesies speaks to men for their upbuilding and encouragement and consolation'. In short, says the Apostle, 'He who prophesies edifies the church' (vs. 4).

Then in 1 Cor. 14:22 Paul is even more explicit when he says 'prophecy is for believers, not unbelievers'. This would seem to distinguish prophecy in its primary meaning from evangelistic preaching and proclamation which is directed at non-Christians.

On the other hand we are to note that prophecy can on occasion result in the conversion of an unbeliever (1 Cor. 14:24–5).

The second New Testament usage of prophecy relates to

revealing something whose evidence has been hidden. For example in Luke 23:64 the chief priests and their henchmen taunt Jesus saying 'Prophesy! Who is it that struck you?'

Not having direct natural, eyesight evidence, the blow coming from behind Him, Jesus is asked to declare the truth of the matter by the supernatural means of prophecy – i.e. revealing something whose evidence or origin is hidden.

The third use is that of foretelling the future. This is its sense in Matthew 11:13 ('All the prophets and the law prophesied until John'); in Matthew 15:7 ('Well did Isaiah prophesy of you') and in 1 Peter 1:10 ('The prophets who prophesied of the grace that was to be yours searched and inquired about this salvation').

Drawing together the threads we have thus far assembled, it would seem then that prophecy is that process whereby a believer under the inspiration or special anointing of the Holy Spirit may declare forth or confirm the mind and will of God, relating either to the past, present or future, in such a way as to edify and upbuild Christians or on occasion convince and convict the outsider.

This being the case the Word need not come as from God in the first person singular 'I, the Lord, say to you . . .'. In fact I suspect this should be the exception rather than the rule, but perhaps it cannot be eliminated as a possibility.

In any event, if prophecy is declaring the word and will of God then it is no wonder in 1 Corinthians 14 that Paul can begin (vs. 1) and end (vs. 39) saying: 'earnestly desire to prophesy'. Indeed, he says this gift or ability is to be sought above all (1 Cor. 14:1).

FOR ALL

This leads us on to make the rather obvious observation that prophecy in the Old Testament was for the few select giants, like Moses, Ezekiel, Jeremiah and Daniel, but in the New Testament it is for all. Every Christian is potentially a prophet. The pouring out of the Spirit on all flesh has this consequence: 'And they shall prophesy' (Acts 2:18).

Likewise Paul can tell the Corinthians: 'I want you ALL to speak in tongues, but even more to prophesy' (1 Cor. 14:5).

Indeed he says: 'Desire to prophesy' (1 Cor. 14:39), and seemingly sets this as the most important of the gifts of utterance and perhaps of all gifts. What else can one conclude from his exhortation: 'Make love your aim, and earnestly desire the spiritual gifts, ESPECIALLY that you may prophesy' (1 Cor. 14:1)?

MINISTRY OF THE PROPHET

On the other hand while he recognises that all may and perhaps should prophesy, not all will have the ministry of the prophet as the activity in which they are primarily or totally engaged. This one sees from his question: 'Are all prophets?' (1 Cor. 12:29), where clearly he expects the answer No.

Ephesians 4:11 also speaks of only 'Some' being prophets. Clearly the New Testament Church set apart a special group of people known as prophets. So the Church at Antioch has in its number both 'prophets and teachers' (Acts 13:1).

Agabus, one of the few prophets named for us, had notable gifts of prediction, prophesying first that there would be a great famine (Acts 11:28) and then that Paul would be bound in Jerusalem and handed over to the Gentiles (Acts 21:10–11).

On the other hand the general use seems to *combine* the triple ingredients of proclamation, prediction and the setting forth of the divine mind or will on a subject.

An interesting comment on this comes in Bob Slosser's biography of the Episcopal minister Terry Fullam. Speaking of Fullam's teaching on prophecy he writes:

Fullam explained that the New Testament teaches all Christians may prophesy as the Holy Spirit wills, depending upon the need of the moment. But, he said, not all Christians are called to be prophets; not all are called to that ministry. It has a special function. In that special sense, viewing it as an office, several passages of Scripture shed light. In Exodus 4, there is the dialogue after God tells Moses He will equip him for leading the people of Israel out of Egypt. Moses cowers, says he's not eloquent and so on. The Lord becomes exasperated and says, in effect, 'Okay, Moses, I'll use your brother Aaron.' In verse 16, God adds that Aaron 'shall speak for you to the people; and he shall be a *mouth* for you, and you shall be to him as God.' Further on, in verse one of chapter seven, God says of the Moses–Aaron relationship, 'Aaron your brother shall be your prophet.' So we see the Scripture likening Moses to God and likening Aaron to a prophet or a mouth. A prophet was like a mouth. Thus a prophet of God is a mouth or mouthpiece for God.

'You can see,' said Fullam, 'a prophet is one who speaks, or delivers, the word of the Lord.'[1]

PURPOSE AND REGULATION

The purpose of the gift then, to come back to 1 Cor. 14:3, is threefold – the 'upbuilding and encouragement and consolation' of the Church, although it may on occasion be used for the conversion of an unbeliever (1 Cor. 14:24–5), but this is not its normal purpose, being 'not for unbelievers but for believers' (1 Cor. 14:22).

However, in its general use, the gift has to be exercised within the biblical controls.

REGULATIONS

Two regulations control prophecy. Both are in 1 Cor. 14:29: 'Let two or three prophets speak, and let the others weigh what is said.'

Firstly, only two or three are to speak during a worship service, or confusion would result.

Secondly, others are to weigh or discern what is said in the light of their knowledge of God and His Truth. One could perhaps say that there are two tests to apply – firstly the experience of other prophets present. Says Paul in 1 Cor. 14:32: 'The spirits of prophets are subject to prophets.' And secondly there is the overall test of apostolic truth. 'If anyone thinks that he is a prophet, or spiritual,' the apostle writes, 'he should acknowledge that what I am writing to you is a command of the Lord. If any one does not recognise this, he is not recognised' (1 Cor. 14:37–8).

In other words the prophets were not sources of new truth to the Church, but expounders and developers and elaborators of truth already given.

Only this way could the Church be on guard against false prophets and teachers who come 'speaking perverse things, to draw away the disciples after them' (Acts 20:28–30).

All this would indicate that prophecy is the cooperative working together of the Holy Spirit with the human spirit either to declare the present mind and will of God and truth of God in a given situation, or to reveal the future intention, plan or purpose of God in the unfolding course of events. As this is declared, there is to be the witness of the Spirit among other discerning believers who will weigh the utterance in the light of Scripture.

We repeat then that if prophesy is hearing, discerning or discovering the mind, will or purpose of God, and then declaring it, it is no wonder that Paul sets this gift as the primary one. After all, what does God want more for us, His children, than to know and do His will?

If prophecy is key to this, we should indeed *all* 'earnestly desire to prophesy'.

Fullam puts it this way:

> It is more important for people to hear the word of God than anything else. It is not mere human advice. And it is not always introduced by some stentorian proclamation of 'thus said the Lord' or 'the word of the Lord came unto me today'. It is merely speaking the words of the Lord into a situation, quietly and humbly.[2]

SUMMARY

Drawing the full range of threads together we could perhaps present a summary definition of prophecy in these terms:

Prophecy is the exercise of that gift and ministry of the Spirit which takes place when a believer who knows the mind, will, purpose or righteousness of God declares it, whether to the Church or the world. The knowledge on which this utterance is based is received not only by understanding the Written Word and abiding in the Living Word, but sometimes by supernatural discernment, or by listening and hearing, or even by direct revelation of the Spirit received by faith. The twofold test of prophetic authenticity lies firstly in whether it is consistent with the revealed Word of God, the apostolic deposit, and secondly in whether it receives the positive affirmation of the Body of Christ, especially other prophets.

Appendix Ci

This list of spiritual gift definitions is used by permission from *Your Spiritual Gifts Can Help Your Church Grow* by C. Peter Wagner, Ventura CA/USA: Regal Books – a Division of G/L Publications, © 1979.

SPIRITUAL GIFTS

These twenty-seven spiritual gifts are here listed in the order in which they were presented in Chapter 2.

1. *Prophecy:* The gift of prophecy is the special ability that God gives to certain members of the Body of Christ to receive and communicate an immediate message of God to His people through a divinely-anointed utterance.
2. *Service:* The gift of service is the special ability that God gives to certain members of the Body of Christ to identify the unmet needs involved in a task related to God's work, and to make use of available resources to meet those needs and help accomplish the desired goals.
3. *Teaching:* The gift of teaching is the special ability that God gives to certain members of the Body of Christ to communicate information relevant to the health and ministry of the Body and its members in such a way that others will learn.
4. *Exhortation:* The gift of exhortation is the special ability that God gives to certain members of the Body of Christ to minister words of comfort, consolation, encouragement and counsel to other members of the Body in such a way that they feel helped and healed.
5. *Giving:* The gift of giving is the special ability that God

gives to certain members of the Body of Christ to contribute their material resources to the work of the Lord with liberality and cheerfulness.

6. *Leadership:* The gift of leadership is the special ability that God gives to certain members of the Body of Christ to set goals to others in such a way that they voluntarily and harmoniously work together to accomplish these goals for the glory of God.

7. *Mercy:* The gift of mercy is the special ability that God gives to certain members of the Body of Christ to feel genuine empathy and compassion for individuals, both Christian and non-Christian, who suffer distressing physical, mental or emotional problems, and. to translate that compassion into cheerfully-done deeds that reflect Christ's love and alleviate the suffering.

8. *Wisdom:* The gift of wisdom is the special ability that God gives to certain members of the Body of Christ to know the mind of the Holy Spirit in such a way as to receive insight into how given knowledge may best be applied to specific needs arising in the Body of Christ.

9. *Knowledge:* The gift of knowledge is the special ability that God gives to certain members of the Body of Christ to discover, accumulate, analyze and clarify information and ideas that are pertinent to the growth and well-being of the Body.

10. *Faith:* The gift of faith is the special ability that God gives to certain members of the Body of Christ to discern with extraordinary confidence the will and purposes of God for the future of His work.

11. *Healing:* The gift of healing is the special ability that God gives to certain members of the Body of Christ to serve as human intermediaries through whom it pleases God to cure illness and restore health apart from the use of natural means.

12. *Miracles:* The gift of miracles is the special ability that God gives to certain members of the Body of Christ to serve as human intermediaries through whom it pleases God to perform powerful acts that are per-

ceived by observers to have altered the ordinary course of nature.

13. *Discerning of spirits:* The gift of discerning of spirits is the special ability that God gives to certain members of the Body of Christ to know with assurance whether certain behavior purported to be of God is in reality divine, human or satanic.

14. *Tongues:* The gift of tongues is the special ability that God gives to certain members of the Body of Christ (a) to speak to God in a language they have never learned and/or (b) to receive and communicate an immediate message of God to His people through a divinely-anointed utterance in a language they have never learned.

15. *Interpretation:* The gift of interpretation is the special ability that God gives to certain members of the Body of Christ to make known in the vernacular the message of one who speaks in tongues.

16. *Apostle:* The gift of apostle is the special ability that God gives to certain members of the Body of Christ to assume and exercise general leadership over a number of churches with an extraordinary authority in spiritual matters that is spontaneously recognized and appreciated by those churches.

17. *Helps:* The gift of helps is the special ability that God gives to certain members of the Body of Christ to invest the talents they have in the life and ministry of other members of the Body, thus enabling the person helped to increase the effectiveness of his or her spiritual gifts.

18. *Administration:* The gift of administration is the special ability that God gives to certain members of the Body of Christ to understand clearly the immediate and long-range goals of a particular unit of the Body of Christ and to devise and execute effective plans for the accomplishment of those goals.

19. *Evangelist:* The gift of evangelist is the special ability that God gives to certain members of the Body of Christ to share the gospel with unbelievers in such a

way that men and women become Jesus' disciples and responsible members of the Body of Christ.

20. *Pastor:* The gift of pastor is the special ability that God gives to certain members of the Body of Christ to assume a long-term personal responsibility for the spiritual welfare of a group of believers.

21. *Celibacy:* The gift of celibacy is the special ability that God gives to certain members of the Body of Christ to remain single and enjoy it; to be unmarried and not suffer undue sexual temptations.

22. *Voluntary poverty:* The gift of voluntary poverty is the special ability that God gives to certain members of the Body of Christ to renounce material comfort and luxury and adopt a personal life-style equivalent to those living at the poverty level in a given society in order to serve God more effectively.

23. *Martyrdom:* The gift of martyrdom is the special ability that God gives to certain members of the Body of Christ to undergo suffering for the faith even to death while consistently displaying a joyous and victorious attitude that brings glory to God.

24. *Hospitality:* The gift of hospitality is the special ability that God gives to certain members of the Body of Christ to provide open house and warm welcome for those in need of food and lodging.

25. *Missionary:* The gift of missionary is the special ability that God gives to certain members of the Body of Christ to minister whatever other spiritual gifts they have in a second culture.

26. *Intercession:* The gift of intercession is the special ability that God gives to certain members of the Body of Christ to pray for extended periods of time on a regular basis and see frequent and specific answers to their prayers to a degree much greater than that which is expected of the average Christian.

27. *Exorcism:* The gift of exorcism is the special ability that God gives to certain members of the Body of Christ to cast out demons and evil spirits.

GIFTS OF THE HOLY SPIRIT

I. MINISTRY GIFTS	Acts 6:4, 21:8. Rom. 12:7. 1 Cor. 12:28. Eph. 4:11, 4:12. Col. 4:17. I Tim. 1:12. II Tim. 4:5, 4:11.
	Apostles
	Prophets
	Evangelists
	Pastors
	Teachers
II. KNOWLEDGE GIFTS (Knowing)	(i) *Word of Wisdom* I Cor. 12:8.
	(ii) *Word of Knowledge* I Cor. 12:8, 13:8, 14:6.
III. GIFTS OF POWER (Doing)	(i) *Faith* I Cor. 12:9, (Acts 13:16)
	(ii) *Healing* I Cor. 12:9, 12:28.
	(iii) *Working of Miracles* I Cor. 12:10, 12:28, 12:29.
	(iv) *Discerning of Spirits* I Cor. 12:10.
IV. GIFTS OF UTTERANCE (Saying)	(i) *Prophecy* Acts 2:17, 18, 19:6, 21:19. Rom. 12:6. I Cor. 11:4, 5, 12:10, 13:2, 8, 9, 14:1, 3, 4, 5, 6, 22, 24, 31, 39. I Tim. 1:18, 4:14.
	(ii) *Diverse kinds of Tongues* Mark 16:17. Acts 2:4, 2:11, 10:46, 19:6. I Cor. 12:10, 28, 30, 13:1, 8, 14:2, 4, 5, 6, 13, 14, 18, 19, 22, 23, 26, 27, 39.

        (iii) *Interpretation of Tongues* I Cor.
12:10, 30, 14:5, 13, 26, 27, 28.

V. OTHER GIFTS   (i) *Helps* I Cor. 12:28

        (ii) *Administration* I Cor. 12:28

       (iii) *Service* Rom. 12:7. II Cor. 8:4,
9:1. I Pet. 4:11

       (iv) *Exhortation* Acts 13:15. Rom.
12:8. I Cor. 14:3. I Tim. 4:13.
Heb. 13:22.

        (v) *Giving* Rom. 12:8. II Cor. 9:7.
Phil. 4:15.

       (vi) *Leading* Rom. 12:8. Heb. 13:7,
17, 24. I Tim. 5:17.

      (vii) *Showing Mercy* Rom. 12:8.

     (viii) *Revelation* I Cor. 14:6, 26.
II Cor. 12:1, 7. Gal. 2:2.

NOTES

1. 'The Practice of Truth', Francis Schaeffer, in *One Race, One Gospel, One Task*, World Wide Publications, Minneapolis, Minnesota, 1967, p. 453
2. *Fire in the Fire Place*, Charles Hummel, Inter-Varsity Press, Downers Grove, Illinois, 1978, p. 25
3. ibid., p. 26
4. *One in the Spirit*, David Watson, Hodder & Stoughton, London, 1973, p. 67
5. *Look Out, the Pentecostals are Coming*, Peter Wagner, Creation House, Carol Stream, Illinois, 1973, p. 152
6. ibid., p. 153
7. ibid., p. 153
8. *Hammered as Gold*, David Howard, Harper and Row, New York, 1969, p. 146
9. Wagner, op. cit., p. 159
10. *Era of the Spirit*, Rodman Williams, Logos Publishing House, Plainfield, New Jersey, p. 23
11. ibid., p. 23
12. *Church Dogmatics*, M. I., Karl Barth, T. & T. Clark, Edinburgh, 1962, p. 828
13. *The Misunderstanding of the Church*, Emil Brunner, Lutterworth Press, London, 1952, p. 48
14. ibid., pp. 47–9
15. ibid., p. 52
16. 'The New Pentecostalism: reflection by a well wisher', Clarke Pinnock, *Christianity Today*
17. *The Descent of the Dove*, Charles Williams, Collins – The Fontana Library, London and Glasgow, 1939, p. 17
18. *The Go Between God*, John V. Taylor, S.C.M. Press, London, 1972, p. 199
19. *The Dynamics of Spiritual Life*, Richard Lovelace, Inter-Varsity Press, Downers Grove, Illinois, 1979, p. 16
20. ibid., pp. 16–17
21. ibid., pp. 20–1

22. The full story is chronicled in *Prisoners of Hope*, by Michael Cassidy, Africa Enterprise, Pietermaritzburg, 1974

23. ibid., p. 146

24. ibid., p. 147

25. ibid., pp. 151–2

26. *I Believe in the Church*, David Watson, Hodder & Stoughton, London, 1978

27. *One in the Spirit*. David Watson, Hodder & Stoughton, London, 1973, p. 15

28. 'The Charismatics Among Us', Kenneth S. Kantzer, *Christianity Today*, 22 Feb, 1980, p. 25

29. ibid., p. 28

30. ibid., p. 28

31. 'Theological Reflections on the Charismatic Movement', James Packer, *The Churchman*, vol. 94, no. 2, 1980, p. 119

32. 'A Catholic Assesses the Charismatic Renewal in His Church', Ralph Martin, *Christianity Today*, 7 March 1980, p. 18

33. ibid., p. 19

34. ibid., p. 19

35. ibid., p. 19

36. *This is the Day*, Michael Harper, Hodder & Stoughton, London, 1979, p. 106

37. *The Evangelicals*, John C. King, Hodder & Stoughton, London, 1969, p. 68

38. ibid., pp. 70–1.

39. 'Critics Corner – Aggressions & Charismatics', *The Christian Ministry*, Sept. 1977, pp. 81–3

40. ibid., p. 82

41. 'The Power of the Holy Spirit', Michael Griffiths in *The New Face of Evangelicalism*, Hodder & Stoughton, London, 1975, p. 245

42. Green, op. cit., p. 208

43. *The New Charismatics*, Richard Quebedeaux, Doubleday, New York, 1976, p. 127

44. Lovelace, op. cit., pp. 262–3

45. *Commentary on St John's Gospel*, Edwin Hosken,

46. 'Theological Reflections on the Charismatic Movement', James Packer, *The Churchman*, vol. 94, no. 2, 1980, p. 104

47. *Evangelism – Now and Then*, Michael Green, Inter-Varsity Press, London, 1979, p. 43

48. *A Man Called Mr Pentecost*, David du Plessis, Logos International, Plainfield, New Jersey, 1977, p. 78

49. ibid., p. 78
50. *God's New Society*, John Stott, Inter-Varsity Press, London, 1970, p. 52
51. ibid., pp. 53–4
52. *How To Be Filled with the Holy Spirit*, A. W. Tozer, Christian Publications, Inc., Harrisburg, Pennsylvania,
53. Watson, *One in the Spirit*, op. cit., p. 67.
54. ibid., p. 69
55. Taylor, op. cit., p. 120
56. *The New Face of Evangelicalism* (Article by Michael Griffiths on *The Power of the Holy Spirit*) in Symposium Volume on Lausanne Congress, ed. Rene Padilla, Hodder & Stoughton, 1976, p. 251
57. *This is the Day*, Michael Harper, Hodder & Stoughton, London, 1976, p. 47
58. *Church Dogmatics*, (Gifts in the Community) Karl Barth, T. & T. Clark, Edinburgh, 1936–9, p. 828
59. *Your Spiritual Gifts*, C. Peter Wagner, Regal, Glendale, California, 1979, p. 32.
60. ibid., pp. 49–50
61. ibid.
62. *I Believe in the Holy Spirit*, Michael Green, Hodder & Stoughton, London, 1975, pp. 155–6
63. *When God Moves*, Festo Kivengere, African Enterprise, Pasadena, 1973, p. 11
64. *The Calvary Road*, Roy Hession, Christian Lit. Crusade, London, 1950, p. 16
65. ibid., pp. 52–3
66. ibid., p. 53
67. ibid., p. 54
68. *The Way*, E. Stanley Jones, Hodder & Stoughton, London, 1947, p. 9
69. *Hitler's Interpreter*, Paul Schmidt, William Heinemann Ltd., London, 1951, pp. 278–9
70. *Saints in Politics*, E. M. Howse, George Allen & Unwin, London, first pub. 1953, reprinted 1971, p. 7
71. *Christian Mission in the Modern World*, John Stott, Falcon, London, 1975, p. 32
72. *Wilberforce*, John Pollock, Lion Publishing, Berkhamsted, 1977, p. 143
73. *Together in One Place*, Michael Cassidy, Evangel Press, Nairobi, 1978, pp. 215–6
74. Taylor, op. cit., p. 4

75. ibid., p. 80
76. *I Believe in the Great Commission*, Max Warren, Hodder & Stoughton, London, 1976, p. 31
77. *In the Gap*, David Bryant, Inter-Varsity Missions Press, Madison, 1979, pp. 71–4
78. ibid., p. 74
79. *Rethinking Missions*, W. B. Hocking, 1932
80. *Christian Message in a Non-Christian World*, Hendrik Kraemer, Kregel, 1938,
81. *Story of Philosophy*, Will Durant, Simon & Schuster, New York, 1959, p. 1
82. *The Celebration of Discipline*, Richard Foster, Hodder & Stoughton, London, 1980, p. 23
83. *The Other Side of Silence* (*A Guide to Christian Meditation*), Morton T. Kelsey, S.P.C.K., London, 1977, p. 207
84. Lovelace, op. cit., pp. 305–6
85. 'Thoughts on the Revival in New England', Jonathan Edwards in C. C. Goen ed., *The Great Awakening*, Yale University Press, New Haven, 1972, p. 418
86. Lovelace, op. cit., p. 246
87. Edwards, op. cit., pp. 421–2

APPENDIX A

1. *I Believe in the Holy Spirit*, Michael Green, Hodder & Stoughton, London, 1975, p. 39
2. *The Baptism & Fullness of the Holy Spirit*, John Stott, Inter-Varsity Press, London, 1964, p. 19
3. ibid. p. 15
4. *One in the Spirit*, David Watson, Hodder & Stoughton, London, 1973, p. 67
5. *A New Pentecost*, Léon Cardinal Joseph Suenens, The Seabury Press, New York, 1974
6. op. cit.
7. Personal letter to the author (15 Oct. 1981)
8. ibid.
9. *The Go-Between God*, John V. Taylor, SCM Press, London, 1972, p. 199
10. *This is The Day*, Michael Harper, Hodder & Stoughton, London, 1979, p. 57
11. op. cit. (One in the Spirit – Hodder, '73) p. 69

12. op. cit., p. 120
13. op. cit., p. 65
14. *Gospel & Spirit*, published by The Fountain Trust and the Church of England Evangelical Council, London, 1977

APPENDIX B

1. *Miracle in Darien*, Bob Slosser, Logos International, Plain Fields, New Jersey, 1979, pp. 177–80.
2. ibid., p. 180